Dana Ziegel

Entstehung, Auswirkungen und Vor- und Nachteile von Massenproduktion am Beispiel Ford

GRIN Verlag

DEPARTMENT OF THE INTERIOR

BULLETIN

OF THE

UNITED STATES

GEOLOGICAL SURVEY

No. 180

SERIES A, ECONOMIC GEOLOGY, 11

WASHINGTON
GOVERNMENT PRINTING OFFICE
1901

UNITED STATES GEOLOGICAL SURVEY

CHARLES D. WALCOTT, DIRECTOR

THE

OCCURRENCE AND DISTRIBUTION

OF

CORUNDUM IN THE UNITED STATES

BY

JOSEPH HYDE PRATT

WASHINGTON

GOVERNMENT PRINTING OFFICE

1901

CONTENTS.

5

6   CONTENTS.

ILLUSTRATIONS.

8 ILLUSTRATIONS.

OCCURRENCE AND DISTRIBUTION OF CORUNDUM IN THE UNITED STATES.

By JOSEPH HYDE PRATT.

INTRODUCTION.

In obtaining data for this paper many corundum localities were visited, especially those that were thought to carry the mineral in commercial quantity. Although all the occurrences of corundum can not be described in detail, they are all mentioned in the tabulated list of localities, page 79.

Considerable activity in corundum mining has sprung up within the last few years, and several new occurrences of corundum in quantity have been brought to light, those of special note being in Ontario, Canada, where the corundum occurs in a syenite, and in North Carolina and Georgia, where it occurs in a gneiss or a quartz-schist.

The corundum localities in the United States are, with the exception of those in Montana, Colorado, and California, limited to the Appalachian region, the mineral having been found at various points throughout nearly its entire length. The mining of corundum has been, however, confined to a narrow section of the southern portion of that region, i. e., to northeastern Georgia and southwestern North Carolina, with the exception of the emery mines at Chester, Mass.

Often a distinction is made between emery and corundum, many persons not recognizing emery as a variety of corundum. There are three names in constant use to designate the varieties of corundum: (1) Sapphire, which includes all corundums, of whatever color, that are transparent to semitransparent; (2) corundum, including the translucent to opaque varieties of all colors; (3) emery, which is a mechanical admixture of corundum and magnetite or hematite. The last two varieties are those used in the arts for abrasive purposes, emery being used in very much larger quantities than corundum. It is of course the presence of corundum in the emery that gives to it its abrasive qualities and makes it of commercial value, and the abrasive efficiency of emeries varies according to the percentage of corundum they contain.

Any corundum that is transparent is included under the head of sapphires, although many of these have distinct names in the gem trade. The blue sapphire is known as the oriental sapphire, the red

9

sapphire as the oriental ruby, the green sapphire as the oriental emerald, the yellow sapphire as the oriental topaz, and the purple sapphire as the oriental amethyst. There are also pink and white sapphires. The corundum gem or sapphire localities are usually distinct from the corundum localities, although very handsome gems have been found where the corundum was mined for abrasive purposes, notably at the Corundum Hill mine, Cullasagee, N. C.

Corundum as it is mined for abrasive purposes occurs as (1) sand, (2) crystal, or (3) gravel and block corundum. Sometimes all three types are found in the same deposit. The sand corundum consists of small grains or fragments of the mineral scattered through the vein. The crystal corundum consists of crystals up to 3 inches in length. Often these crystals have parting planes so thoroughly developed that, in crushing, the corundum breaks up into regular rhombohedrons, this breaking continuing to even the finer sizes and causing the grains of corundum to crumble when in use. This persistent regular breaking of the corundum destroys its cutting efficiency, for it is the irregular fracture that produces the best cutting edge. The block variety often occurs in masses of almost pure corundum from 10 to 1,000 pounds in weight. Again it occurs in large masses intimately associated with hornblende, feldspar, etc., making a rock which is tough and is difficult to work. Frequently the only way to break the masses is to build fires over them and then suddenly cool them by pouring water upon them. The parting planes are at times very noticeable in the block corundum, and are, as in the crystal corundum, detrimental to the commercial product. The parting planes are not lines of cleavage, but are planes developed in the mineral by synthetic twinning, usually parallel to the unit rhombohedron.

It is the hardness of corundum that makes it of so great value as an abrasive. Next to the diamond it is the hardest mineral known, having a hardness of 9, while the diamond has a hardness of 10. Garnet, which is sometimes used as an abrasive, has a hardness of but 7 to 7.5. Corundum varies slightly in hardness; the sapphire varieties are generally considered the hardest, and of these the blue stands at the head. Some corundum has been observed that was readily scratched with a knife, as that from Acworth, Ga. The hardness of a corundum is often misjudged because, when made into a wheel, it does not cut so well as another, when in reality the degree of hardness may be the same in both cases, but the cutting efficiency of one surpasses that of the other.

The theoretical composition of corundum is alumina (Al_2O_3); but with one or two exceptions all corundums that have been examined vary from this by containing a small percentage of other constituents, principally silica (SiO_2), water (H_2O), and ferric oxide (Fe_2O_3). Nearly all corundums contain water, the amount varying from a trace to 2 per cent or more. The amount of silica and ferric oxide varies also, some corundums containing neither of these constituents and some

OUTCROP OF PERIDOTITE AT BUCK CREEK, CLAY COUNTY, N. C.

containing as much as 5 per cent of one or the other. The purest forms of corundum that have been analyzed are the sapphire or gem varieties, which sometimes show over 99.5 per cent of alumina.

All corundums do not behave alike when heated to the high temperature necessary for the manufacture of vitrified wheels. While most corundums can, if properly cleaned, be used in the manufacture of these wheels, some will, when heated, crumble to a powder. It is, therefore, very essential, before beginning to mine a corundum deposit, to thoroughly test the ore and ascertain its adaptability to the manufacture of vitrified and other wheels.

MODES OF OCCURRENCE OF CORUNDUM.

Corundum was formerly regarded as occurring sparingly in nature, and in only a few types of rocks, but it is now known to occur rather widely, and instead of being in quantity in the basic magnesian or peridotite rocks only, it.has been found in abundance in syenites, in gneisses, and in schists. Although occurring in many of the crystalline rocks, it has been observed as a rock constituent in only a few of them. In some cases it is an original constituent of the rock, and in other cases it has been formed later, during the process of metamorphism.

In the United States corundum is known to occur in the following rocks: In peridotite (dunite and saxonite), in biotite contact on saxonite, in enstatite, in serpentine, in chlorite-schist, in amphibolite, in norite, in basic minette, in andesite, in syenite, in amphiboleschist, in gneiss, in mica-schist, in limestone, and in cyanite. These modes of occurrence are described below in the order in which they are mentioned.

CORUNDUM IN PERIDOTITES.

Extending from Tallapoosa County in east-central Alabama to Trenton, N. J., there is a narrow belt which contains disconnected outcrops of peridotite rocks; north of New Jersey (in New York, Connecticut, Massachusetts, New Hampshire, and Maine) the outcrops are fewer and do not form a continuous belt. It is in the southern portion of this belt that these rocks have reached their greatest development, in some localities outcropping over an area of several hundred acres. In North Carolina and in the more southern portion of the belt the prevailing type of the rock is dunite, while in the northern portion the secondary rocks, serpentine and talc, are prominent. Pl. I is a reproduction of a photograph of an outcrop of dunite at Buck Creek, Clay County, N. C.

Throughout nearly the entire southern portion of the belt the peridotite rocks show a freshness to almost the surface of the exposures, and there are few localities where there is any considerable area of peridotite entirely altered to serpentine. Under the microscope thin sections of the dunite show an alteration to serpentine between the particles of dunite. These peridotite rocks have been shown to be of igneous origin.[1] The blunt lenticular form in which they are found would be difficult to associate with any origin but that of an intruded igneous mass, which would also account for the apophyses that have been observed extending into the inclosing gneiss. At Webster, Jackson County, N. C., a large block of gneiss is completely inclosed by the peridotites in such a manner as could be attributed only to the intrusion of the latter while in a molten condition. The line of separation of the peridotites and the gneisses is always sharp, and there is no transitional zone from the acid gneiss to the basic peridotite. Under the microscope the latter rock shows the granular structure characteristic of plutonic origin, the grains fitting perfectly into one another without cementing material.

Associated with all these peridotites is the mineral chromite, which occurs as disseminated particles near the borders of the lenticular masses of the peridotites. There is very little carbon found associated with these rocks, and what has been observed is unquestionably of secondary origin.

Until recently the common occurrence of corundum (not including emery), and the occurrence in which the mineral had been found in commercial quantity, was in association with these basic magnesian rocks, peridotites, principally dunite. The country rock that is commonly in contact with the peridotite is a hornblende-gneiss, but these peridotite formations have also been found in contact with a biotite-gneiss and with a mica-schist. Where the country rock is a gneiss it is usually considerably decomposed near the contact, and, while retaining the appearance of the unaltered rock, it readily crumbles to pieces when handled. The peridotite is also more or less altered, the change being usually to serpentine.

The corundum is not an accessory mineral in these peridotites, but is either concentrated near the contact of the peridotite with the other country rocks or in pockets within the peridotite formation. A series of alteration products has been developed in this contact zone, so that the corundum is not found in direct contact with the peridotite, but is separated by intermediate zones of chlorite, enstatite, etc. Chlorite and vermiculite are usually developed between the corundum and the gneiss. For convenience, the occurrences of the corundum in these alteration products between the peridotite and the gneiss are designated contact veins, and those wholly within the peridotite dunite veins.

In a cross section of a contact vein extending from the gneiss to the peridotite (dunite) the following sequence is often observed:

a. Gneiss, hornblendic or micaceous, apparently unaltered.

b. Gneiss with same general appearance as *a*, but so decayed that the particles readily separate from one another.

---

[1] Elisha Mitchell Sci. Soc. Jour., Part II, 1895, p. 35, and Am. Jour. Sci., 4th series, Vol. VI, 1898, p. 50.

c. Yellowish vermiculites, varying considerably in thickness, the maximum being 6 to 8 inches; in places absent, so that *b* comes directly in contact with *d*; where present, *c* often merges into *d*.

d. Green chlorite, varying in thickness much like *c*, and in places absent.

e. Chlorite and corundum, sometimes with a little vermiculite. In places this mass may be largely corundum, and it is what is called the "corundum vein," varying in thickness from a few inches to 12 or 15 feet.

f. Green chlorite: so far as observed always present, and varying in width from 1 to 12 inches.

g. Enstatite; in places hard and compact, and in widths of several feet; usually merges into *h*.

h. Talcose rock, usually fibrous, varying in thickness from a few inches to several feet.

j. Dunite, more or less altered, friable, and stained with ferric oxide.

k. Dunite, apparently unaltered, quite extensive.

Between *h* and *j* a seam of yellowish clay (*i*) is sometimes observed which often contains a narrow seam or fragments of chalcedony.

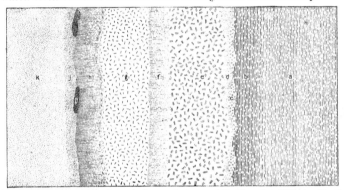

FIG. 1.—Ideal cross section of a corundum contact vein at the Corundum Hill mine, North Carolina. *a*, fresh and unaltered gneiss; *b*, decayed and unaltered gneiss; *c*, vermiculites; *d*, green chlorite; *e*, corundum-bearing zone; *f*, green chlorite; *g*, enstatite; *h*, talcose rock; *i*, clay; *j*, altered dunite; *k*, unaltered dunite.

From what could be learned by actual observation and inquiry among the miners, *c* and *d* are sometimes absent, and when this is the case, *e*, a mixture of chlorite, vermiculite, and corundum, is seemingly in direct contact with *b*. The chlorite, however, on the dunite side of the section is constant. The thickness of the several zones (*a*, *b*, *c*, etc.) in such sections varies greatly at different places, and the distance across the sections may be said to vary at different points, even in the same region, from a few feet to 30 or 40 feet. The accompanying diagram (fig. 1) represents the cross section of a contact vein observed at the Corundum Hill mine, Cullasagee, Macon County, N. C.

In the diagram *a* represents gneiss, apparently fresh and unaltered, passing into *b*, which has somewhat the appearance of the unaltered gneiss, but is so decayed that the particles readily separate from

one another; *c* represents a narrow zone of vermiculites that is sometimes entirely lacking; *d*, a green chlorite (clinochlore) partially
decomposed and forming the vermiculites of *c; e*, the corundum-
bearing zone, a mass of the green chlorite with crystals and fragments of corundum disseminated through it; *f*, another zone of the
green chlorite; *g*, a mass of grayish, interlocking, crystalline sheaves
of enstatite that merge into *h; h*, a fibrous talcose rock which passes
into *j; j*, an altered dunite that is somewhat friable and stained with
ferric oxide; *k*, a hard and apparently unaltered dunite. Between *h*
and *j* is a mass of soft, yellowish clay (*i*) containing fragments of
chalcedony.

The line of contact between the zone of alteration products and the
gneiss was very sharp and distinct in all the contact veins examined.
The minerals developed between the corundum-bearing zone and the
dunite are in great abundance and differ from those between that
zone and the gneiss.

In a cross section of a dunite vein at a shaft near the southern part
of Corundum Hill, in a distance of from 20 to 25 feet, the following
has been observed:

 1. Dunite, hard and apparently unaltered.
 2. Dunite, somewhat friable and discolored, passing into 3.
 3. Talcose rock, fibrous, merging into 4.
 4. Enstatite, grayish and somewhat fibrous.
 5. Green chlorite, 6 to 15 inches in width.
 6. Green chlorite, corundum, and spinel, 6 to 8 feet wide.
 7. Chlorite. same as 5.
 8. Enstatite, same as 4.
 9. Talcose rock, same as 3.
10. Dunite. same as 2.
11. Dunite, same as 1.

The similarity of the two parts of the vein separated by the corundum zone, as already described and as illustrated in fig. 2, is very
apparent.

In fig. 2, 1 and 11 represent the apparently unaltered dunite; 2 and
10 represent dunite somewhat friable and stained and passing into
3 and 9—a fibrous talcose rock, often carrying a green actinolite and
some green chlorite; 4 and 8 represent a grayish, rather fibrous enstatite rock, which merges into 3 and 9; 5 and 7 represent a green chlorite,
which passes into 6—a mass of chlorite, corundum, and spinel.

Although the section just described is a special case, it was observed
that all of the dunite veins had the same character on both sides of
the corundum-bearing zone. As has been already stated, either a
talcose or a serpentine rock may be the limit of the cross section.
In one of the dunite veins at Corundum Hill near the west end of the
outcrop, the zone of corundum, chlorite, and vermiculites is in direct
contact, both on the hanging and on the foot wall, with a serpentine
rock. This zone is divided—in one place almost pinched out—by a
mass of serpentine.

At all of the corundum localities examined a careful search has been made to find the corundum directly surrounded by the peridotite, but it has been thus observed at only one locality—the Egypt mine, on the western slope of the Sampson Mountains, in Yancey County, N. C. The few specimens obtained were collected by Mr. U. S. Hayes, who developed the corundum property in that section. One specimen shows a prismatic crystal of the corundum surrounded by a granular peridotite (dunite), but with none of the chlorite minerals which usually intervene. The dunite is not quite fresh, but is stained a yellowish brown by iron oxide and is rather friable. On the basal surfaces of the corundum a little muscovite is developed. This has been observed on corundum from other localities.

Spinel has been found at a number of the corundum veins, and in

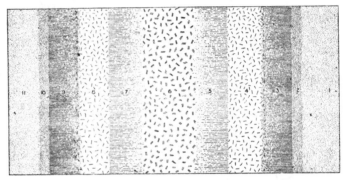

FIG. 2.—Ideal cross section of a corundum-dunite vein at the Corundum Hill mine, Macon County, N. C. 1, hard and unaltered dunite; 2, friable and discolored dunite; 3, talcose rock; 4, enstatite; 5, green chlorite; 6, green chlorite, corundum, and spinel; 7, green chlorite; 8, enstatite; 9, talcose rock; 10. friable and discolored dunite; 11, dunite.

a few cases it is very intimately associated with the corundum. At the Carter mine, near Democrat, Buncombe County, N. C., the corundum is found, in masses of a white and pink color, intergrown with a greenish-black spinel. The masses of corundum and spinel are partially surrounded by a deep-green chlorite, which has also been developed in places between the corundum and the spinel, although this contact of the corundum and the spinel is usually very sharp and distinct. A massive, coarsely to finely granular spinel is found at the Corundum Hill mine, Macon County, N. C., which has disseminated through it small grains and fragments of pink and white corundum.

The mineral chromite, which has always been found associated with these peridotite rocks, occurs sparingly in many of the corundum veins. It is a well-observed fact[1] that where there is any quantity of

---

[1] Am. Inst. Min. Eng., Vol. XXIX, 1899; February meeting.

corundum found in the peridotite rocks there is a scarcity of chromite, and where there is a large quantity of chromite there is a scarcity of corundum.

In a recent paper[1] I have discussed the origin of the corundum in the peridotite rocks, and have accepted the theory that the corundum was held in solution in the molten mass of the peridotite when it was intruded into the country rock, and that as the mass began to cool it was among the first minerals to separate. In these molten magmas the more basic minerals, corundum and spinel, would be the first to

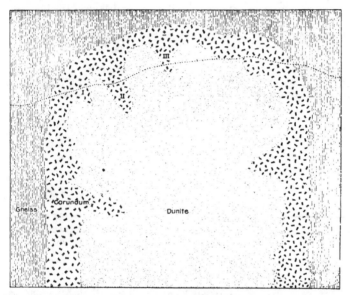

FIG. 3.—Ideal vertical cross section of a mass of peridotite soon after its intrusion in gneiss. The corundum zone is greatly exaggerated.

separate, and this separation would take place along the outer border of the mass, for there it would first cool. Convection currents would then tend to bring into this outer zone a new supply of material carrying alumina, and when this zone was reached crystallization would take place and the alumina would be deposited as corundum.

Fig. 3 represents an ideal appearance of a vertical cross section of a mass of dunite holding corundum in solution, soon after its intrusion into a gneiss. In this figure the corundum zone has been greatly exaggerated, in order to illustrate better the cross section. The corundum would be concentrated toward the borders of the

---

[1] Am. Jour. Sci., 4th series, Vol. VI, 1898, p. 49.

dunite, and would make a sharp and nearly regular contact with the gneiss. The contact with the dunite would be in some places sharp and regular and in other places very irregular, and masses of the corundum would penetrate the dunite. In some cases there would be a somewhat gradual transition from the corundum to the peridotite, as represented in fig. 4. The rapid erosion to which rocks in a moun-

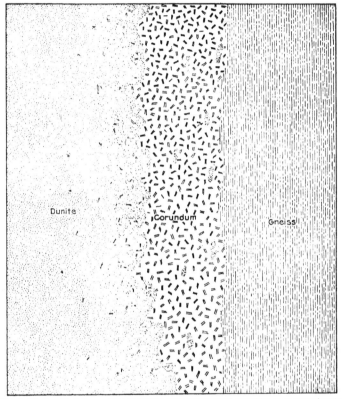

FIG. 4.—Ideal vertical cross section showing a somewhat gradual transition from corundum to peridotite.

tain region are subjected would readily wear them down to their present condition, represented by the dotted lines in fig. 3.

The corundum veins, I, II, and III, in fig. 3, which at the present time have no connection with one another, but are each separate and distinct, were at the time of their formation part of the corundum concentrated along the border of the dunite. Some of these veins would soon be worked out, while others might be explored for a hundred or more feet without any apparent change in their width.

The most important observations leading to the adoption of this theory are: The occurrence of the corundum surrounded by granular dunite and also by serpentine; its occurrence with and surrounded by spinel; the sharp contact between the gneiss and the alteration products of the contact vein; the development, on both sides of a corundum vein penetrating dunite, of the same sequence of alteration products, which are almost identical with those on the dunite side of a contact vein; the usual narrowing and pinching of the dunite veins, the trend of which is toward the center of the mass of peridotite, while the contact vein seems to extend down indefinitely.

At a number of the corundum veins in these peridotite rocks, feldspar, which is undoubtedly one of the original minerals of the rock and not a secondary product, is found associated with the corundum. There is a marked difference in the associated minerals when the feldspar is present; the chlorite is not so thoroughly developed, and enstatite is not so common, while margarite is rather abundant and zoisite is not uncommon. These last two minerals are rarely met with free from feldspar in the corundum veins.

The separation of alumina from these peridotite magmas has given rise to some interesting problems, which I have treated in a paper[1] published a short time ago. A summary of the conclusions reached is given here, as they bear directly upon the occurrence of the associated minerals, spinel, chromite, and feldspar, in a corundum vein.

From what has been observed in nature and from the experiments that have been made in the laboratory, it seems that the separation of alumina as corundum from molten magmas is dependent upon the composition of the chemical compounds that are the basis of the magma, upon the oxides that are dissolved with the alumina in the magma, and upon the amount of alumina itself.

1. When the magma is composed of a magnesium silicate without excess of magnesia, all the alumina held by such a magma will separate as corundum.

2. Where there is an excess of magnesia in the magma just described, it will unite with a portion of the alumina to form spinel, and the rest of the alumina will separate as corundum.

3. Where there is chromic oxide present in a magma composed essentially of magnesium silicate (as the peridotite rocks), and only a very little alumina and magnesia are present, these, uniting, separate with chromic oxide to form the mineral chromite, and no corundum or spinel is formed.

4. When peridotite magmas contain, besides the alumina, oxides of the alkalies and alkali earths, as soda, potash, and lime, a portion of

---

[1] Am. Jour. Sci., 4th series. Vol. VIII, 1899, p. 227.

the alumina is used in uniting with these oxides and with silica to form feldspar.

5. There is a strong tendency for the alumina to unite with the alkali and the alkali-earth oxides to form double silicates like feldspars, whether such silicates form the chief minerals of the resulting rock or are present in relatively small amount. There is, however, little tendency for the alumina to unite with magnesia to form double silicates when the magma is a magnesium silicate.

CORUNDUM IN BIOTITE, CONTACT ON SAXONITE.

At the asbestos quarry near Pelham, Mass., there is a large lens of the igneous saxonite variety of the peridotite rocks penetrating the acid gneiss of the country. The saxonite is very much altered to a depth of 3 to 12 feet, when the hard nearly fresh rock is encountered, which is of a dull-black color and is made up of grains of olivine and the orthorhombic pyroxene, bronzite. The black color of the rock is due to disseminated particles of chromite and magnetite. Part of the magnetite may be due to the alteration of the grains of olivine, similar to that observed in the dunites of North Carolina, where, at the beginning of its alteration, there is a deposition of magnetite in fine grains, which forms a network of black lines often outlining the grains of olivine.

Professor Emerson has made a petrographical examination of this rock and describes it as follows: [1]

This is a very fresh mixture of olivine and enstatite, both dusted through with black ore, largely chromite. It is a dull-black rock of very great toughness. The olivine grains have often many crystalline faces. The enstatite is in rare, small plates, with parallel sides and irregular ends. and with a fine wavy lamination, which is often marked by lines of black ore, generally concentrated in some part of the plate, especially the center. Although nearly colorless or pale bronzy in common light, it has marked pleochroism. It is plainly rhombic, and grades into the asbestiform decomposition product in veins running through the section.

None of the anthophyllite that is so abundant in the decomposed portion of the saxonite were observed in the fresh rock.

From the fresh rock to the surface and the contact with the gneiss the saxonite is more or less completely altered, and penetrating through this there is a network of veins of anthophyllite, which are more or less asbestiform. These veins vary in width from very thin seams to 8 inches, with some that are very much wider, from which fibrous masses have been obtained 20 to 30 inches long. It is these veins of fibrous anthophyllite that constitute the asbestos quarry of Pelham.

The saxonite is separated from the gneiss by a band of bronze-colored biotite, usually 4 to 8 inches thick, but in places reaching a thickness of 4 feet. In this wider portion there are nodules or imperfect crystals of corundum of a grayish color mottled with blue.

---

[1] Mon. U. S. Geol. Survey Vol. XXIX, p. 52.

These are often wrapped with chlorite. Nodules of a black-green hornblende and an emerald-green actinolite are also found in the biotite. There has been no great quantity of the corundum found.

This zone of biotite is probably the result of contact metamorphism of the saxonite on the gneiss, and the inclosing corundum was formed at the same time. This is similar to the large quantity of corundum occurring in biotite at the contact of saxonite and gneiss at the Bad Creek mine, Sapphire, N. C. (See page 62.)

CORUNDUM IN ENSTATITE.

Enstatite is rather common as a secondary product at many places where the corundum occurs in peridotite, and is thus an associate of corundum at these localities. Occurrences are rare, however, of corundum in an enstatite that is the original rock. Where thus found the rock is made up chiefly of the orthorhombic pyroxene, enstatite, in bladed interlocking crystals of a grayish color. It is always more or less decomposed into talc.

At the Rattlesnake mine, Sapphire, Jackson County, N. C., and on the West Fork of the French Broad River, in Transylvania County, N. C., corundum has been found sparingly in the borders of an enstatite rock.

Enstatite rocks are somewhat common in North Carolina, but accessory minerals in them are rare, and the most common one observed is chromite, in small grains.

CORUNDUM IN SERPENTINE.

At a number of peridotite localities in North Carolina and Georgia crystals and fragments of corundum have been found that were surrounded by serpentine, but nowhere in this southern section of the peridotite belt has corundum been found associated with the larger masses of serpentine. In Chester and Delaware counties, Pa.,[1] there is a long belt of serpentine rocks, part of which, at least, have been derived from peridotite rocks, and in connection with these, in the eastern part of Chester County and the western part of Delaware County, corundum has been found. In this, as in the peridotite, the corundum occurs near the contact of the country rock. Considerable plagioclase feldspar is associated with the corundum in the vein in a manner somewhat similar to the occurrence of this mineral at the Cullakeenee mine, Buck Creek, Clay County, N. C. In the South corundum has not been found as constantly associated with the serpentines as it is with the peridotites, but chromite is found very abundantly with many of them.

Cutting through the serpentines on the eastern slope of Spanish Peak, Plumas County, Cal., are white, coarse-grained dikes composed of corundum and oligoclase.

---

[1] Geol. Survey Pennsylvania, C⁴, 1883, p. 351.

CORUNDUM IN CHLORITE-SCHIST.

Besides being associated with chlorites in the peridotites just described, corundum is found in the long belts of chlorite-schist that traverse the country 10 or 12 miles southeast of Webster, Jackson County, N. C. These chlorite rocks, which sometimes attain a width of several hundred feet, are traceable for miles across the country. Almost the only constituent of these rocks is a green scaly chlorite, though sometimes there are present small grains of feldspar, and occasionally needles of amphibole. The chlorite is in small scales, never very coarse, as is sometimes the case in the zones about the peridotite, and often these are so minute as to give the rock a very compact appearance.

In one of these belts, on Caney Fork of Tuckasegee River, Jackson County, N. C., corundum is disseminated through the chlorite in small rounded masses, ranging in thickness from an inch to minute grains, and there the chlorite is not so compact as elsewhere. The corundum is usually wrapped with a white coating of mica, which is a secondary mineral derived from the corundum. The mica is often in radiating scales perpendicular to the outer surface of the corundum, and while in some cases it is very thin, in other cases it has replaced nearly all of the corundum, leaving but a grain of that mineral in the center.

CORUNDUM IN AMPHIBOLITE.

The occurrence of corundum in amphibolite is important, as the large deposits of emery corundum at Chester, Mass., are found in this rock. Under the head of amphibolite are included all those rocks that are composed entirely or chiefly of amphiboles. These rocks occur rather widely, including, as they do, those of Massachusetts, Georgia, and North Carolina, but with the exception of those that contain the emery they have not, up to the present time, been important in the production of corundum.

Associated with the peridotite rocks of Clay County, N. C., and the adjoining Towns County, Ga., are dikes of amphibolite, which are, for the most part, between the peridotite and the gneiss, although in some places they cut directly across the peridotite formation, but close to the contact of that rock with the gneiss. These dikes vary in width from 25 to over 300 feet, their average width being from 75 to 100 feet. The relation of these amphibolite dikes to the peridotite formation at Buck Creek, Clay County, N. C., is shown in fig. 5.

The groundmass of this amphibolite is a grass-green amphibole, containing 17 per cent of alumina, nearly 12 per cent of lime, and one-half of 1 per cent of magnesia, which is best classified under the edenite variety of aluminous amphiboles. The rich green color of the edenite is undoubtedly due to the presence of a small amount of chromic oxide, the analysis showing the presence of 0.38 per cent of this oxide. Many microscopic grains of picotite or chromite are scattered through the groundmass of the edenite. There is also present, in widely varying proportions, the plagioclase feldspar anorthite. The feldspar is not constant in all of the amphibolites, and where it does occur it varies in size from minute particles to masses as large as a pea.

The rock has often a very strikingly laminated structure, and grades from that to one which shows no lamination at all. It is exceedingly tough and very fine grained. The corundum, which occurs in the amphibolite as an accessory mineral, varies in size from minute particles to masses several inches in diameter, in which there are usually developed parting planes parallel to the unit rhombohedron. In color it varies from almost white to a deep ruby red, but the prevailing color is a deep pink.

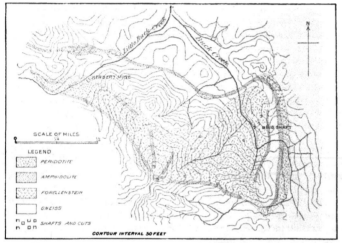

Fig. 5.—Map of the Buck Creek peridotite area, showing the relation of the amphibolite dikes.

On account of the exceeding toughness of the rock, and more particularly on account of the low percentage of corundum, these amphibolites are not of commercial value as a source of corundum; they do, however, make handsome mineral specimens.

On the eastern slope of the Blue Ridge, in the vicinity of Statesville, Iredell County, N. C., corundum has been found associated with an amphibolite composed of a dark-green hornblende. On account of the thickness of the soil and the depth to which these rocks have been decomposed, there are few places where the fresh rocks are exposed, and little is known of their extent. At Hunters, 7 miles west of Statesville, the amphibolite was exposed during

_____

[1] Bull. Geol. Survey North Carolina No. 11, 1896, p. 59.

exploration for corundum, which, according to Lewis,[1] was found to occur in fine brown vermiculite, developed in zones along the borders of and penetrating the amphibolite, and varying in thickness from a few inches to 3 or 4 feet.   Fig. 6 is an ideal illustration of the occurrence of corundum in the amphibolite at Hunters.   In this figure, *a* represents a feldspar vein that is sometimes encountered in the midst of the vermiculites, *b;* the feldspar is more or less altered to kaolin, and often bears corundum, although most of it was found in the vermiculite zones.   *b* represents the vermiculite zones carrying the corundum, which is in crystals and in rounded masses of crystals clustered together.   Margarite sometimes accompanies it, and large masses made up almost entirely of these two minerals have been found on the surface in this region.   *c* represents radiating borders of actinolite that inclose large masses of what was once amphibolite, but which

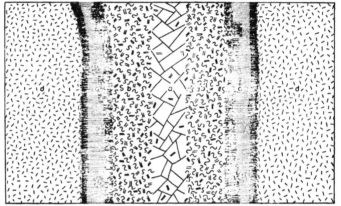

FIG. 6.—Ideal vertical cross section of corundum in amphibolite at Hunters, Iredell County, N. C.

is now nothing but a mass of ocherous clay, bearing occasional needles of hornblende and scales of vermiculite. The outer portions, *d*, are dark-green amphibolite.

CORUNDUM (EMERY) IN AMPHIBOLITE AT CHESTER, MASS.

The most widely known occurrence of corundum in amphibolite is that of the emery at Chester, Mass., an elaborate description of which is given by Prof. B. K. Emerson[1] in his exhaustive work on the geology of old Hampshire County, Mass.

Extending almost continuously across the State, north and south of Chester, there is a band of amphibolite that is conformable throughout its entire extent with the sericitic schists of this section of the

---

[1] Mon. U. S. Geol. Survey Vol. XXIX, 1898.

State. The strike of this band of amphibolite is dependent upon the windings of the schists, and its dip is approximately 90°. Its width will average only a few rods, but in the vicinity of Chester, a few miles both north and south of the town, it is three-quarters of a mile wide, and it is in connection with this broad band that the emery is found. It occurs on the eastern side of the amphibolite and is separated from the sericitic schists by a narrow band of amphibolite, varying in width from an inch or two to nearly 18 feet. Sometimes there has been considerable serpentinization of the amphibolite, and the emery is separated from the schists by serpentine. Across the Westfield River from the point where the emery is first encountered, the amphibolite is replaced by serpentine, and it is in this bed of serpentine that crystals of this mineral, pseudomorphous after olivine, are said to occur, specimens of these being in the geological collection at Amherst College.

The amphibolite is in appearance a finely laminated rock made up of interrupted thin sheets of feldspar grains and of jet-black needles of hornblende, and usually contains more or less green epidote.

The sericitic schists on the west of the amphibolite, which are described by Professor Emerson under the head of the "Rowe schist," [1] are biotitic and feldspathic, and often contain garnets that are more or less altered to chlorite. The schists on the east are described as the "Savoy schist," [2] and are chloritic sericite-schists, mostly of a light-gray color, with a shade of green, due to the chlorite that is mixed with the muscovite. When the chlorite can not be seen with the eye it is readily detected under the microscope. In some places the proportion of the chlorite has increased until there are considerable aggregations of this mineral along the planes of lamination. Garnet and pyrite are also abundant in certain portions of the schist.

The emery vein can be followed for a distance of nearly 5 miles, starting from the point where it is first encountered, at the north end of the broad band of amphibolite, on the left bank of the Westfield River, just above the railroad bridge of the Boston and Albany Railroad. The general strike of the vein is a little east of south and runs for the most part parallel to the line of contact of the amphibolite and schist. Emery is not found throughout the vein, but can be almost continuously followed by means of streaks of chlorite. The vein varies in width from a few feet to 10 or 12 feet, the average width of the emery being about 6 feet. Upon both sides of the emery there are usually developed thin seams of chlorite varying from 1 inch to 6 inches or more in width. During the early history of the mine a seam of feldspar was encountered, about 12 inches wide, lying to the east of the emery and bordered on both sides by chlorite 3 or 4 inches wide. There is also more or less chlorite developed in the mass of the ore body, which varies from some portions that are an almost pure mag-

[1] Mon. U. S. Geol. Survey Vol. XXIX, 1898, p. 76.   [2] Ibid., p. 156.

netite to others where there is an intimate admixture of magnetite and corundum. At the Sackett mine (described on page 68) the corundum, of a bronze color and luster, is coarsely crystallized, giving the ore a porphyritic appearance. Sometimes the corundum has crystallized out in blue and white crystals and in masses of a pound or two in weight.

ORIGIN OF THE EMERY.

It is a perplexing question to decide from the examination of this and the surrounding rocks whether the amphibolite is of sedimentary or igneous origin, for there are many indications that point to one and to the other. It is not improbable that some portions of this band of amphibolite, which extends across the State, may have been formed in one way and other portions in the other. Professor Emerson has examined this belt of rocks for practically its entire distance across the State, and while he is inclined to consider this band of amphibolite of sedimentary origin, he does not, if I understand him correctly, see anything antagonistic to the view that at least a portion of this amphibolite is an intrusive igneous rock. I have examined only that portion of the amphibolite adjacent to the emery vein, and from my observations I had come to the conclusion that this part of the amphibolite band was an igneous rock that had been intruded into the schists along their line of weakness, and that the magnetite and emery had been the first minerals to separate out from this magma. The reasons that have led me to this conclusion are given briefly below.

The position of the amphibolite, with a dip of practically 90°, lying between the Rowe and Savoy schists, which would have been a line of least resistance, suggests an igneous origin. What seems to me opposed to the acceptance of a sedimentary origin for this broad band of amphibolite is the separation of the vein of emery and magnetite from the sericitic schist on the east by a band of the amphibolite varying in width from a few feet to 18 feet, which, as far as can be judged superficially, is identical in every way with the amphibolite on the west of the vein. Yet, if the amphibolite and emery are of igneous origin, it would naturally be expected that emery would occur on the west side of the amphibolite, but none has been found there, although it is not certain that it does not occur.

Only a small amount of carbonates has been found in connection with the amphibolite and emery—no more than could readily be accounted for as secondary minerals.

Then, again, chromite has been found in connection with the serpentine that is associated with the amphibolite, some of which is undoubtedly an alteration of this rock. The presence of the chromite in the serpentine is to me a very good indication of its igneous origin, and its being the alteration product of a basic magnesian rock. This, then, would indicate the existence of former masses of a basic magnesian rock which have been changed into serpentine, the serpentinization continuing into the amphibolite for some distance.

The emery is not continuous along the strike of the vein, but occurs in a series of pockets in the vein that dip about 30° to the north. In going from one pocket to another along the strike there is often nothing to indicate the vein but a small seam of chlorite. The pockets are almost continuous in the direction of the so-called dip and hold this dip very constantly.

It seems to me that this portion of the amphibolite band was an igneous mass intruded after the formation of the sericitic schists, and either after or at the time these schists were tilted to their present position, and that the emery bed is the result of the differentiation of components of the mass that were held in solution by the igneous magma.

The theory that Professor Emerson[1] proposes is also probable, viz:

That the emery-magnetite vein was originally a deposit of limonite which was formed by the replacement of limestone and into wh ch alumina was carried by infiltrating solutions and deposited as allophane and gibbsite. The subsequent metamorphism of the bed, although it may well have been intimately connected with the extremely violent mechanical forces to which the strata have been subjected, was largely completed before these forces had ceased their activity, as is shown by the jointing and brecciation of the magnetite and emery. * * * The less altered ferruginous limestone below was changed into the epidotic amphibolite.

Many points that can be noticed support this conclusion, but these also indicate an igneous origin for the amphibolite. No fresh peridotite rocks have been observed in this section, and the nearest are probably across the Connecticut River at Pelham, where an igneous mass of saxonite is encountered. The presence, however, of chromite in the serpentine associated with this amphibolite is to me very good evidence for believing that the serpentines have an igneous origin, and it is very probable that they are alterations of former masses of an intruded peridotite.

If any deep mining is undertaken on the emery, new evidence may be brought to light that will determine decidedly what may have been the origin of these amphibolites and emery deposits.

CORUNDUM IN NORITE.

In the vicinity of Peekskill, Westchester County, N. Y., corundum has been found associated with norites, which have been described by G. H. Williams.[2] These rocks belong to the Cortland series, of which the prevailing rock type is one that is characterized by the presence of the mineral hypersthene. But though this mineral is

---

[1] Mon. U. S. Geol. Survey Vol. XXIX. p 145.
[2] Am. Jour. Sci., 3d series, Vol. XXXIII, 1887, pp. 135, 191.

there so abundant, a normal norite, containing nothing but a plagioclase feldspar and hypersthene, is extremely rare. There is more
or less biotite, hornblende, or augite developed in nearly all rocks of
this class, so that there is a gradual transition from normal norite to
mica-diorite, hornblende-diorite, and gabbro. The intermediate varieties are much more common than the extremes, and they have been
classified by Williams according to the prevailing nonfeldspathic
mineral. Where hypersthene prevails the rocks are grouped as
norites, being subdivided into normal norite, horneblende-norite, mica-
norite, and augite-norite, according to the presence of these different
minerals in the rock. These so grade into each other that no sharp
line can be drawn between them.

Associated with the norites, 3 and 4 miles southeast of Peekskill,
N. Y., are deposits of magnetite and emery. It is not at all unlikely
that these veins are the products of the differentiation of the molten
norite magma, by which the basic portion of the magma has been concentrated near its outer surface, a gradual transition occurring toward
the center to the more acid norite. This occurrence would be similar
to that of the pyrrhotites which have separated out from the norites
of Norway, as described by Vogt.[1] In that case the pyrrhotite was
concentrated toward the border of the norite, and there is at some
places a gradual transition from the pure pyrrhotite through a pyrrho-
tite-norite to the pure norite, while at others there is a sharp contact
between them. The deposits of magnetite and emery are not in a continuous vein, but are more like segregated masses. Attempts have been
made to work these for both iron and emery, but as iron-ore deposits
they were soon abandoned. They are still being worked to a certain
extent for emery by the Jackson Mills Company, of Easton, Pa.; the
Tanite Company, of Stroudsburg, Pa.; and H. M. Quinn, of Philadelphia, Pa. An examination of the emery ore by J. D. Dana[2] and G. H.
Williams,[3] has shown that the corundum component is often scattered
rather sparingly through the ore, and what had formerly been supposed to be green chlorite was found to be the iron-magnesian spinel,
pleonaste. The corundum in the emery varies from small, colorless
grains to crystals 7 mm. in diameter, which show a hexagonal outline.
In other parts of the emery the corundum grains are larger and of a
bluish color.

The pleonaste, which is so commonly associated with the emery,
has been found at the Cruger iron mine, in the eastern part of the
township, as veins in a nearly normal norite, into which it passes by
gradual transitions. The most compact specimens of the ore at this
mine are found to contain the various mineral components of the
norite, i. e., hypersthene feldspar, biotite, and garnet, no corundum
having been observed here.

[1] Zeitschr. für Prakt. Geol., Nos 1.4. and 7.1893.
[2] Am. Jour. Sci., 3d series, Vol. XX. 1880, p. 199.
[3] Idem, Vol. XXXIII. 1887. p. 194.

This gradual transition of the pleonaste and iron ore into the normal norite and the occurrence of the norite minerals in the compact ore are strong evidence that these ore bodies were formed by the differentiation of the molten norite magma.

In the vicinity of these norites there are small masses of peridotite, but no corundum has been found associated with them.

CORUNDUM IN BASIC MINETTE.

Near the entrance of Yogo Gulch, in Fergus County, Mont., two parallel dikes of igneous rock have been observed cutting through the limestones. These dikes are about 800 feet apart, and can be followed for over a mile in a nearly east-west course. Their general width is from 6 to 20 feet, but they are occasionally 75 feet wide. They are much decomposed near the surface, but in working them for the sapphires which they contain the nearly unaltered rock has been encountered.

The rock has a dark-gray, decided basic appearance, and is very tough, breaking with an uneven fracture. Scattered through it are light-green and white fragments, which are by far the most conspicuous of any of the mineral components of the rock. These are a pyroxene that is more or less decomposed and calcite. Some of these white fragments are probably the barium carbonate witherite, for in the concentrates obtained from washing the decomposed portions of the dike a considerable quantity of this mineral was found. Numberless crystals of pyrite, not over a millimeter in diameter and almost perfect trapezohedrons, were also found in these concentrates. A few scattered tablets of biotite, from 2 to 3 mm. in diameter, were observed. The sapphire variety of corundum is found rather sparingly in this rock in well-formed, flat, tabular crystals, some of which are half an inch in diameter.

Professor Pirsson, of the Sheffield Scientific School, has made a petrographical examination of this rock, and describes it as follows: [1]

In the section the rock at once shows its character as a dark, basic lamprophyre, consisting mainly of biotite and pyroxene. There is a little iron ore present, but its amount is small and much less than is usually seen in rocks of this class. The biotite is strongly pleochroic, varying between an almost colorless and a strong, clear, brown tint. It occurs in ragged masses, rarely showing crystal outline, and it contains a large amount of small apatite crystals. The pyroxene is of a pale-green tint, with the habit of diopside, and is filled with many inclusions, now altered, but probably originally of glass; in some crystals these inclusions are so abundant as to render the mineral quite spongy. The grains sometimes show crystal form, but are mostly anhedral and vary in size, though the evidence is not sufficient to show two distinct generations.

These two minerals lie closely crowded together, and no feldspars are seen in the rock. The interstices between them consist of a small amount of a clouded, brownish, kaolin-like aggregate, which appears to represent some former feldspathoid

[1] Am. Jour. Sci., 4th series, Vol. IV, 1897, p. 421.

component, possibly leucite, perhaps analcite. * * ° Some calcite in agglomerated granules is also seen in the section.

This calcite does not appear to be of secondary origin, and is probably due to fragments of limestone that were picked up as the igneous mass forced its way up through the limestones and were converted into calcite.

As has been indicated by Professor Pirsson [1] in his paper, the amount of biotite in this rock shows that it is closely related to the minettes, and although it is lacking in feldspar it has the biotite and pyroxene of these rocks. It is a more basic type of these and is also similar to the shonkinites from the Highwood Mountains, Montana, described by Weed and Pirsson.[2]

The sapphires, which are all of some shade of blue, occur but rarely in the rock, and from their sharp, distinct crystals and their general distribution it is very evident that they have crystallized out of the molten magma at the time of its intrusion, similarly to crystals of feldspar in porphyry. The alumina of the sapphires was not an original constituent of the magma, but, as has been shown by Pirsson,[3] was due to inclusions of clay sediments taken up from the strata through which it passed. The Belt formation, consisting of clay shales of great but unknown thickness, undoubtedly underlies the limestones, and the included fragments of these shales were the source of the alumina of the sapphires. These included fragments would be dissolved by the molten magma and thus form local areas that would be very rich in alumina. As the magma began to cool corundum crystals would separate out in these alumina-rich areas.

CORUNDUM IN ANDESITE.

The occurrence of corundum in andesite in the United States was first described by Kunz.[4] He described a dike of andesite at Ruby Bar, near Eldorado Bar, on the Missouri River, 12 miles northeast of Helena, Mont. As described by him, this rock is in a dike cutting the slates of the country and is a vesicular mica-augite-andesite, which is made up of a groundmass of feldspar microlite and a brownish glass, in which are many particles of biotite and crystals of augite.

A similar occurrence has been observed by myself on the river 6 miles above Eldorado Bar, at French Bar, which is nearly 12 miles due east of Helena. At this locality a narrow dike, 3 to 6 feet wide, was found cutting through the slates in this section. The trend of the dike is N. 5° to 10° E., and it dips about 45° E. It was encountered by miners who were working the gravels of the bar for sapphires, and it has been exposed at but one point, so that its extent is not known.

[1] Am. Jour. Sci., 4th series, Vol. IV, 1897, p. 422.
[2] Idem, Vol. I, 1895, p. 467.
[3] Idem, Vol. IV, 1897, p. 423.
[4] Idem, Vol. IV, 1897, p. 418; Min. Mag., Vol. IX, 1891, p. 396; Seventeenth, Eighteenth, Nineteenth, Twentieth Ann. Repts. U. S. Geol. Survey.

The rock is fine grained, of a rather light-gray color, and a decided basic appearance. Biotite is the most conspicuous mineral and occurs in small, flat, tabular plates, sometimes with distinct crystal outline, and up to a millimeter or two in diameter. In some specimens of the rock there are nodules, 5 to 10 mm. in diameter, that appear to be partially decomposed feldspar. The augite, which is prominent in the thin section, is not very apparent in the hand specimen.

Prof. L. V. Pirsson, of Yale University, has kindly examined thin sections of this rock for me and says that the rock is an altered augite-mica-syenite. It contains unaltered phenocrysts of a clear brown biotite which are well crystallized and which sometimes show slight resorption. It also contains phenocrysts of augite of a pale-brown color, variable in size, the largest 2 mm. across, replaced in the majority of cases by pseudomorphs of calcite. Besides this pseudomorphous calcite there is also a considerable amount of this mineral in irregular masses or streaks, which may in part be the filling of steam pores and in part be pseudomorphous after hornblende; this, however, could not be definitely determined. The minerals just mentioned are embedded in a groundmass of a brown glass which is everywhere speckled and dotted with microlites of a lath-shaped plagioclase feldspar. These are small and somewhat altered, so that their determination is not entirely satisfactory, but they appear to be oligoclase.

The rock is thus porphyritic, and the structure of the groundmass is typical for the hyalopilitic structure of Rosenbusch. In many respects it closely resembles the augite-porphyrite of Weiselberg, weiselbergite.[1]

One feature that is brought out in the thin sections is the somewhat laminated character of the rock in one direction, while in the slide cut at right angles to this a well-characterized flow structure is observed, all the longer axes of the minerals pointing in one direction. This indicates movements of flowing lava after the components had formed.

The corundum crystals occur very sparingly in the rock, and those that were observed were not so sharp and distinct as the blue sapphires.

I could obtain no definite information regarding the location of Ruby Bar and no one of the bars is now called by that name. It is possible that the bar described by Kunz is the same as the one now known as French Bar. From the description given of Ruby Bar, it is apparently not so far up the river as French Bar.

CORUNDUM IN SYENITE.

On a high foothill between Gallatin and Madison rivers, in Gallatin County, Mont., corundum has been found in a rock that is

---

[1] Rosenbusch. Mass. Gest., 3d ed., p. 953.

composed essentially of orthoclase feldspar, corundum, and biotite, with the feldspar predominating. This would classify the rock as a corundum-bearing biotite-syenite. The rock, for the most part, has a somewhat gneissoid structure, and in these portions the corundum is more or less finely divided, being in fine grains and small crystals. In other portions, where the corundum is coarsely crystallized, the rock has something of a pegmatitic character, and the corundum is surrounded by the orthoclase. The crystals of corundum vary in size; the largest ones are 1½ inches long and from a quarter to a half an inch in diameter. They are fairly well developed in the prismatic zone, but many of them, especially the larger ones, are rounded. In color they vary from bluish gray to almost colorless. The percentage of the corundum in the rock is large, and from a superficial examination it could be compared to the percentage of quartz in an average granite. The biotite is in small tablets, without definite crystal outline, and the tablets are often so arranged as to give the mass of the rock its gneissic appearance. The orthoclase did not show any crystal outline even in the larger fragments.

This occurrence of corundum was discovered by Prof. F. W. Traphagen, of Bozeman, Mont., to whom I am indebted for the specimens.

From the appearance of the hand specimens, this occurrence of corundum is similar to that in the syenite of Ontario, Canada, recently described by Blue [1] and Miller.[2]

CORUNDUM IN AMPHIBOLE-SCHIST.

At the Sheffield mine, in Cowee Township, Macon County, N. C., corundum has been mined in a saprolitic rock at various times for a number of years. In a shaft sunk to determine the depth of the corundum-bearing saprolite, solid, unaltered rock was encountered. The shaft, which was 87 feet deep, passed through the following rocks: The first 12 feet (*a*) was through the saprolite, in which there were seams of kaolin; the next 2 feet (*b*) were corundum bearing. From 14 to 28 feet (*c*) the same saprolite was encountered; the next 2 feet (*d*) were corundum bearing, followed by 10 feet (*e*, 30 to 40 feet) of the saprolite, and 2 more feet (*f*) that were corundum bearing. From 42 to 63 feet (*g*) the rock began to be less decomposed, and from 63 to 66 feet (*h*) another seam of corundum-bearing rock was encountered. From this point to the bottom of the shaft the rock became more and more solid, until at 77 feet (*i*) the fresh rock was encountered. These various seams in the rock are very pronounced. They dip 30° toward the west near the top, but become nearly horizontal near the bottom

---

[1] Trans. Am. Inst. Min. Eng., Vol. XXVIII, 1898, p. 565, and Rept. Bureau of Mines, Ontario, Vol. VIII, Part II, 1899, p. 240.

[2] Rept. Bureau of Mines, Ontario, Vol. VII, Part III, 1898, p. 238, and Vol. VIII, Part II, 1899, p. 205.

of the shaft. The seams of decomposed feldspar observed in *a* become less and less kaolinized, until in *i* the seams are of pure plagioclase feldspar. In *i* there are two seams of corundum similar to *b*, *d*, and *f*, although in the fresh rock the corundum seams are not as pronounced as in the saprolitic rock. There is often a considerable amount of feldspar bordering the seams of the corundum. The general trend of the rock is about N. 5° to 10° E.

From what could be seen of the solid and the saprolitic rocks, it is evident that the corundum occurs at intervals in the rock in seams a few feet in width. While the corundum may comprise 10 per cent or more of these veins, the amount in the rock that it would be necessary to mine would probably not be over a few per cent. The actual width of the dike is not known, but the saprolitic rock has been cut across for about 100 feet in a direction nearly at right angles to its strike.

The fresh rock at the bottom of the shaft is somewhat varied in appearance, and while it does not show any definite gneissoid structure, it sometimes closely resembles it. There are streaks in the rock a few inches thick, the more finely divided portions of which are distinctly gneissoid.

Some portions of the rock are decidedly porphyritic, and contain phenocrysts of a light-gray amphibole, a centimeter in diameter, in a groundmass of feldspar. A large part of the rock is made up, however, of small, roughly outlined prismatic crystals of an amphibole, probably hornblende, and irregular fragments of plagioclase feldspar. The hornblende is almost black in color, but in thin splinters it has a bronze luster and a deep resinous color. Biotite of a deep-brown color occurs sparingly, and a pink garnet is rather abundant. This part of the rock has a gneissoid structure and contains the corundum. The corundum is of a light to a purplish-pink color and occurs in nodules up to 2 or 3 cm. in diameter. Some streaks in the rock are highly garnetiferous, composed essentially of the garnet and plagioclase feldspar or of garnet and biotite. Chalcopyrite occurs very sparingly in these portions of the rock. Small particles of graphite have been observed in the coarsely crystallized portions.

Professor Pirsson has kindly made a microscopical examination of this rock, the results of which are embodied in the following paragraphs:

In thin section the microscope disclosed the minerals hornblende, plagioclase feldspar, garnet, biotite, muscovite, staurolite, and rutile. Hornblende is the most common, forming about two-fifths of the section, while of the remainder plagioclase and garnet occur in about equal quantities and the others in comparatively insignificant amounts.

The hornblende is formless, but tends to irregular columns, almost invariably extended in the plane of schistosity. It has very rarely a somewhat stringy tendency in its cleavage, but is usually homogeneous in broad plates. Its color is a clear olive brown, and it is somewhat pleochroic, but not strongly so. It is everywhere dotted by the small grains of garnet. which rarely show good crystal form. The garnet occurs as associated also with the plagioclase.

The plagioclase occurs twinned according to the albite law only. In sections perpendicular to 010 the lamellæ show extinction as great as 30°, and the plagioclase is therefore rich in lime and as basic as labradorite, which it probably is. It shows strong evidence of shearing movement in the rock; it is often broken, exhibits rolling extinction, and the albite lamellæ are curved and bent. It runs along the planes of schistosity between the feldspars and forms a mosaic of angular broken grains.

Staurolite was found in rather broad, irregular grains, and rutile in small, irregular grains and well-crystallized prisms.

Professor Pirsson has indicated that the character and structure of this rock, composed chiefly of amphibole, labradorite, and garnet, suggest most strongly that it is a metamorphosed igneous rock of the gabbroid family. During metamorphism the augite of the gabbro would be converted into the brown hornblende; any iron ore that was present would be taken up by the hornblende and garnet. The rutile would have resulted from the titanic acid that is a regular component of the iron ores in these gabbro or diabase rocks. Staurolite is a mineral that would be rather naturally expected, as it is usually a mineral of metamorphism, and its natural home is in the schistose rocks. The feldspar has suffered the least (except the corundum) chemically, and shows only the shearing of dynamic processes.

The corundum does not occur in crystals, but in small fragments and in elongated nodules, which are cracked and seamed and appear to have been drawn out by the shearing processes. The general character and shape of the fragments of corundum would indicate that they were original constituents of the igneous rock and were not formed during its metamorphism.

The exact classification of this rock is not easy, but it is probably an amphibole-schist.

CORUNDUM IN GNEISS.

Corundum has been found in North Carolina in the ordinary gneiss of the same belt of crystalline rocks in which the peridotites occur. A number of occurrences, part of which may be corundum in gneiss, are described under the head of mica-schist; some of the rock that was at first thought to be a gneiss is now known to be a quartz-schist.

In the eastern part of Clay County, N. C., on the southern slope of Gross Ridge of the Chunky Gal Mountains, just above Thumping Creek, corundum has been found in the gneiss at a number of points. The rocks are so covered with soil and decomposed rock that the exact relation of the corundum-bearing gneiss to the normal gneiss can not be determined, but from what can be seen the former appears to be in narrow bands cutting through the latter. In structure the gneiss is distinctly laminated and very fine grained, except the portions immediately surrounding the corundum, where its constituents

are much more coarsely crystallized, especially the biotite. It is a
hornblende-gneiss, showing but little mica except where associated
with the corundum.

The corundum occurs in nodules and crystals, half an inch and
smaller in diameter, sometimes wrapped with muscovite in a manner
similar to that described for the corundum in the chlorite-schists
(p. 21). The crystals are prismatic, with the length of the prism
usually two or three times its diameter. Occasionally they are very
flat, with the prism not over a quarter of an inch in length and half
an inch in diameter, and from their appearance these crystals are
known locally as "button" corundum.

This occurrence of corundum in gneiss is in no way associated with
the peridotite rocks of this section of the country. It is, however,
very similar to the occurrence of corundum in quartz-schist described
below. None of the peridotite rocks in which the corundum is so
commonly found in this section of North Carolina have been found
associated with these bands of gneiss.

CORUNDUM IN MICA-SCHIST.

It has recently been observed that portions or bands of the crystalline rocks of the southwestern part of North Carolina and the northeastern part of Georgia are corundum bearing. The composition of
these rocks varies from those that are a normal gneiss to those that
contain no feldspar and can best be described as quartz-schist composed of biotite, mica, and quartz. Some portions of the rock are
rich in garnet, others are almost entirely free from this mineral, and
occasionally there are also small bands of white quartzite. The rocks
are distinctly laminated and are frequently intersected by granitic
dikes, some of which are coarsely crystallized and of a pegmatitic
character. These dikes are often parallel with the bedding of the
schists, although many of them cut irregularly through them. Where
these dikes are parallel to the bedding of the schists, the laminated
structure of the latter is much more apparent. The general strike of
these crystalline rocks is about northeast to southwest and the dip is
about 30° NW.

Portions or bands of these schists are corundum bearing, but they
are irregularly defined and gradually merge into the normal rock.
They have a similar relation to the normal schists as the garnet-bearing
bands of a gneiss to the normal gneiss in which they occur. These
bands are not veins in any sense of the word, but are simply portions of the same mass of crystalline rocks in which corundum occurs
as a constituent of the rock. They vary in width from a foot or
two to 12 or 15 feet, but in these wider ones the corundum-bearing
portion is not continuous and is intercepted by streaks of barren rock
and granitic dikes. The bands can be traced for a distance of 5 or
6 miles in a northeast-southwest direction, sometimes outcropping

continuously for nearly a mile. There are at least two of these corundum-bearing bands which are parallel to each other and about 2 miles apart. The only variation that has been observed in them is in the percentage of corundum and garnet; otherwise they are identical. The amount of corundum is never large, and from determinations made on samples from various parts of the deposits it will not average over 4 or 5 per cent.

The corundum occurs for the most part in small particles and fragments that have no regular shape and are of a gray, white, and bluish-white color or almost colorless. It is also in crystals which vary in size from some that are very minute to some that are $2\frac{1}{2}$ inches long and about one-half inch in diameter, and which are usually fairly well developed in the prism zone.

It is probable that these schists are the result of the metamorphism of sandstones and shales formed from alluvial deposits many thousand feet in thickness that were once the bed of the ocean. By lateral compression these have been folded and raised into the mountain ranges of this region. That these have been much higher than at the present time is very evident from the granitic dikes, which are of deep-seated origin. By decomposition and erosion the mountains have been worn down to their present condition, thus exposing the schists in contact with the granitic dikes which have aided in their thorough metamorphism. The shales were rich in alumina, and during their metamorphism the excess of the alumina crystallized as corundum along the planes of lamination, so that during the subsequent weathering the corundum has been left in knotty nodules, studding the surface of the rock and giving it the appearance of containing a high percentage of the mineral.

Genth [1] has described an occurrence of corundum in Patrick County, Va., about 2 miles from Stuart, where it has been found in the mica-schists on a knob of Bull Mountain. These schists are talcose and chloritic in character and are intersected by a number of granitic dikes. The portions of the schists in which the corundum occurs are gneissoid in character. This occurrence is decidedly different from that in Clay County, N. C., and more like the corundum-bearing schists near the headwaters of Caney Fork of Tuckasegee River, in Jackson County. The schists are in rather narrow bands that can be followed for some distance across the county. They are not true chlorite-schists like those described on page 21, but are made up largely of an elastic mica (probably muscovite) with some chlorite. The corundum occurs in rough crystals and nodules up to 1 inch in length and half an inch in diameter, of a grayish-white to white color and colorless. It is readily cleaned, and tests made upon the cleaned product show that it is well adapted for the manufacture of the vitrified wheel.

---

[1] Am. Jour. Sci., 3d series, Vol. XXXIX, 1890, p. 47.

CORUNDUM IN LIMESTONE.[1]

Extending from Byram, Sussex County, N. J., to Warwick Township, New York, a distance of about 25 miles, there is a belt of limestone having a general northeast-southwest strike, which widens out toward its northern end. About 1828 a specimen of sapphire corundum was found at Franklin Furnace in a detached piece of rock composed essentially of feldspar, and although search was made no more specimens were found in this vicinity. A few years later sapphire corundum was found in Newton Township, about 6 miles from Franklin Furnace, embedded in a feldspar and partly surrounded by a carbonate. This occurs near the contact of the limestone with the granitic rocks of this section, and it is very evidently the result of contact metamorphism. Dana reports the occurrence of sapphire corundum in these limestones near Newton and Vernon, Sussex County, N. J., and near Amity, Orange County, and Crugers Station, Westchester County, N. Y.

Prof. W. P. Blake[2] has described the occurrence of red sapphire corundum in the white crystalline limestones in Vernon Township, Sussex County, N. J. The finest specimens were ruby red in color and the others were of various shades of purple. The crystals were translucent, but no transparent ones were observed. They were embedded in the limestone and it is not improbable that crystals may occur in the similar rocks of the adjoining counties of New York.

The New Jersey occurrences seem to be well authenticated, but those from New York are not. In the report of the New York State Museum for 1895 on the mineral resources of the State there is no mention of the occurrence of corundum at this locality, and in the report for 1898 it is stated that no sapphire corundum is found in the State.

CORUNDUM IN CYANITE.

The occurrences of corundum associated with cyanite are quite widespread, and at times there are large masses of cyanite in which are numerous hexagonal crystals of corundum. At Litchfield, Conn.,[3] a mass of cyanite containing crystals of a dark, grayish-blue corundum, which was said to have weighed 1,500 pounds, was found. Large masses of cyanite have been found at various points in North Carolina in which there were well-developed crystals of corundum.

All the occurrences that have been noted have been from surface specimens, and the rocks in the vicinity have always been either schists or gneisses. It is without doubt in connection with these rocks that the cyanite and corundum originated. I do not believe that the cyanite is usually an alteration product of the corundum, as has been sug-

[1] Am. Jour. Sci., 1st series, Vol. XXI, 1832, p. 319.
[2] Idem, 2d series, Vol. XIII, 1852, p. 116.
[3] Idem, 1st series, Vol. VI, 1823, p. 219.

gested by Genth,[1] but that they were both formed during the metamorphism of the rocks from which the schists and gneisses have been
derived.

SUMMARY OF CORUNDUM OCCURRENCES.

From the facts presented in the preceding pages, the occurrences
of corundum are seen to be of much greater variety than was
formerly supposed. While the large concentrated masses are still
confined to the basic magnesian rocks, corundum is scattered in small
amounts through a number of other rocks, and in the aggregate is in
very large quantity.

Of the igneous magmas there are two that are very distinct from each
other and that can be designated as the lime-magnesia and the alkaline series. In the first the mineral components of the rock are free
from alumina, and where there has been alumina in solution in the
molten magma it has all separated out either as corundum or spinel.
In the second series, however, it is only the excess of alumina that
has separated out as corundum, by far the larger percentage having
united with the alkaline oxides to form a feldspar. In all the occurrences that have been examined this phenomenon has been constant.

It is very evident that there are magmas that contain an excess of
alumina just as there are magmas with an excess of silica, and it is
evident that the alumina separates out as corundum in the same manner that silica separates as quartz in granitic rocks.

DISTRIBUTION OF CORUNDUM.

Most of the corundum that has been mined for abrasive purposes
has been obtained from the eastern part of the United States, and has
been found associated with the long belt of basic magnesian rocks
extending from Massachusetts to Alabama. It is in the southern portion of this belt, in North Carolina and Georgia, that these rocks have
their greatest extent, and it is in this region that the greatest quantity
of corundum has been found. During the past few years, however,
North Carolina is the only State that has produced any corundum and
Massachusetts and New York the only ones that have produced any
emery.

While the production of corundum has been limited almost entirely
to one locality in North Carolina, it is not because this is the only
known deposit of this mineral in quantity, but because the better
deposits have not been worked. The emery deposit that has proved
of the most economic importance, and which has produced practically
all the emery mined in the United States, is at Chester, Mass. The
amount of corundum that has been mined during the past year is
very much less than the amount of emery, although its market value

---

[1] Am. Philos. Soc., Vol. XIII, 1873, p. 22.

is twice that of the emery and there is a large demand for a well-cleaned commercial product. There are a number of reasons for this condition: the better deposits have been so controlled and tied up that they could not be worked, an imperfectly cleaned product has been put on the market, and other minerals have been substituted for this one.

It is still too soon to predict to what extent recent discoveries of corundum in Canada and India will add to its production. Some of the Canadian deposits in Ontario were granted by the government to the Canada Corundum Company, Limited, of Toronto, and this company began extensive operations on the deposits at the beginning of 1900. This corundum, which occurs in a syenite similar to that described on page 30, has been thoroughly tested and has given fairly satisfactory results. The reports of the bureau of mines at Toronto show that this ore carries 14.7 per cent of corundum and that a very clean product is obtained. If the ore from this extensive Canadian bed continues to carry so large a percentage of the mineral, can be readily cleaned, and shows good abrasive qualities, this deposit should play an important part in the world's production of corundum (see page 88).

The India corundum occurs at Pipra, South Rewah. It is pink in color, with a fine-grained massive structure, and very tough. It is reported that there is an unlimited supply of this material, and it has already been used in this country in the manufacture of certain oilstones (see page 89).

In the following descriptions of localities those that contain sapphires are first taken up, then the corundum, and last the emery.

SAPPHIRE OR CORUNDUM GEMS.

The properties of a mineral that determine its rank as a gem are hardness, color, rarity, index of refraction, and luster. As an illustration of the extent to which the hardness affects the value of a mineral for gem purposes, sphalerite might be cited. This mineral, which has an index of refraction and a luster not far below that of the diamond, has a hardness of only 3.5 to 4, which effectually cuts it off from being a gem mineral.

Corundum has properties that place some of its varieties among the most valuable gems. With the exception of the diamond, it is the hardest mineral known, and the rarity and color of the ruby, the red corundum, has made that gem, when more than a carat in weight, more valuable than a diamond of corresponding weight. Corundum has been found in almost all the colors of the rainbow, and in the following list its gems have been classified according to color. They are very often designated by the prefix "oriental," to distinguish them from gems of the same name whose mineral composition and character are entirely different.

Sapphire or corundum gems.

Oriental or true ruby	Red of various shades.
Oriental sapphire....................	Blue of various shades.
Pink sapphire	Rose or pink.
White sapphire...............	⎰ Colorless.
Diamond spar	⎱
Opaline..............	⎱
Girasol	⎬ Pale blue or bluish white.
Hyaline	⎰
Oriental amethyst ....,..............	Purple.
Oriental emerald	Green.
Oriental topaz	Yellow.
Star sapphire	⎱
Chatoyant	⎬ Opalescent.
Asteria...............	⎰

The gems occur in the mines in three forms: First, as crystals, of which there are two distinct forms, (1) hexagonal prisms terminated by rhombohedrons and pyramids, sometimes with basal plane, the larger crystals being often rounded or barrel-shaped, and (2) flat, tabular crystals, where the basal plane is very largely developed; second, as transparent colored portions of larger massive pieces of corundum; third, as nodules of finer and clearer material in a mass of cleavable corundum, often having the appearance of rolled pebbles when separated from the mass of corundum.

ORIENTAL RUBY.

The most important of the sapphire gems is the oriental ruby, which varies from rose, pinkish, dark-red, and purplish to pigeon-blood color, the most highly prized. The rubies are very likely to be flawed, and when examined many of the cut stones are found to contain flaws of one character or another. The stones are often so cut that these flaws are distinguishable only by the aid of a magnifying glass.

The finest rubies of pigeon-blood color are those found in the Mogok district, about 90 miles north-northeast of Mandalay, in upper Burma. Small but fine rubies, often, however, of a pink color or a purplish tint, are found at Ratnapoora, in Ceylon, and of a dark-red color, similar to that of a garnet, in Siam. The rubies of the Burma district are found in situ in limestones, but the mining is confined almost entirely to the gravels.

At the Corundum Hill mine, Cullasagee, N. C. (see description, page 55), various shades of gem ruby corundum have been found. Two of the best rubies of good color that have ever been found at this mine are in the collection of Clarence S. Bement, of Philadelphia; there are also a number of fine ones in the United States National Museum at Washington. Many of the smaller crystals of various shades of pink to red are transparent near the outer surface and near their extremities, and from these small gems can be cut, but few that are worth $100 have been obtained from them. These smaller crystals are usually well developed and have a clean-cut form. The faces commonly developed on these are the base, c, 0001; the unit prism, m, $10\bar{1}0$; the unit rhombohedron, r, $10\bar{1}1$, and the pyramid, n, $22\bar{4}3$, more rarely observed.

The North Carolina locality for corundum gems which at the present time is attracting the most attention is the tract of land between the Caler Fork of Cowee Creek and Mason Branch, tributaries of the Little Tennessee River.[1] This tract is situated in Macon County, almost 6 miles below (north of) the town of Franklin. The nearest railroad station is Dillsboro, Jackson County, on the Southern Railway, about 12 miles to the east. The bottom of the valleys are about 2,500 feet above sea level, and the mountain peaks or knobs in the immediate vicinity rise to a height of 3,000 or 3,500 feet.

In the gravels of Caler Fork Valley pieces of crystals of red corundum were picked up by the people of the district, which led to the driving of two or three tunnels with the expectation of striking the vein and finding the corundum in sufficient quantity for commercial purposes. Work in this direction was soon abandoned, and for a number of years there were only prospecting and a little mining for the red corundum for gem purposes.

Systematic search was made, which revealed the fact that ruby corundum was to be found in the gravels of Caler Fork Valley for a distance of 3 miles. In 1895 the American Prospecting and Mining Company, of New York, bought out the old claims and began work on a systematic basis. The property owned by the company is a large tract on both sides of Caler Fork of Cowee Creek and nearly all the land in the northern part of the watershed of Mason Branch, a total area of about 5,000 acres.

The gravels in which most of the rubies have been found are covered by soil averaging about 2 feet in depth, but varying from 1 to 5, and they are about 3 feet higher than the present alluvial gravel of the stream. Pl. II, *A*, is a view of one of the gravel beds that is being worked for rubies, just west of the company's office. The gravel in this part of the valley, which is overlain with 3 to 5 feet of soil, is composed of waterworn masses of quartz and small pebbles of gneiss and quartz, and is much cleaner in appearance than the gravels a mile farther up the creek, at In Situ Hill, where most of the mining was carried on during 1898. Fifty feet above the level of this gravel another bed was discovered at In Situ Hill which carried ruby corundum.

In washing these gravels for the rubies, hydraulic processes have been used very similar to those used in the West in washing gold-bearing gravels. All the soil, as well as the gravel, is washed into a short line of sluice boxes (*a* of Pl. II, *B*) which lead into a large sieve

----

[1] Am. Jour. Sci., 4th series, Vol. VIII, 1899, p. 370.

.1 BED OF RUBY-BEARING GRAVEL AT CALER FORK, COWEE VALLEY, MACON COUNTY, N. C.

RUBY MINE AT COWEE VALLEY N. C

Plant for washing the gravels is shown in the foreground, *a*, sluice box, *b*, sieve boxes, *c*, rocker.

bo
re
an
cl
do

m
th
h

as
th
de
at

v
it
b
p
k
s
g
u
a
g

box (b of Pl. II, B), where the large pieces of rock and bowlders are removed and most of the dirt and fine gravel is washed out. They are then shoveled into a rocker (c of Pl. II, B), where they are further cleaned and concentrated, the final concentration of the rubies being done by hand.

No basic magnesian rocks or serpentine derived from them, in which most of the corundum of North Carolina occurs, have been found in this valley. Corundum Hill and the Ellijay corundum region are, however, less than 10 miles to the south.

Although, in many respects, the occurrence of the rubies and their associate minerals in the Cowee Valley is similar to the occurrence of the ruby in Burma, no limestone has been found near the alluvial deposits, the nearest point at which limestone has been found being at Cullowee Gap, about 8 miles to the southeast.

The country rock of the district is a gneiss, of a gray, fine-grained variety, which has a great many small garnets disseminated through it. The rock for the most part is in a highly decomposed condition, but there are small exposures of the undecomposed rock in many places. The gravels in which the rubies are found rest on a soft rock known as saprolite, which is the result of weathering of the basic silicate rocks in place. By means of shafts and the workings at the gravel washings it has been shown that at a depth of 35 feet or more these saprolitic rocks contain fragments of the undecomposed rock and pass into such rocks as eclogite-amphibolite and a hornblendic gneiss.

A narrow dike of hornblendic eclogite a few feet in width is exposed near the present workings of the company and can be traced for about 100 yards.

No rubies have been found in the undecomposed rock, but at In Situ Hill small rubies of a rather pale color were found in a narrow band of saprolitic rock. This band was, however, cut off by slickenslides so that it could not be followed in any direction. There are four parallel slickenslides that have been exposed at one place in the workings, the general direction of the slides being N. 75° E. Some of these are 70 feet in length and of unknown depth. It is very evident that there has been a great deal of disturbance in this immediate vicinity through the breaking of the rock masses by faulting, the ready influx of water having caused the reduction of the rocks to their saprolitic condition.

In washing the gravels and masses of saprolite, masses of undecomposed rock have been uncovered, and in the center of these nodules of the pure hornblende rock have been found. The saprolite bordering these nodules often contains particles and crystals of corundum.

Less than 2 miles to the east of In Situ Hill, beyond Betts Gap of the Cowee Mountains, corundum of a gray to bluish color, but highly crystallized, has been found in hornblende-gneiss. One mile a little north of west, at the Sheffield mine, pink corundum has been found in amphibole-schist (see pages 31 and 58).

An association of corundum peculiar to this locality is with the garnet, rhodolite. Corundum and garnet occur not only constantly together in the saprolitic material and in the gravels, but corundum crystals have been found that bear the impression of the garnet. By means of wax a mold was taken of these impressions, and they were shown to be either the dodecahedron or trapezohedron. Then again some of the ruby crystals when broken are seen to have a garnet inclosed, and the garnet can often be seen in the transparent ruby crystal and the cut gem.

As has been said, there is no limestone in this immediate vicinity, and these rubies were probably derived from an amphibolite or eclogite. The usual flat tabular form of the crystals is one that seems to be characteristic of the gem corundum when found in igneous rock.

The Cowee Creek rubies frequently contain inclusions, some of which are very minute, known to jewelers as "silk," and these give rise to a cloudiness or sheen in the polished gem. Rutile and menaccanite often occur in the rubies and greatly mar their beauty and value. Some gems that were 3 or 4 carats in weight have been cut, which were free from inclusions, of fine color, and transparent. A great many smaller ones have been cut that are perfect gems. In color and brilliancy these gems are equal to the Burma ruby, and if the percentage of the unflawed transparent material increases but little this new field will be a worthy rival to the Burma field.

A considerable percentage of the transparent material is often very badly flawed by cracks due to parting, and by the inclusions of rutile or menaccanite, so that the percentage of perfect stone from this mine is small. This, however, is true of the rubies from the Burma field, for a large proportion of the rubies on the market to-day are usually more or less flawed with the parting cracks.

The pleochroism exhibited by the Cowee rubies is very marked, some of them being a very rich pigeon-blood red in the direction of the vertical axis—that is, looking down upon the basal plane—and changing to an almost pinkish-white color when viewed at right angles to this or looking through the prism. The pleochroism which nearly all the deep-colored varieties of corundum gems exhibit is one of the means of identifying a corundum gem; this often interferes with the cutting.

The ruby crystals [1] from the Cowee Valley show a very wide variation in their development. Although many of the crystals are so striated that no crystallographic measurements were possible on the reflecting goniometer, the faces were readily identified by means of the contact goniometer. On some of the crystals the faces were bright

---

[1] Am. Jour. Sci., 4th series, Vol. VIII, 1899, p. 379.

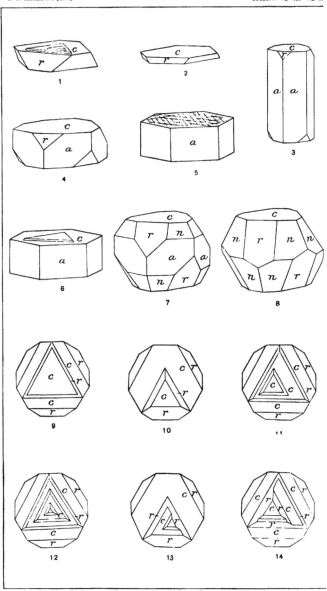

RUBY CRYSTALS FROM COWEE VALLEY, MACON COUNTY, N. C.

and smooth, making them well adapted for measurement on the reflecting goniometer. These crystals are shown on Pl. III.

In the crystals examined two common habits were noticed; one is shown in figs. 1 and 2 of Pl. III, and is a combination of the base c (0001) and the unit rhombohedron r (10$\bar{1}$1); the other is represented by figs. 3–6 of Pl. III, where the prism a (11$\bar{2}$0) is very prominently developed. The rhombohedral crystals vary from those in which the base and the rhombohedron are disproportionately developed, the base having a diameter of 12 mm. and the rhombohedron of only 1.5 mm., to some (fig. 1 of Pl. III) in which the base and the rhombohedron are nearer one size. The majority of these crystals have, however, the base more largely developed, thus giving the crystals a flat, tabular appearance. This rhombohedral development is very similar to the sapphires from Yogo Gulch, Montana, described on page 52.[1]

On some of the prismatic crystals the prism reaches a length of nearly 15 mm. in the direction of the c axis, and has the rhombohedron r but slightly developed (fig. 3 of Pl. III), while on others the prism is very short and the rhombohedron is sometimes wanting, as represented in figs. 4 and 5 of Pl. III.

Another habit of these crystals is shown in figs. 7 and 8 of Pl. III, where the pyramid n (22$\bar{4}$3) is well developed. This face was identified by means of the contact goniometer, the measured angles approximating closely to those calculated. The usual form of these crystals is shown in fig. 7 of Pl. III, where the faces c (0001), a (11$\bar{2}$0), r (10$\bar{1}$1), and n (22$\bar{4}$3) are nearly equally developed. On some of the crystals the prism is very prominent, being 8 mm. in length in the direction of the c axis, while the pyramid is only 1.5 mm.; on others the pyramid is only very slightly developed. A few crystals were examined which showed only the presence of the base, the rhombohedron, and the pyramid, as represented in fig. 8 of Pl. III. The crystals, measuring up to 7 mm. in diameter, were doubly terminated and nearly perfect in their development.

The crystals represented by fig. 7 of Pl. III are similar to those described by Bauer[2] from the Burma district, and are almost identical in form with the sapphire crystals figured by me, from Emerald Bar, Canyon Ferry, Meagher County, Mont. (p. 50).

Although both the basal and rhombohedron planes are very often striated, it is only on the basal planes that the striations are sharp and distinct and can be measured. The striations are parallel to the three intersections of the base c and the rhombohedron r as shown in fig. 5 of Pl. III.

A very common development that was noticed on nearly all the flat rhombohedral crystals and on many of the prismatic crystals is a

[1] Also Am. Jour. Sci., 4th series, Vol. IV, 1897, p. 424.
[2] Neues Jahrbuch für Min., Geol., und Pal., Vol. XI, 1898, p. 209.

repeated growth on the basal plane of the rhombohedron r (10$\bar{1}$1) and
the base c (0001), as represented in figs. 1–6 of Pl. III.

To illustrate better the variation in these growths, a series of
drawings, figs. 9–14 of Pl. III, have been made in basal projection.
In figs. 9 and 10 of Pl. III, which represent the more common development of these repeated growths, there is but one secondary rhombohedron and base, which sometimes has one of its rhombohedron faces
a continuation of one of the rhombohedron faces of the crystal.
Figs. 11 and 12 of Pl. III represent the repeated growths, the faces of
which are separate and distinct from one another and from the faces
of the main crystal. In the crystals represented by fig. 12 of Pl. III,
the basal plane of the crystal has the appearance of being striated
with triangular markings when the secondary growths are but slightly
developed. In figs. 13 and 14 of Pl. III is represented a series of
growths where a number of the rhombohedron faces coincide.

Some of the pyramidal crystals (figs. 7 and 8 of Pl. III) also show
the development of the secondary growth of rhombohedron and base.
The thickness of the rhombohedron of the secondary growth varies
greatly: some are so thin that they appear like striations; some are 2
mm. in thickness. A few crystals were observed on which there was
a secondary growth parallel to the prism 11$\bar{2}$0. This same style of
development has been described by Bauer[1] as occurring in the Burma
rubies.

The sapphire crystals from Montana, described on page 53, are
strikingly similar in this respect to the Cowee rubies. Among the
most noticeable associated minerals of these Cowee rubies is a delicate
rose-colored garnet of great brilliancy, to which the name rhodolite[2]
has been given. The rhodolite usually occurs in waterworn pebbles,
but it has been found in very small dodecahedrons, and its close connection with the rubies in the small crystals of rhodolite inclosed by
the garnet has already been mentioned.

The other accompanying minerals are: Quartz, rarely as pseudomorphous dodecahedrons; corundum crystals, of pale-blue, amethystine,
and pink shades; spinel (pleonaste); gahnite, in octahedral crystals;
chromite (rare); rutile; menaccanite; bronzite (transparent); tremo-
lite; hornblende; iolite (colorless); cyanite; fibrolite; staurolite in perfectly transparent fragments of a garnet-red color; monazite in small
crystals; zircon, small, brilliant crystals, and also the variety cyrto-
lite; pyrite; chalcopyrite; pyrrhotite; sphalerite; sperrylite in minute
crystals; and gold.

Much of the work that has been done in Cowee Valley has been in
the nature of prospecting to locate the extent of the ruby-bearing
gravel and if possible to locate the origin of the rubies themselves.
No work was done in the valley during the past year, but it is stated

---

[1] Loc. cit., p. 209.
[2] Am. Jour. Sci., 4th series, Vol. V, 1898, p. 294.

upon good authority that work will be begun again in the coming spring.

At the Mincey mine, Ellijay Creek, ruby corundum has been found from which several small stones could be cut. This occurs at the same locality as the bronze corundum, described below.

Another locality that is worthy of mention, and one that gives some promise of making a satisfactory showing in course of development, is the so-called gem mine on the property of Dr. C. Grimshawe, of Montvale, Jackson County, N. C. Rubies of good color, from which a number of fine but very small stones have been cut, have been found in the gravels of the stream. Blue and yellow corundum of gem quality is associated with the rubies. By following up the gravels the corundum was located in a small vein in the decomposed peridotite.

At the Cullakeenee mine, Buck Creek, and near Elf, on Shooting Creek, Clay County, N. C., masses of emerald to grass-green amphibolite are found, through which are disseminated particles of pink and ruby corundum, ranging in size from that of a pea to some as large as hickory nuts. The corundum is not of gem quality, but the combination of the green amphibolite and pink corundum makes very beautiful specimens, and if the rock is hard enough to admit of a good polish, this occurrence might furnish a decorative or ornamental stone of some value.

At the Mincey mine, on Ellijay Creek, Macon County, and about 2½ miles northeast of Corundum Hill, there occurs a peculiar brown or bronze corundum, known locally as "pearl corundum," which shows distinct asterism, both by natural and artificial

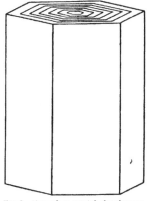

FIG. 7.—Corundum crystal, showing concentric hexagons on basal plane.

light, when the stone is cut en cabochon. In natural light these corundums all show a bronze luster and are somewhat similar to the cat's-eye, but in artificial light the star is more distinct. Most of the bronze corundum is in rough crystals, but some have been found that have the prismatic faces smooth and well developed, and these are often dark, almost black, in color.

Asterism has been noticed in many of the rubies and sapphires from Cowee Valley and in a few of the sapphires from the Montana deposits. This asterism, according to Von Lasaulx, is sometimes produced by rifts due to the basal parting. These rifts, when examined with the microscope, are seen to be very thin, sharp, and rectilinear, and are parallel to the edge of the prism onto base.

In other cases asterism is undoubtedly due to the rutile or other mineral that is inclosed in the sapphires, which intersect each other at angles of 60°, and form a "sagenite web" or similar structure.

On many of the corundum crystals, especially of the sapphire variety, concentric hexagons were observed on the basal plane, as represented in fig. 7. The edges of the hexagon are parallel to the edges of the prism faces onto base, and the plane of the hexagon is parallel to the base. In a few of the transparent crystals this hexagon was observed as a web in the midst of the crystal, the plane of the web being parallel to the basal plane.

ORIENTAL SAPPHIRES.

The finest sapphires that are known are found in Burma and Ceylon, and have the rich, deep-blue color for which the oriental stone is noted. Sapphires of a rich, velvety blue and some very good stones of a lighter color have been obtained from Simla Pass, in the Himalaya Mountains. Siam has also produced some sapphires of very good color. The sapphire corundum from Australia is generally of an opaque, milky-white color.

NORTH CAROLINA SAPPHIRES.

No corundum gems were found in the United States until the opening of the Corundum Hill corundum mine at Cullasagee, Macon County, N. C., in 1871. This corundum is mined for abrasive purposes, but in certain parts of the deposit crystal corundum is occasionally found that is of a decided gem character, and, again, many of the fragments of the corundum have certain portions that are transparent. A number of very handsome dark-blue sapphires from this mine are in the United States National Museum, one of which weighs a carat.[1]

Yellowish and blue colors in the same specimen are rather common, and are sometimes sharply separated into consecutive bands, while in other specimens the colors merge into one another.

Sapphire gems of all the different colors have been found at Corundum Hill, and I have in my collection cut gems representing all these various colors. Many of them are, however, very small.

During the past ten years but few gems have been obtained from this mine, for the reason that the portion of the deposit from which these crystals were formerly obtained has not been worked. In the alluvial deposits below this portion of the mine many handsome crystals can be obtained by washing the gravel.

The green sapphire, which is the oriental emerald, is one of the rarest of gems. The Corundum Hill mine is the only place in this country at which the emerald-green sapphire has been found, and it

---

[1] Kunz: Gems and Precious Stones of North America, 1890, p. 40.

7

n
i-
s
t
:.
),
e

),
..
k

8
8
3

min
ang
O
ety,
sen
of t
to t
obs
bei

T
and
not
of
lay
goo
an

N
opo
Cor
pos
occ
ma
aro
fro
wh
T
anc
oth
S
du
van
I
thi
the
all
cry

rar
cou

occurs very sparingly here, although the yellowish and light-green colors are not uncommon. What is probably the finest known specimen of the oriental emerald in the world came from this mine, and is now in the Bement collection. It is a crystal 4 by 2 by 1¼ inches; part of it is transparent, and several very fine gems could be cut from it.

At the Sapphire and Whitewater corundum mines, near Sapphire, Jackson County, N. C., fragments of sapphire of a fine blue color have been found, from which small but good gems have been cut.

Associated with the green amphibolite rock near Elf post-office, Clay County, N. C., deep-blue sapphires have been sparingly found. These bear the same relation to the amphibolite as the red and pink sapphire described on page 45.

MONTANA SAPPHIRES.

The only systematic mining that has been undertaken for sapphires is in Montana. Sapphires were first found in this State by miners who were washing the gravels of the bars on the Missouri River, to the east of Helena, for gold. These were first described in 1873 by J. Lawrence Smith,[1] but it was not until 1891 that actual mining was begun. During that year a number of companies were organized to work these bars for sapphires.

These bars are located from 12 to 18 miles east and northeast of Helena, and have been followed for a distance of about 12 miles from Canyon Ferry down the river to American Bar. At various intervals these bars have been worked for the sapphires and are designated by the following names, starting with the one that is farthest up the river: Emerald Bar, Cheyenne Bar, French Bar, Spokane Bar, Metropolitan Bar, Ruby Bar, Eldorado Bar, Dana Bar, and American Bar. The location of these bars is shown on the map (Pl. IV).

A few sapphires have been found as far down the river as Beartooth, but sapphires have not been found in large quantity below American Bar.

Above Emerald Bar there have been no sapphires found on any of the bars, but in the gravel of Magpie Gulch, less than a mile above Emerald Bar (at Canyon Ferry), many sapphires have been found by miners who were washing the gravel for gold. No sapphires have been found in situ in this gulch, but Kunz[2] has noted the occurrence of sapphires that were found in a dike of vesicular mica-augite-andesite which was about 6 feet wide and cut through the green slate below the gravels. In the gravel deposits at French Bar, about 3 miles below Canyon Ferry, a narrow dike was encountered last summer, 3 to 6 feet in width, that had greenish sapphires scattered sparingly through it.

This dike was encountered about 50 feet above the river and its

---

[1] Am. Jour. Sci., 3d series, Vol. VI, 1873, p. 185.
[2] Min. Mag., Vol. IX., 1891, No. 44, p. 396.

strike as it cuts through the slate is N. 10° E., the dip being about 45° W.

This rock is undoubtedly of the same character as that described by Kunz as occurring at Ruby Bar. From the occurrence of these two corundum-bearing dikes of andesite it would seem that the source of the sapphires found in the various bars along the Missouri River is a series of small parallel dikes with a slight northeast-southwest trend, like those described. As the sapphires are scattered so sparingly through these dikes, the amount of decomposition and erosion that was required to liberate those that are now found in the gravels must have been simply enormous.

The beds of gravel in which the sapphires occur are from 10 to 50

FIG. 8.—Spokane Bar sapphire deposits, Lewis and Clarke County, Mont.

feet thick and rest for the most part upon slate, in bluffs that rise nearly 50 feet above the river. At Emerald Bar the gravel beds are nearly 130 feet above the river and rest upon granite rock.

Most of the mining has been done at Spokane and Eldorado bars. The former locality is near the center of the sapphire deposits and on the west side of the river about 16 miles due east of Helena. In 1895 these beds of gravel, which are 8 to 18 feet thick, were extensively mined by an English company known as the Montana Sapphire and Ruby Company. The gravels were washed by hydraulic methods and a great many gems were obtained, most of which were sent to England. This company also controlled or owned French Bar and Dana Bar on the west side of the river and Eldorado Bar on the east side.

It was reorganized in 1897 as an American company, known as the Eldorado Gold and Gem Company, with A. N. Spratt, of Oakland, Cal., president, and Frank Spratt, of Helena, Mont., manager. No work has been done at any of the bars by the present company. This bar is shown in fig. 8, the bluff rising from the river being 30 to 50 feet high.

Directly across the river from Spokane Bar, but about three-fourths of a mile from the river, is Metropolitan Bar, which has been worked during the summer of 1899 by different men who have staked out individual claims. The gravels are from 6 to 20 feet thick, and are washed in hand rockers, the water being obtained from shallow wells. Several of the claims are owned by Robbin Bird, Charles Johnson, and John Durrant, of Helena, Mont.

Above Spokane Bar, French Bar, Cheyenne Bar, and Emerald Bar no regular mining has been done during the last few years, but frequently different persons have worked in the old drifts for a few days at a time, washing by hand the gravel obtained.

A large part of the work done at Emerald Bar has been under ground, by means of shaft and drifts. Henry Crittenden, of Canyon Ferry, has done a large part of the work here, and still controls the deposits.

Below Spokane Bar, at Dana Bar, Eldorado Bar, and American Bar there was no mining for sapphires during 1899.

Most of the gems that have been obtained from these bars during 1899 have been put on the market through the Helena Lapidary Company, of Helena, Mont., of which William Knuth is manager. Mr. Knuth has done considerable work on these bars, and has been instrumental in the development of the Montana gem fields.

As mining investments these sapphire deposits have not thus far been financially successful, partly on-account of the heavy capitalization of the companies who have bought the mines and partly on account of the-color of the stones. They are, for the most part, of a pale-greenish or greenish-yellow color, and do not command a very high price in the market. Occasionally pink and yellow ones have been found that have cut good gems. Stones approaching a red or blue color are, however, extremely rare.

There are still a great many sapphires in the gravels that have not been worked, but on account of their color it is rather doubtful whether under the most favorable conditions it will pay to mine them.

The crystals from all these bars show the same development, and are prismatic in habit. The prism, a ($11\bar{2}0$), is always present, and is usually in combination with the base, c (0001), and the unit rhombohedron, r ($10\bar{1}1$), as represented in fig. 9, A. Some of the crystals have the prism very short and the rhombohedron is wanting, giving the crystal a very tabular appearance (fig. 9, B). A pyramid of the second order, n ($22\bar{4}3$), was observed on some of the crystals in addition to the base and unit rhombohedron, and is represented in fig. 9, C.

The crystals are usually rough and more or less striated, so that no measurement could be made upon the reflecting goniometer, but sufficiently accurate measurements could be obtained with the contact goniometer to identify the faces.

The largest crystal that has been observed from any of these bars was one from Eldorado Bar that was nearly an inch long and three-eighths of an inch in diameter.

A repeated growth was observed on some of these crystals, but not in the variety of forms seen in the Cowee rubies (p. 43) and the Yogo Gulch sapphires (p. 52). Only one form of growth was observed, represented in fig. 9, *A*, which is a combination of the unit rhombohedron and the base.

Since the discovery and mining of sapphires from the Missouri River bars sapphires have been found at three other localities in Montana—at Rock Creek, Granite County; at Cottonwood Creek, Deerlodge County; and at Yogo Gulch, Fergus County.

The first two localities are about 80 and 30 miles southwest of those on the Missouri River, and the last one is about 80 miles to the north-

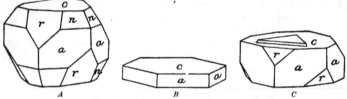

Fig. 9.—Sapphire crystals from Missouri River bars, Montana.

east. From these sapphire deposits stones of deeper colors have been obtained, those from the first two being of all colors from blue to red, while those from the last are all blue.

ROCK CREEK SAPPHIRES.

For information concerning the sapphire deposits of Rock Creek, I am indebted to Mr. William Knuth, of Helena. All the sapphires that have thus far been found in this section are in the gravel deposits on the West Fork of Rock or Stony Creek, in the southern part of Granite County, about 35 miles southwest of Phillipsburg, the county seat, and 30 miles nearly west of Anaconda, Deerlodge County. (Pl. IV.)

The sapphires are found in rather a limited area, which is bounded roughly by the gravels of Cold Creek, Myers Creek, tributaries of the West Fork of Rock Creek, and that portion of Rock Creek lying between them.

These gravels were extensively worked during the summer of 1899, principally by William Knuth, of Helena, and William Moffitt, of Phillipsburg. Altogether about 200,000 carats of rough sapphires were obtained. Of these about 12,000 carats are fit for cutting. In color they are much more varied than those from the Missouri River bars, and the prevailing color, which is greenish to bluish green, is deeper. No deep-blue sapphires like the oriental stones have been found, but paler blue ones have been obtained, from which very handsome sapphires 2 or 3 carats in weight have been cut. Some of the finest yellow sapphires (oriental topaz) that I have ever seen have been found at Rock Creek. One of these weighed close to 2 carats when cut. Pale green and bluish green are among the common stones, some cutting gems of 5 to 8 carats in weight. A number of beautiful pink sapphires have also been found.

Few red and ruby-colored crystals have been found and none that would cut a gem over a twelfth of a carat in weight. These colors are extremely rare in the Montana sapphire deposits.

The crystals and fragments of sapphires that are found in these gravels do not show as much abrasion as those from the Missouri River, probably because they have been carried a shorter distance from where they originated.

In habit the crystals are very similar to those already described from the Missouri River, and fig. 9 will also illustrate very well the character of the Rock Creek crystals. One type that is very noticeable is a short prismatic crystal, whose diameter nearly equals its length. A parallel growth on the basal plane is only occasionally observed, and is composed of the basal plane and unit rhombohedron.

No sapphires have as yet been found in situ, but a few have been found in the gravels that were embedded in the original matrix. Mr. Knuth, to whom I showed a specimen of the andesite containing sapphires from French Bar, said that it very closely resembled the small fragments of rock carrying sapphires that he had found at Rock Creek. It is not at all improbable that these sapphires originated in the same type of rock as those of the Missouri River and that small dikes of andesite will be found in the divide between Myers, Cold, and Quartz creeks. A very few sapphires have been found on Quartz Creek.

While the sapphire gems from Rock Creek do not command so high a price as the ruby and the deep-blue sapphires, and are regarded more as fancy stones, they are coming to be quite highly prized by many who are acquainted with them. As yet but few of the Rock Creek sapphires have been put on the market except locally at Helena, and it seems to me that it can be confidently predicted that these sapphires will become important in the jewelry trade when they are once known.

COTTONWOOD CREEK SAPPHIRES.

The sapphire deposits on Cottonwood Creek are in Deerlodge County, about 30 miles southwest of Helena and 10 miles east of Deerlodge, the county seat. There has not been a great deal of work done on this creek, so that the extent of the sapphire-bearing gravels is not known. The sapphires are similar in character to those of Rock Creek, but they are apt to be of lighter color and not of such a variety of colors. What little work was done on the creek during the past summer was by Franz Cobalt, of Helena, and according to him there were but few sapphires taken out of the gravels. Future development at this locality may show these deposits to be of considerable importance and extent.

YOGO GULCH SAPPHIRES.

The sapphires that are the most widely known and that have attracted the most attention have been obtained in Fergus County near the entrance of Yogo Gulch, on the Yogo Fork of Judith River. This locality is on the eastern slope of Prospect Ridge of the Little Belt Mountains, about 75 miles northeast of Helena and 15 miles a little south of west of Utica, which is the nearest town, and which is on the Judith stage line. The sapphires were first found in the gravels of Yogo Fork, and in following these up the creek their original source was located in dikes that extend across the county for a mile and a half.[1]

There are two parallel dikes about 800 feet apart, with a general east-west trend, which vary in width from 15 to 75 feet. The mineralogical composition of the rock shows that it has a close affinity with minette and shonkinite, as described on page 28.

The alluvial deposits below these dikes have been pretty thoroughly worked for the sapphires, and mining operations are now confined almost entirely to the dikes themselves. These dikes, the upper portion of which is thoroughly decomposed, have been worked by means of open cuts, the limestone making fairly firm walls. By hydraulic processes the decomposed rock was readily broken up and washed into sluice boxes. As the mining extended deeper the rock was much less altered and it was necessary to leave a great deal of it exposed to the atmosphere from one season to the next, before it could be broken up and run through the sluice boxes. At a number of points the almost perfectly fresh rock has been encountered, and from this it will be a difficult problem to separate the sapphires. The percentage of sapphires in the rock is small and if it were the unaltered rock that had to be worked for them the deposit would not be of economic importance.

The sapphires occur embedded in this rock in distinct crystals from less than a millimeter in diameter to some that were over 15 mm. Their color, as far as I have observed them, is always a blue, varying from light blue to a very few that showed the dark blue of the Ceylon stone. The prevailing color is a bright blue.[2]

---

[1] The geology of the district and a full description of the mines and workings, by W. H. Weed, will be found in the Twentieth Ann. Rept. U. S. Geol. Survey, Part III, 1899, pp. 454-460.
[2] Kunz: Am. Jour. Sci., 4th series, Vol. IV, 1897, p. 420.

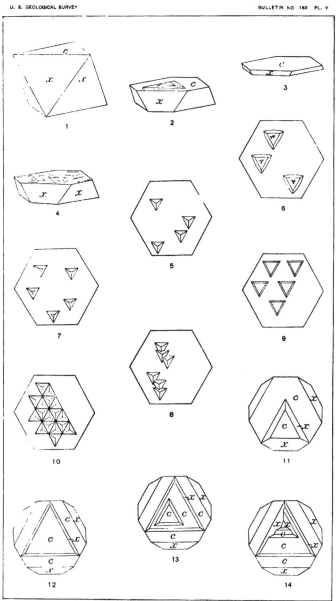

SAPPHIRE CRYSTALS FROM YOGO GULCH, FERGUS COUNTY, MONT.

While the color of these sapphires is not as dark as the highly-prized Ceylon stones, they show a richness and brilliancy not equalled by the oriental stone. They not only show a strong rich color by transmitted light, but their color is almost as good by reflected light. Then again, while many blue sapphires make beautiful day stones but are dull at night, the Yogo sapphire is a very brilliant night as well as day stone.

The crystallography of these sapphires is markedly different from that of the sapphires of the Missouri bars and Rock Creek (page 50). The latter all show a prismatic development, while the former are all rhombohedral crystals, none of which show the presence of any prism face.[1]

The crystals are etched and striated to such a degree that no crystallographic measurements on the reflecting goniometer were possible; but sufficiently accurate angles were obtained with the contact goniometer to permit the identification of the faces. The only two faces that could be identified were the base c (0001) and the rhombohedron x (30$\bar{3}$2) which is a new face for corundum. On one crystal two very small faces were observed which were too small to be measured with the contact goniometer, but were probably the faces of a pyramid of the second order.

In determining the rhombohedron, ten or more independent measurements were made of $c \wedge x$. These varied from 66° to 68°, but approximated closely to 67°, which agrees very well with the calculated value, 67° 3′, for 0001 $\wedge$ 30$\bar{3}$2. These crystals are represented on Pl. V.

The crystals are developed, as shown in figs. 1, 2, and 3 of Pl. V, the prevailing type being like fig. 3 of Pl. V. The crystals vary from those where the base is very largely developed, having a diameter of 8 mm., while the rhombohedron is only 1 mm., to those that have the base and the rhombohedron equally developed (fig. 1 of Pl. V). Where the faces are more equally developed, the rhombohedral faces are generally rounded.

The basal plane often shows characteristic striations which are parallel to the three intersections of the base c and the rhombohedron x, as shown in fig. 4 of Pl. V. These lines are sharp and distinct and on the very flat crystals can easily be measured when examined under the microscope. The rhombohedral faces are very roughly striated without showing any distinct parallel lines.

One very common development of these crystals is a repeated growth on the basal plane of the rhombohedron x (30$\bar{3}$2) and the base c (0001), as represented in fig. 2 of Pl. V. These growths are exceedingly varied, as is shown in figs. 11–14 of Pl. V, where they are drawn in basal projection. In fig. 11 of Pl. V there is but one secondary rhombohedron and base, which has one of its rhombohedron faces a continuation of one of the rhombohedron faces of the crystal.

---

[1] Am. Jour. Sci., 4th series, Vol. IV, 1897, p. 424.

Fig. 12 of Pl. V represents a repeated growth, each face of which is entirely distinct from the faces of the main crystal. In fig. 13 of Pl. V there are represented two, and in fig. 14 of Pl. V a series of such growths, where a number of the rhombohedral faces coincide. These growths occur most frequently on the flat crystals. The thickness of the rhombohedron rarely reaches 1 mm. and often they are so thin that they appear like striations.

This repeated growth is very similar to that described as occurring on the Cowee rubies (p. 43). Bauer,[1] in an article entitled "Ueber das Vorkommen der Rubine in Birma," has described this same style of development as occurring on the Burma rubies, but it is not so general as on the Montana corundums.

Etching figures.[2]—The etching figures which were observed on nearly all the crystals examined were on the basal plane. The figures are very perfect, and although showing many different forms, they all have a rhombohedral symmetry. Fig. 5 of Pl. V represents the common etching figure, which is a rhombohedral depression terminating in a point. The edges of the depression are sharp and well defined, as are also the intersections of the rhombohedral faces of the depression. These rhombohedral faces were smooth and gave fair reflections of the signal on the reflecting goniometer. In measuring them the entire crystal except the depression to be measured was covered with a thin coating of wax. Two different crystals were measured, which gave for rhombohedron on rhombohedron 22° 30'; this corresponds to the rhombohedron $10\bar{1}7$, for which the calculated value is 21° 50'. Figures of the same style were observed whose edges were parallel to those of the negative rhombohedron; these, however, are not common in isolated forms.

Another common form is represented in figs. 7 and 9 of Pl. V, where the depression is bounded by the basal plane, which at times is so large that the rhombohedral plane is hardly visible. Fig. 6 of Pl. V represents etching figures, where, on the basal plane of a shallow depression, there is one additional etching figure and sometimes two. These second etching figures are like the common ones shown in fig. 5 of Pl. V. The outer rhombohedral contour of these figures is generally rounded. This is also usually the case with the deeper depressions.

Often the etching figures are intergrown, fig. 8 of Pl. V, and when many of these occur together they have the appearance of raised figures rather than of depressions. This raised appearance is very striking when there is a combination of the plus and minus rhombohedron in parallel position and without overlapping, fig. 10 of Pl. V.

The figures vary considerably in size, but most of them are near 1 mm. in diameter. A few were observed that were nearly 2 mm. in diameter.

[1] Neues Jahrbuch für Min., Geol. und Pal., Vol. XI, 1896, p. 209.
[2] Am. Jour. Sci., 4th series, Vol. IV, 1897, p. 428.

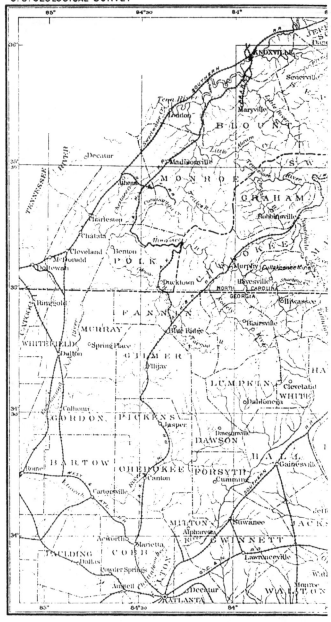

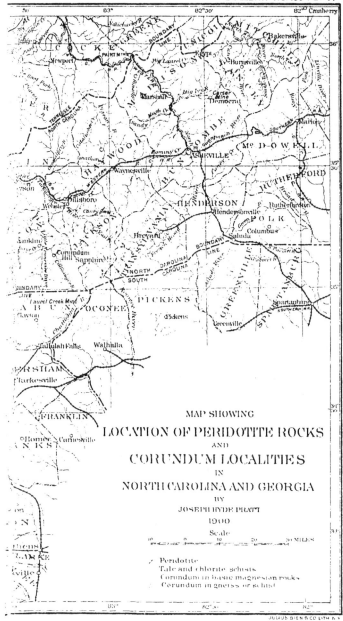

MAP SHOWING
LOCATION OF PERIDOTITE ROCKS
AND
CORUNDUM LOCALITIES
IN
NORTH CAROLINA AND GEORGIA
BY
JOSEPH HYDE PRATT
1900
Scale

10   0   10   20   30 MILES

Peridotite
Talc and chlorite schists
Corundum in basic magnesian rocks
Corundum in gneiss or schist

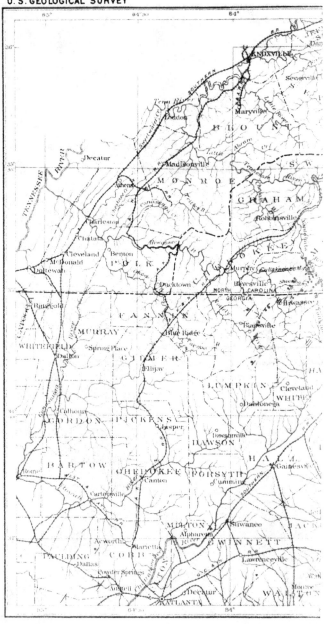

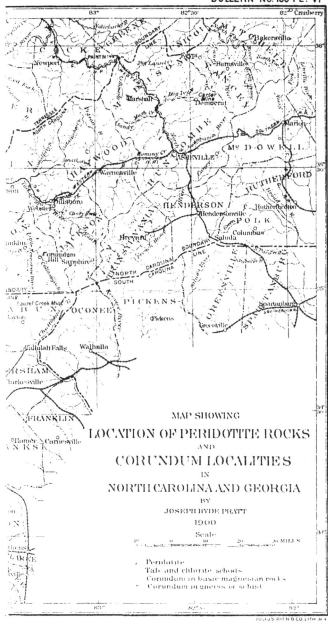

MAP SHOWING
LOCATION OF PERIDOTITE ROCKS
AND
CORUNDUM LOCALITIES
IN
NORTH CAROLINA AND GEORGIA
BY
JOSEPH HYDE PRATT
1900
Scale

Peridotite
Talc and chlorite schists
Corundum in basic magnesian rocks
Corundum in gneiss or schist

Bauer[1] has described etching figures that he observed on the base 0001 and the pyramid $22\bar{4}3$ of the Burma rubies. Those on the base are similar to the figures in fig. 5 of Pl. V, except that the outside contour of the rhombohedron is rounded.

These sapphire deposits are now controlled by the New Mine Sapphire Syndicate of Utica, Fergus County, Mont., and London, England, of which Mr. George A. Wells, of Great Falls, Mont., is president. Mr. S. S. Hobson, of Lewiston, Mont., one of the directors of the company, states in a recent letter that 130,000 carats of cuttable material were taken out last season. Besides this there is a large amount of very small crystals and badly flawed larger crystals that are not capable of being cut into gems and that are sold by the ounce. The largest rough stones that have been found weighed 11 to 12 carats, and from these were cut gems weighing 5 to 6 carats. One of the better stones taken out the season of 1899 weighed 4 carats when cut and is valued at over $75 a carat. All of the material is shipped to London.

That the American gems are being appreciated is shown by the large orders that are received for them from Paris, London, and New York.

CORUNDUM.

Under this head are included all the translucent to opaque varieties of all colors, subdivided into block, crystal, and sand corundum. While a sharp line can be drawn between corundum and emery, no such distinction can be made between corundum and sapphire, for many pieces of the former are found that have transparent portions. Many sapphire gems have been found in masses of corundum that were being mined for abrasive purposes.

In the following descriptions corundum deposits have been taken up by States in the order of supposed importance. Many of the beds are briefly noticed, but the larger and more important deposits are described in detail.

NORTH CAROLINA.

Most of the corundum localities in North Carolina are, in a general way, indicated on the map (Pl. VI), except the very few that are east of the Blue Ridge. In the following descriptions only those deposits have been considered which have been mined for corundum or which hold out a promising prospect for the mineral. These will be taken up by counties, the more important ones first.

MACON COUNTY.

Corundum was first discovered in this county in 1870 at what is now known as the Corundum Hill mine, and mining was begun here about a year later. This mine has become one of the most important

---

[1] Loc. cit., p. 213.

corundum deposits in this country.   It is situated about 8 miles southeast of Franklin, the county seat, on the northeast side of Cullasagee Creek, a tributary of the Little Tennessee River.

The corundum found at this mine occurs in peridotite rock, and this has been worked very extensively, especially near the contact of this rock with gneiss.   Pl. VII gives a general view of this peridotite formation, and shows to a certain extent the number of openings that have been made in it.   The hill is about 350 feet high, the summit being about 500 feet above the level of Cullasagee Creek.   Fig. 10 is

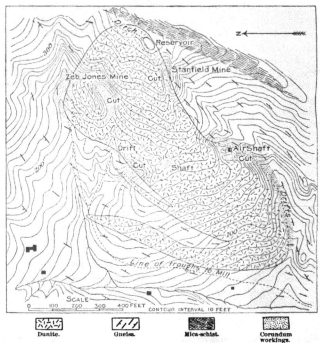

FIG. 10.—Map of the peridotite formation at Corundum Hill, Macon County, N. C.

a topographic map of this same peridotite formation, and shows the location of the various mines.   The formation is a rather blunt lens-shaped mass of the dunite variety of peridotite, and has about 10 acres of surface, over most of which the rock is exposed.   As is seen from this map, most of the mines are located near the contact of the dunite with the gneiss or schist, and follow contact veins of corundum.   A number of dunite veins have been worked within the formation, but with the exception of the one marked "Shaft" on the map, they have all soon pinched out.

GENERAL VIEW OF THE PERIDOTITE FORMATION AT CORUNDUM HILL, MACON COUNTY, N. C.

THE BIG VEIN BETWEEN THE PERIDOTITE AND THE GNEISS AT CORUNDUM HILL, MACON COUNTY N. C.

Most of the mining has been done on the south side of the formation, where was encountered what is known as the Big vein. This was first mined by means of open cuts and later by tunnels, the last one being about 300 feet below the summit of the hill. Pl. VIII is a view of the entrance to this tunnel, and shows the peridotite rock on the left and the gneiss on the right beyond the cut. For nearly the whole distance of the southern boundary of the dunite formation a cut has been made following the contour of the hill. This cut was sometimes wholly within the gneiss, at other times wholly within the peridotite, and again cutting directly on the contact. The tunnels are all to the left of the cut, and they have encountered corundum almost continuously for a distance of 1,280 feet, reaching nearly to the southeast boundary of the formation. Pl. IX is a view of the upper or southeastern end of this cut, showing the peroditite on the left and the gneiss and schist on the right. The upper part of this cut is known as the Stanfield mine. A tunnel has been run into the hill near the contact, at the head of which the vein of corundum is 8 to 10 feet wide. No work has been done at this mine for a number of years.

On the northeast side of this formation is what is known as the Zeb Jones mine, where there was exposed (July, 1899) a bench of ore 25 feet in depth and 2 to 5 feet in width, uncovered for a distance of 50 feet, which averaged very close to 50 per cent corundum. This vein carries what is known as "buckwheat" corundum, which, as its name suggests, is made up of small, irregular particles of corundum about the size of buckwheat grains.

Numerous dunite veins have been found and worked, but they can be mined profitably only when they are large contact veins, for the reason that they are very likely to pinch out after being worked for a short time.

From these various openings, collectively known as the Corundum Hill mine, block, crystal, and sand corundum ores have been obtained, all of which can be readily cleaned and will make a commercial product that can be used in the manufacture of any kind of corundum wheel. A small amount of garnet is occasionally found associated with the corundum in the vein along the southern contact, but this portion of the ore can be readily eliminated by hand cobbing at the mine. This is the only mine that produced any quantity of corundum during 1899. It is now owned by the International Corundum and Emery Company, of New York, N. Y.

The water of Cullasagee River is utilized for the washing and cleaning machinery of the mill, which is located about a mile and a half below the mine, at Cullasagee. A line of sluice boxes connects the mine with the mill, and all the corundum ore that can be readily broken to pieces is carried down to the mill in these boxes.

There are many outcrops of peridotite on Ellijay Creek, a few miles north of Cullasagee, and at many of them corundum has been found.

The most work that has been done is at the Mincey mine, which is 2 miles northwest of the Corundum Hill mine. At this locality a considerable quantity of corundum has been taken out, which was carried to the mill at Cullasagee and cleaned. Pl. X is a view of this open cut, which was entirely within the formation. Judging by the amount of corundum obtained and by that found near the contact of the dunite with the gneiss, there are good indications of the existence of corundum in quantity along the contact. The corundum that was obtained at this mine was hauled by wagons to the Corundum Hill mine, where it was cleaned. This property is owned by the International Corundum and Emery Company, of New York, N. Y.

Between the Corundum Hill and Mincey mines there is a bold outcrop of dunite on the Gray property, covering about the same surface as that at Corundum Hill. Although there has been no mining here, the little prospecting that has been done has shown corundum to be very thickly scattered along the lower borders of the formation, and many small pits that have been sunk within the formation have encountered corundum. This, in my opinion, is one of the most promising prospects for corundum in Macon County.

A great many of the peridotite formations along Ellijay Creek have been worked a little at different times, and these are mentioned in the lists of corundum localities (p. 83).

Sheffield mine.—This mine is in Cowee Township, about 7 miles northeast of Franklin, the county seat, just north of Cowee Creek. The corundum occurs here in amphibole-schist, and is described on page 31. On account of the depth to which decomposition has extended, the solid rock was only observed in the lower portions of the 87-foot shaft, so that nothing definite is known of this corundum-bearing amphibole-schist. The corundum, which is pink in color and which occurs in oval-shaped nodules up to an inch in diameter, has been pretty thoroughly mined down to the hard rock. The corundum is of good quality, and some preliminary tests have shown that it is well adapted to the manufacture of the vitrified wheel. On account of the low percentage of corundum in the rock, it is not at the present time a profitable corundum ore.

The saprolitic ore is readily cleaned, and furnishes a nearly pure commercial product. A small mill has been erected here. This property is owned by the National Abrasive Manufacturing Company, of New York, N. Y.

CLAY COUNTY.

Buck Creek or Cullakeenee mine.—This mine is in the Buck Creek Valley, about 20 miles southwest of Franklin, Macon County, and 21 miles a little north of east of Hayesville, the county seat of Clay County. These corundum deposits are associated with a compact mass of peridotite, covering about three-quarters of a square mile, the largest

UPPER END OF BIG CUT AT CORUNDUM HILL MINE, MACON COUNTY, N. C.

Peridotite is shown on the left and gneiss and schist on the right

OPEN CUT ON DUNITE VEIN AT THE MINCEY MINE, MACON COUNTY, N. C.

mass that is known in the Appalachian belt. Fig. 5 (page 22) is a topographic map of this formation, and shows the relation of the amphibolite to the peridotite and the location of the various openings that have been made for corundum. There has been but very little systematic mining for corundum in this locality, and most of the work has been in the nature of prospecting. Numerous cuts and pits have been made at a great many points on the formation, most of which have shown the presence of corundum. The principal work is at the east end of the formation, near the contact of the dunite with the gneiss, where a shaft 40 feet deep was sunk partially on the contact vein. A number of open cuts in this same vicinity have penetrated into the same vein. This vein is different from most of the corundum veins in the peridotite rocks, in that it is composed essentially of plagioclase feldspar and hornblende, which bear a similar relation to each other as the feldspar quartz and mica in the pegmatitic dikes. Pl. XI, A, is a general view of the Buck Creek formation, showing the shaft mine and the location of the contact vein that has been opened. With this exception all the pits and cuts that have been made are within the formation itself, and where they encountered corundum it was in small pockets, the remains of larger dunite veins. Pl. XI, B, shows one of these dunite veins. From the amount of corundum exposed by prospecting and the work done in the shaft, there is without doubt a large amount of corundum associated with these peridotite rocks, and if the mine were more accessible to the railroad it would offer one of the best corundum prospects in the country. At the present time, however, the nearest shipping point is Murphy, which is over 40 miles to the west. The nearest point on the Murphy branch of the Southern Railway is only 18 miles, to which a good road can be built that would not cost much more than the first 18 miles of the road to Murphy. Buck Creek offers ample water supply for running a mill sufficient to clean whatever corundum would be mined here. This property is also owned by the International Corundum and Emery Company, of New York. The ore is not difficult to clean, and, as far as can be judged from a superficial examination, should make a commercial product that can be used in the manufacture of the vitrified wheel.

Blue Ridge corundum tracts.—Under this head are included the long bands of corundum-bearing quartz-schist that have been found in the southeastern part of the county and in the adjoining county of Georgia (Rabun County). Parallel bands of this corundum-bearing schist have been followed for a number of miles close to the summit of the Chunky Gal and the Yellow mountains. As is stated on page 35, the amount of corundum in this schist is probably not over 5 per cent, and with such a low percentage of corundum these rocks are not to be considered, at the present time at least, as a source of this mineral.

There are four tracts included under this head, which are described below.

The Scaly Mountain tract is near the headwaters of Beech Creek, a prominent eastern tributary of the Tallulah River, on the southern and southwestern slopes of Scaly Mountain, at the elevation of about 4,500 feet. The corundum-bearing bands of schist have been traced for the distance of about 2 miles, with a general strike of N. 40° E. and with a dip approximately 20°–30° NW. Considerable prospecting has been done in tracing this band of schist, but experiments show that there is less than 5 per cent of corundum in this schist, although some specimens have yielded 12 per cent. The latter were probably pieces broken off along planes of lamination of the schist, while the rest of the piece from which they were broken off carried but little corundum.

The Foster tract is in Georgia, about 1¼ miles from Scaly Mountain, and the State line forms its northern boundary. It is on both sides of Falls Branch, one of the smaller western tributaries of the Tallulah River, and is about 3,500 feet above sea level. Here a number of pits have been made and samples of corundum have been obtained which have assayed on an average about 5 per cent of this mineral. There is more garnet associated with the corundum in this ore than in that from any of the other localities.

The Yellow Mountain tract is on the north of Scaly Mountain, on the northern slopes of the Yellow Mountains. No prospecting has been done here, and from the indications the ore is the same grade as at the other localities.

The Chunky Gal tract is at the summit and along the western slopes of the Chunky Gal Mountains, near the headwaters of Sugar Cove Creek. With a few interruptions, the corundum-bearing schist has been traced for over 2 miles, with a strike and dip approximately the same as on the other tracts. A number of pits and cuts have been made, from which considerable ore has been taken out and tested, and the tests show the percentage of corundum to be practically the same as at the others.

The corundum bands of the schist in all the tracts vary considerably in width, some being not over a foot or two wide, while others are 18 feet. In these wider bands, however, there are apt to be bands of the normal schist. More or less garnet has been found associated with the corundum in all the schist, and if in any amount would have to be eliminated or it would prevent any commercial corundum obtained from these ores being used in the manufacture of the vitrified wheel.

From the extent of the corundum-bearing schist, there is undoubtedly a large quantity of corundum in this section, but the low percentage of corundum in the rocks makes it very questionable whether they can be profitably worked.

The Corundum Mining and Manufacturing Company, of Philadel-

IN OF CORUNDUM IN THE PERIDOTITE FORMATION A
CLAY COUNTY, N. C.

phia, Pa., has recently been organized to work the deposits on the Scaly Mountain and Foster tracts. The only mining that has thus far been done consists of an open cut extending 35 feet on the band of corundum-bearing quartz-schist. About 1,000 tons of ore have been taken out, a small portion of which has been crushed and cleaned. The point at which mining was begun is on the southwestern slopes of Scaly Mountain at an elevation of nearly 4,500 feet. The crushing plant has been erected close to the cut. The cleaning mill is about 2,000 feet lower on Scaly Mountain, the crushed ore being conveyed thither in a flume.

No definite method of cleaning has as yet been decided upon. Experiments have been made with jigs and a Bartlett table, but they have not proved very satisfactory. The garnet and magnetite in the ore are to be separated by the electro-magnet. No corundum has as yet been cleaned for the market.

JACKSON COUNTY.

Perhaps the most important corundum locality in this county is in the extreme southeastern portion, in the vicinity of Sapphire, extending over into the adjoining county, Transylvania. In this section there is a series of about 30 outcrops of peridotite, which extend in a general northeast-southwest direction. All these outcrops are small, and corundum has been found associated with many of them. The location and relative size of the larger of these outcrops and the places where corundum has been mined are represented on the map, fig. 11. Most of this has been at the Bad Creek and Socrates mines, but the greater part of the work done at any of them has been in the nature of prospecting.

At the Burnt Rock mine, which is located about 5 miles northeast of Sapphire, all the mining has been done within the peridotite formation, and about 10,000 to 12,000 pounds of corundum have been taken out. It is of good quality and occurs in white crystals and knotty nodules. The ore is free from garnet and can be readily cleaned. From the amount of work done here the indications are that there is a considerable quantity of good corundum associated with the peridotite near its contact with the gneiss. The mining at the Brockton mine was also within the peridotite, and about the same amount of corundum was taken out as at the Burnt Rock mine. The corundum occurs in dull-gray crystals, which are easily cleaned and separated from the gangue. These two mines are in Transylvania County. Just below this mine, on the slopes of Poplar Ridge, a vein of corundum was exposed in October, 1900, by workmen who were making a new road. The corundum is massive, and gives good indications of occurring in quantity.

The little work that was done at the Sapphire mine shows a considerable quantity of white and gray corundum, often speckled with blue,

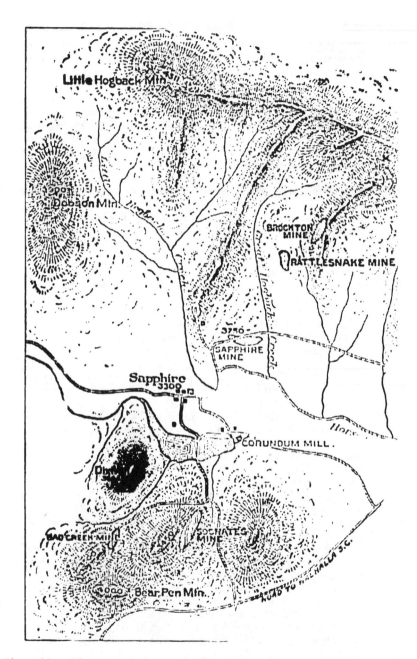

FIG. 11.—Map of the peridotite areas in the vicinity of ?
the location of the different cc

the garnet can be entirely eliminated this ore will not make a product that can be used for making the vitrified wheel. The vein has an average width of nearly 9 feet, and will carry from 15 to 20 per cent of corundum. All these mines just referred to belong to the Toxaway Company, Sapphire, N. C.

Corundum has been found at a number of the peridotite outcrops between the Bad Creek and the Whitewater mines; and while this does not by any means indicate that there are large deposits of this mineral in these rocks, it does indicate, taking into consideration the corundum deposits already found northeast and southwest of these, that there is a possibility of such deposits, and it makes this section a promising one for systematic prospecting.

GEORGIA.

The corundum localities of this State are shown on the map (Pl. VI), which also gives the general location of the peridotite formations that have been observed in this section. Although there is considerable peridotite occurring in the northern portion of the State, it is at but few places thus far that corundum has been found in any quantity, and these are at the extreme northern part, not far from the North Carolina line.

Georgia corundum is well known, and perhaps has the best reputation of any on account of that obtained from the Laurel Creek mine, which, with the exception of the Track Rock mine, is the only one that has produced any considerable quantity of corundum. The peridotite formations are not so large as in North Carolina, nor are the corundum localities so numerous, and it is not probable that there is as much corundum in this State as in North Carolina, although the Laurel Creek mine may be superior to any one thus far located in North Carolina.

Laurel Creek mine.--This mine, which is owned by the International Corundum and Emery Company, is located at Pine Mountain, Rabun County, Ga., and is 18 miles from Walhalla, S. C., the nearest point on the railroad. At this locality there is a large outcrop of peridotite, covering several hundred acres, and along the contact of this with the gneiss large deposits of corundum have been found. Several openings have been made, some of which have been worked very extensively. Fig. 12 is a topographic map of this peridotite formation, showing the general location of the cuts and shafts that have been made. As is seen from the map, the formation extends over two small hills, which, on account of their rough and barren nature, offer a sharp contrast to the surrounding country. There is a large open cut (1 in fig. 12) on the east side of the formation, which follows for the most part along the contact, is 200 feet in depth at the lower end, and gradually rises until at the upper end the surface is reached.

s lower end this cut encountered what

of massive corundum, the cut having

of crystal corundum. Pl. XII is a photog

the gneiss very distinctly on the left and

with the shaft house in the foreground.

Big vein of massive corundum, for whic

the foot of the south slope of the hill, and l

wer end of the cut (1, fig. 12) for a dist

sented by the dotted lines, with the shaft

estern end. Although this vein is near t

OPEN CUT ON PERIDOTITE-GNEISS CONTACT AT LAUREL CREEK, GEORGIA.

Shaft house in foreground.

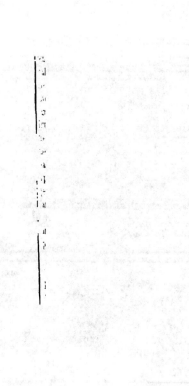

a little work was done farther to the east which showed the corundum vein to extend on the south side of the block of gneiss, and it is not at all improbable that this vein continues as represented by the dotted line 3. Open cuts on the east and west side of this block of gneiss have followed contact veins of corundum. Pl. XIII, *A*, is a photograph of the peridotite formation near the cut on the east side. Little work has been done at Laurel Creek except on contact veins, the principal exception being a small dunite vein (6 in fig. 12) near the west end of the formation, from which considerable corundum was obtained, but the vein soon began to pinch out. Pl. XIII, *B*, is a photograph of this vein, showing both the hanging and foot walls of peridotite. At 5, fig. 12, considerable work has been done, and some large crystals, for which this mine is noted, were obtained here.

This is perhaps the most famous corundum mine in this country, and has furnished ore from which an exceptionally good commercial product has been obtained.

It has not been worked since 1894, when the tunnels and shafts of the Big vein were cut off by the slipping of a large block of the peridotite formation, nearly a 200-foot cube. It is that portion of the formation represented on the map (fig. 12) between the open cut (1) and the cut to the west of the block of gneiss (2).

Track Rock mine.—The location of this mine is in the northeastern part of Union County, Ga., on the south side of Track Rock Gap. The corundum occurs in a peridotite formation, which is very much decomposed on the surface, there being very little visible but a mass of chlorite-schist containing more or less actinolite. A tunnel, having its upper end 75 feet below the surface, has been run in on the formation for about 200 feet, with short branching tunnels at several points. From the material cut through by the tunnel, which was examined by King,[1] of the Georgia geological survey, the rock was found to be an altered peridotite, made up of small grains of chrysolite surrounded by actinolite, and containing many grains of magnetite. It may be that the original of this rock was the peridotite amphibole-picrite.

All the work that has been done at this mine has been entirely within the formation, and the best results would be obtained near the contact of this rock with the surrounding country rock.

Foster mine.—This mine, which is located in the northeastern part of Towns County, Ga., just over the North Carolina line, has been described with the other mines occurring in this vicinity under the head of "Corundum in North Carolina," on page 60. The corundum occurs in a quartz-schist, and the property is owned by the Corundum Mining and Manufacturing Company, of Philadelphia, Pa.

---

[1] Bull. Geol. Survey Georgia No. 2, 1894, p. 93.

SOUTH CAROLINA.

In the northeastern part of York County, from 3 to 4 miles west of the Catawba River, on the land between Allison and Crowder creeks, corundum has been found in a belt about 200 to 300 yards wide which skirts along the western slopes of Nannies Mountain. This locality is about 12 miles northeast of Yorkville, S. C., and 25 miles southwest of Charlotte, N. C.

Mining operations have been carried on at two distinct portions of this belt, one a mile north of the summit of; Nannies Mountain, on the property of Alexander Rickard. The work done here consists of a shaft about 35 feet deep, from which several drifts have been run, which penetrate what is probably a light-gray granite, but it is much decomposed and of a sandy constituency. The only solid material encountered were irregular masses of black cleavable corundum associated with muscovite mica. In the surrounding fields float corundum ranging in size from small particles to masses of several pounds in weight are abundant, and many tons of this have been picked up and shipped.

A little to the west of the south end of Nannies Mountain, about 1½ miles from the Rickard mine, there is a similar occurrence of corundum. There have been a number of shallow cuts, ditches, and pits made in prospecting for corundum, but apparently none was found in place. The corundum that was found is often wrapped in mica.

The mode of origin of this corundum has not been determined, for up to the present time the exact nature of its occurrence is not definitely understood, as no exposure of the corundum can be seen which shows its relation to the rock in which it occurs. Neither can it be stated whether it is to be found in quantity.

PENNSYLVANIA.

The corundum in this State, so far as can be learned, is all associated with the serpentine rocks in Chester and Delaware counties and occurs near the contact of this rock with the gneiss. Considerable feldspar (plagioclase) similar to that described from the Big vein at Buck Creek, N. C., is usually crystallized out with the corundum.

Corundum has been found more abundantly near Unionville, in Newlin Township, Chester County. It is found here in a mass of serpentine rock, with an average width of about 800 feet and a length of 1 mile. A number of tons of corundum have been obtained from this mine, but during the last ten years little or no work has been carried on here. Associated with the corundum are tourmaline and spinel.

MONTANA.

Most of the corundum that has been found in Montana has been of the sapphire variety, but at one locality near Bozeman, Gallatin

PERIDOTITE FORMATION AT LAUREL CREEK, GEORG

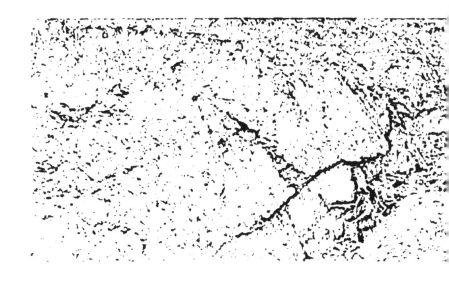

and extensively.

ometimes associated with the emery and
l it is largely in excess of the corundum
nto what might well be called a " spinel en

MASSACHUSETTS.

eposit of emery that has been found in
y of Chester, where the emery vein has b
s.   The vein is first encountered about 2
village of Chester, in a ledge that projec
rom its left bank.   The vein can be fol
along the line of the strike—south to a
tends across the east slope of Gobble (Nor
nto and crosses the narrow valley of Walk
t crosses South Mountain and can be foll
south.   The map (fig. 13) shows the gene
in, the places that have been opened alor
e different emery mills.   The emery occurs i
s been described on page 23.
at the southern end of the vein the first w
alf a mile north of where the vein disappe
Wright mine.   About twenty years ago
vas being carried on here, the work consisti
400 feet long that was worked to a depth o
and about 30 feet at its northern, with

average depth of 20 feet for the entire distance. Emery varying in width from 3 to 20 feet was encountered throughout nearly the entire length of the cut.

This mine was reopened in 1899, a shaft 87 feet deep having been sunk on the vein near the southern end of the cut and drifts run out from this. Margarite is the most conspicuous accessory mineral, and specimens that can rarely be excelled have been found here.

Continuing nearly half a mile to the north on the vein and near the top of the mountain is the Melvin mine. There is a shaft here 40 feet deep, from which drifts are being run. This shaft is but 1,250 feet from the head of the upper tunnel of the Old mine, the next

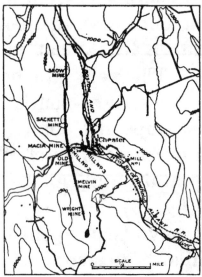

Fig. 13. - Map showing the location of the emery deposit at Chester, Mass.

one to the north. It is in this Old mine that the most extensive work has been done. Fig. 14 is a cross section of its underground workings. The mouth of the lowest tunnel is but 8 feet above Walker Brook and 75 feet to the south of it. As is seen from the diagram, the emery does not occur continuously throughout the vein, but in pockets or chimneys which dip into the vein about 30° N. From the work already done these seem to hold this direction rather constantly, so that the pockets can be approximately located at a given depth. It was in the first chimney of emery (see map, fig. 13) that the beautiful specimens of diaspore, for which this mine is noted, were found.

North of Walker Brook and about 500 feet from the Old mine is the Macia mine, where a small amount of surface work has been done. Near the head of a small ravine a tunnel was started on the west of the vein to intercept it, but work was discontinued before the vein was reached.

The next opening is near the highest point of the vein on the eastern slope of Gobble (North) Mountain, about three-fourths of a mile north of the Macia mine, and is known as the Sackett mine. At this part of the vein there was a considerable quantity of magnetite that was practically free from corundum and was mined as an iron ore. This mine was worked very extensively over twenty years ago, but had been abandoned until 1899, when it was reopened. The old works were near the highest point of the vein, on the slope of the mountain, and were worked for about 30 feet. The new work was started 117 feet below the mine, and a tunnel from the east side was run 114 feet to the vein. When this was reached a shaft and tunnels were started. At this mine the corundum occurs in what might be called porphyritic crystals of a bronze color, which are from 5 to 15 mm. across. Here blue and white masses of corundum weighing several pounds have been found, and small, well-formed blue crystals are also frequent. A little north of this mine, in an old opening, a cross vein of chlorite was encountered which carried a great many almost perfect cubes of pyrite and radiating groups of black tourmaline.

The last opening on the vein where there has been any work is at the Snow mine, over a mile north of the Sackett mine. A small open cut was made that exposed the vein, 3 feet in width. Between these two mines and also from the Snow mine north to the river the vein can be followed almost continuously.

While the vein can be followed nearly the whole distance, the emery does not occur throughout its entire length, for it is

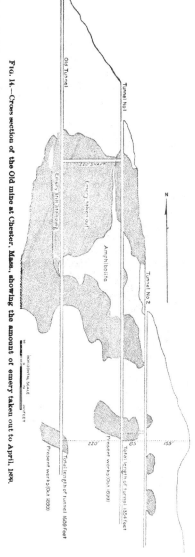

FIG. 14.—Cross section of the Old mine at Chester, Mass., showing the amount of emery taken out to April, 1899.

often in a series of pockets that are frequently connected with each other along the strike by a thin streak of chlorite and have a general dip in the vein of about N. 30°.   In the direction of the dip, however, the emery is more or less continuous.   The width of the vein varies from a few feet to 10 or 12, with an average width for the emery of about 6 feet.   This is the most extensive deposit of emery known in this country.

Emery has also been discovered in the vicinity of Huntington, Mass., but no development work has as yet been done.

NEW YORK.

The emery deposits of this State occur associated with the norite rocks in Westchester County that have been described on page 26. Deposits of magnetite and emery have been found at a number of places 3 to 4 miles southeast of Peekskill.   These deposits vary considerably in character, some being a nearly pure magnetite, others containing magnetite and spinel, and still others magnetite, spinel, and corundum.   Those within a mile north and northeast of Crugers Station have been worked for iron ore, while those worked for emery are in the southeastern part of Cortland Township.   The principal openings have been made on a ridge running north from Colabaugh Pond and it is here that the ore has been mined.   While the iron ore and emery appear to be very rich it was found upon examination that there was more or less of a dark-green mineral mixed with magnetite, and this mineral was shown by Williams[1] to be the pleonaste variety of spinel.   There is also considerable spinel in the emery, and even when this is quite abundant it can not be distinguished in the hand specimens from that in which there is almost none of this mineral.

At the emery deposits in the southeastern part of Cortland Township the percentage of corundum varies considerably at different openings, and it is sometimes observed in small blue, white, and colorless crystals.   Associated with most of the corundum there is spinel, and considerable of the ore that has been mined for emery has contained little or no corundum and has been made up of magnetite and spinel.   An ore of this sort would have most of the requisite properties of a true emery except the high degree of hardness due to the corundum; and when made up into a wheel it would not have the cutting efficiency of a true emery wheel.   The spinel, which is 8 in hardness (corundum being 9), would play the same part in this ore as corundum in the true emery, and while not so hard as corundum it has the cutting qualities which would give the ore considerable value as an abrasive.   For many purposes wheels made from this could be used fully as well as emery or corundum wheels and for some purposes they might be used to better advantage.   The spinel would not interfere at all in the manufacture of a vitrified wheel.

---

[1] Am. Jour. Sci., 3d series, Vol. XXXIII, 1882, p. 194.

Some of the ore that has been mined here carries a very high percentage of garnet.

The analyses that have been made of this ore all show a high percentage of alumina, which was to be expected, as the spinel is an alumina mineral, $(MgFe)O.Al_2O_3$, containing about 50 per cent of this oxide. An error is very often made in judging the percentage of corundum in an ore by calculating as corundum the total percentage of alumina obtained in a chemical analysis, which would represent, however, the alumina contained in all the aluminous mineral components of the ore.

Some of the ore at these mines is undoubtedly a true emery, but a considerable portion of it is a mixture of spinel and magnetite, which, while not a true emery, will make a useful abrasive. This whole ore body might be called a spinel-emery.

From what has been said regarding the occurrence of the emery in these Peekskill deposits, their pockety nature is what would be naturally expected and this has been characteristic of all the mining that has been done in this district.

The Jackson Mills Company, of Easton, Pa., is now the largest miner in this section. It has leased the emery deposits on the land of Isaac McCoy, 3 miles southeast of Peekskill. Its principal work is on the summit of a hill about one-half mile south of McCoy's house and consists of an open cut 40 to 50 feet deep, 40 feet long, and 12 to 20 feet wide. The emery ore is from 4 to 6 feet wide, but is broken up by bands of serpentine and chloritic rocks. In some of the ore the corundum is very distinct, occurring in elongated bluish white crystals up to 5 mm. long. This ore is very free from garnet.

Another deposit of emery has been encountered 50 feet below the summit, and still another 25 feet farther down. No mining has been done at either of these localities.

The ore is hauled by teams to Peekskill, where it is shipped by rail to Easton, Pa.

On a hill 1 mile east of the McCoy mine H. M. Quinn, of Philadelphia, Pa., has mined on the land of John H. Buckby. Pockets of emery were encountered on the summit of the hill and at a number of points on its western slope, but they soon pinched out. About 50 feet below the summit a face of rock 15 to 20 feet high and 40 feet across has been exposed. The only emery seen here is the remnant of a pocket.

As far as could be learned the emery deposits of the Tanite Company of Stroudsburg, Pa., are also leased. They are on the lands of Henry Heady, Oscar Dalton, and David Chase, and are for the most part similar to the deposits just mentioned. The ore on the land of Henry Heady is composed largely of garnet, and a considerable portion of it has been shipped by the Tanite Company to their mill at Stroudsburg.

NORTH CAROLINA.

While corundum has been known to occur in quantity in this State for over thirty years, emery has until recently only been known from one locality, and here the quantity was not apparently sufficient to be worthy of any development. This deposit has been described by Genth[1] as occurring at the McChristian place, 7 miles south of Friendship, Guilford County.

During the past few years emery has been found in Macon County in what appears to be considerable quantity. Nothing definite can be stated regarding the rock in which it occurs, as it is greatly decomposed as far as it has been exposed by the excavations. It does have, however, very much the appearance of a decomposed basic magnesian rock. There are a number of small outcrops of this saprolitic rock about 5 miles southwest of Franklin, the county seat, and emery in varying quantity occurs at all of them.

These outcrops, as far as could be judged, are isolated and in no way connected with one another. They are lenticular in form and but a few hundred feet wide, the longer axis being sometimes two or three times this. While the general direction of the strike of these outcrops is nearly the same, they are not in even an approximate line as regards one another. For nearly 15 miles south of these and following the valley of the Little Tennessee River small isolated outcrops of peridotite are numerous. The country rock through which these have forced their way is a hornblende-gneiss.

Considerable mining was done two years ago by Dr. H. S. Lucas, of Franklin, at the Fairview mine near North Skeener Gap, about a hundred tons of ore having been taken out and cleaned. The vein has been tapped at intervals for a distance of nearly 200 feet, good emery being encountered at each opening. All the work done was near the summit of Fairview Knob.

One mile N. 25° W. of the Fairview mine, on the southwest slopes of Dobson Mountain, another opening has been made for emery in an outcrop of the same rock on the land of J. A. Waldroop. A vein of emery ore was uncovered here that was 15 feet wide. No mining has been done here, all the work being in the nature of prospecting.

Emery has been found in similar outcrops on the lands of William Mann, three-fourths of a mile south, and of James Ledford, one and one-fourth miles S. 30° E. of the Fairview mine.

Preliminary fire tests were made upon the cleaned product of this ore, which proved it to be well adapted for use in the manufacture of the vitrified wheel.

METHODS OF MINING CORUNDUM.

In considering the methods used in mining corundum, it must be borne in mind that up to the present time it has been obtained in quan-

---

[1] Bull. U. S. Geol. Survey No. 74, 1891, p. 30.

tity only where it has been associated with peridotite rocks. These rocks, as will be shown later, present certain difficulties which, if not overcome, will cause considerable delay and danger in mining. The emery occurring in amphibolite presents these difficulties in only a slight degree.

Nearly all of the peridotite formations in which the corundum deposits occur are bold outcrops on the mountain sides and hilltops, having almost perfect natural drainage. At all the localities where there has been no mining the little prospecting has been usually by means of open cuts supplemented by tunnels. While at first mining by means of cuts may seem to be the most advantageous, it is soon found to be the cause of considerable extra expense. These cuts, or any other openings made over the surface of the peridotite, offer a much greater opportunity for surface water and frost to penetrate the mass of the rock formation. These rocks are more or less seamed or cracked, usually to the depth that alteration can extend, and thus offer opportunities for the infiltration of water. As most of the alteration products of this peridotite formation are slippery hydrous magnesium minerals, such as serpentine and talc, and as these are developed in the seams and cracks of the peridotite, anything that is done to disturb them will make them very liable to slip. At the Corundum Hill mine there are large masses of peridotite that have become loosened and gradually slipped down and closed up some of the tunnels, and there is constant danger that fragments of the rock will fall into the cuts and some of the tunnels. At the Laurel Creek mine, a mass of peridotite with soil, etc., nearly a 200-foot cube, has become loosened and slipped downward, effectually closing up the tunnel and shaft of the Big vein.

In mining corundum associated with peridotite rocks it is therefore advisable not to break the surface of the formation any more than is absolutely necessary and to do no work at all along the contact by means of open cuts, but to confine the mining to a system of tunnels and shafts. This method of mining will be found the cheapest in the end. Then, again, all the tunnels and shafts should be well timbered and the mine kept as thoroughly drained as possible.

A large amount of the material that must be handled is easily worked with pick and shovel, as it consists of the crystals and fragments of corundum in the zone of chlorite and vermiculite. In those veins in which the corundum is associated with feldspar, as at Laurel Creek and Buck Creek, and those where there is considerable amphibole or enstatite, as at Corundum Hill, blasting is necessary. Most of the corundum deposits in peridotite are so located that there need be but little hoisting of the ore for some time. By drifting from a shaft at the upper end of a tunnel that has been run into the vein at the lowest level possible the ore can be removed with a minimum of hoisting and the mine will be kept dry.

If the mill is located some distance from the mine and a line of sluice boxes can be built, the more or less finely divided ore may be carried to it by means of these.   In this way the ore is partially cleaned by the time it reaches the mill.   This is the method employed at the Corundum Hill mine.

Where the corundum occurs in a gneiss, quartz-schist, or syenite, there should be no difficulty in mining by means of open cuts.

METHODS OF CLEANING CORUNDUM.

The difference between the commercial product and the ore as it comes from the mine is that the latter has been freed as far as possible of all impurities, so that the resulting product is or should be nearly pure corundum or emery.   Most of the impurities are easily removed by conveying the crushed ore into boxes through which a stream of water runs, which is so regulated that the corundum readily settles to the bottom of the trough and the lighter minerals are carried off.   Before this, however, the crushed ore is sieved, and all that will not pass through a No. 12 screen is recrushed and passed between rollers until it is reduced to the desired size.   This washing process will remove only the impurities that are entirely separated from the particles of corundum, but there are usually some of the impurities attached to the particles or grains that have to be removed by another process.   The product is passed through a machine known as the screw or scouring machine, in which there is a coarse worm similar to the screw conveyer.   This grinds out almost all of the impurities, and these are separated by again subjecting them to the washing process.   The final impurities are separated from the particles of corundum by means of a machine called the "muller" or "chaser" (see Pl. XIV).   The principle of this is to cause each grain of corundum to rub against another and thus wear away the adhering foreign substances.   The machine consists of a shallow tub, in which are two heavy wooden rollers which move around its circumference. The freshly ground corundum on being thrown into these tubs is kept constantly stirred up and then pressed down by the rollers being passed over it.   In this way the scouring motion is kept up between the grains.   The impurities are thus gradually worn away and are carried off by a stream of water that flows continually through the tub.   The corundum in the tub is kept stirred up by men with hoes or by plow-shaped iron blades in front of the wooden rollers.   It usually requires from four to eight hours, according to the nature of the impurities that are attached to the corundum grains, to obtain a clean product.

There are two methods of drying this product, by either of which it is removed from the mullers and allowed to lie overnight on inclined floors.   By one method this product is conveyed by elevator belts to the second floor of the mill and dropped vertically for a distance of 20 to 30 feet down the stack of a furnace.   At the bottom it strikes an

. AT CULLASAGEE, MACON COUNTY, N. C.

inclined surface that is just above the flames of the furnace and slides down this surface into an iron box. By the other method the wet product is thrown in at the upper end of an iron cylinder, open at both ends, which revolves about a coil of steam pipes. One end of the cylinder is lower than the other, and the wet mass is alternately carried up by the revolving cylinder and dropped on the hot coil of pipes, and so gradually worked toward the lower end, where it is caught in a hopper and conveyed by elevator belts to the sizing room. Here it is automatically screened to the various sizes.

On Pl. XIV, *A* and *B*, are views of the exterior and interior of the corundum mill at Cullasagee. In the foreground of *B* are the boxes in which the ore is first washed and just beyond these are the mullers.

Only within the last few years has any attempt been made to improve the methods of concentrating and cleaning corundum. There are now a number of companies that have installed complete concentrating mills, similar to those used in concentrating gold ores, but modified to suit corundum ore. While all are using jigs for the coarser sizes of the crushed ore, some are using Frue vanners and others Bartlett or Wifley tables for the finer sizes. This method works very satisfactorily for concentrating the corundum, and if, during the crushing and rolling of the ore, the corundum is largely separated from the associated minerals, a nearly cleaned product is obtained. It is necessary, however, to subject the larger part of the concentrates to some process similar to that performed by mullers, to free the grains of corundum from other minerals attached to them.

A new machine—the Hooper pneumatic concentrator—can also probably be used to advantage in concentrating corundum ores.

Any other minerals that will be likely to remain with the corundum in the concentrates, as garnet, pyrite, etc., can undoubtedly be separated by means of the Wetherill magnetic concentrator. Unless these minerals are unattached to the particles of corundum there will be a considerable loss of corundum by this separation.

USES OF CORUNDUM.

Corundum is used for only two general purposes, as gems and as an abrasive.

The varieties of corundum that are of value as gems have been described on page 39, and the many uses that are made of the cut stones in the jewelry trade are too well known to need more than a passing notice here. One use of the corundum gem that is perhaps worthy of notice is in supplying jewels for watches. In a recent notice from the Swiss agency of precious stones for watches, Aarburg, Switzerland, it said that 75,000,000 watch jewels are required annually. With the increase of production of gem corundum in this country a great deal of the smaller fragments could and should be utilized in the manufacture of watch jewels.

Both corundum and emery are used in the manufacture of abrasive materials, and these are on the market in three forms, as wheels and blocks of various shapes and sizes, as emery paper, and as grains or powder. The last two need no further explanation, but a description of the first is of importance.

The shapes of the corundum and emery wheels and bricks or stones are extremely varied, being adapted to all kinds of grinding. The principle of these wheels is the same as that of the rotary files, and as the points of a file become dull from using, so also do the grains or points of the emery and corundum in the wheel. In making a wheel it is necessary, therefore, to make it of such a temper or grade that when these grains become dull or rounded they will fall away or will be readily removed by a truing tool, leaving fresh, sharp grains exposed. The grade of a wheel depends upon the character of the work for which it is to be used, and the bond should be such that it will wear away a little faster than the corundum or emery, and thus always leave the sharp edges ready for cutting. The greatest economy is effected when the bond does not wear away until the grains of emery or corundum have become rounded or dulled, thus permitting the wheel to do its greatest amount of work.

Before leaving the factory all wheels should be thoroughly tested to a higher strain than that to which they are to be subjected in actual use; as the wheels have to be run at a very high velocity in order to secure the greatest efficiency, there is at times but little reserve strength, and a sudden blow will often cause them to fly to pieces.

To give an idea of the number of different wheels that the larger emery-wheel companies are prepared to make, I can not do better than to mention what I saw and what was told me at the Norton Emery Wheel Company, of Worcester, Mass. The wheels are manufactured for the special work for which they are intended, and vary in shape, in bond, and in grain of corundum. The sizes of corundum that are used are Nos. 12, 14, 16, 20, 24, 30, 36, 40, 50, 54, 60, 70, 80, 90, 100, 120, 150, 160, 180, 200, and 6 grades of flour corundum. The bond has 26 degrees of hardness, represented by the letters of the alphabet, although a bond is seldom used softer than E or harder than M. There are 408 different sizes of circular wheels, so that the different grades of wheels possible are almost unlimited.

There are three types of wheels known to the trade, the vitrified, chemical, and cement, the names being derived from the process by which they are manufactured. In the manufacture of all, the corundum or emery used is in grains of uniform size, but varies with the grade of wheel that is to be made. The vitrified wheel is the most important and most generally used, although for some work one of the others is preferable, and for very large wheels the chemical is especially adapted.

VITRIFIED WHEEL.

In the manufacture of this wheel more care is necessary in the selection of the corundum, for in the vitrifaction of the bond the foreign minerals containing water are very likely to cause the wheel to burst. The corundum grains are mixed thoroughly in a paste of prepared clay and other fluxes, and the mixture is then poured into paper molds and set aside in a drying room until hard enough to be readily handled. When the molds are sufficiently dry, they are subjected to a dressing or trimming process and shaped to approximate dimensions on a potter's wheel or shaving machine, and are then further dried.

The excess of mechanical water having evaporated, they are then ready for the kilns. The kilns are cone shaped and the inside measurements vary from 12 to 20 feet in height and 10 to 18 feet in diameter. When the kiln is filled the entrance is closed and sealed and the fires are started. The temperature is allowed to rise slowly, until all the water of mechanical admixture and of crystallization in the foreign materials is driven off, when the temperature is raised to about 3,000°, or to a white heat, this heating process requiring several days. Where the foreign minerals mixed with the corundum contain water of composition that is driven off only at a very high temperature, the wheels are apt to be broken by this water coming off when the temperature of the kiln is raised to the fusing point of the clay. The clay and other fluxes fuse and form a porcelain setting for each grain or fragment of corundum, which makes a very strong bond. The kilns are allowed to cool very slowly, several days being required for this. The kiln is then opened and the wheels are brought to a lathe, called the "truing machine," where they are turned to the exact dimensions desired, the hole is bushed to the exact size, and the wheel is then trued and balanced ready for shipping.

The heat necessary for the fusion in making the vitrified wheel apparently has no effect upon the corundum beyond a partial decolorization and the expulsion of the slight percentage of water in the corundum.

CHEMICAL WHEEL.

In this process, which is also called the silicate process, silicate of soda is used as the binding material. The silicate is thoroughly mixed with the emery or corundum and some drying material and tamped into molds. It is then subjected to an "oven" heat for twenty-four hours, after which it is removed and finished according to the method described above for the vitrified wheels after they are removed from the kilns. Wheels have been made by this process that were over 2,000 pounds in weight.

CEMENT WHEEL.

In the cement wheel, shellac, rubber, linseed oil, and other substances are used as the binding material. This makes a soft wheel that is well adapted for roll and surface grinding when made with shellac, and for saw gummers and thin wheels when made with oils.

Although an examination of a corundum property may show the existence of considerable quantity of the mineral, no mining should be undertaken until satisfactory tests have been made upon the corundum to prove that it has those properties that will make it of value as an abrasive.

The value of a corundum deposit as an ore for abrasive purposes depends upon that property of the mineral which enables it to retain a sharp edge, known as a cutting edge, when it is crushed to grains. All corundums do not have this property, and while many exhibit this in the first stage of the crushing, the finer fragments and grains do not. This is more apparent when the corundum has been made into a wheel, for when first used the wheel may do good work, especially if it is a coarse-grained wheel, but as it wears away, the grains of corundum become rounded, instead of breaking to a cutting edge. In estimating the value of a corundum deposit, it is therefore very essential to determine the abrasive qualities of the corundum. Neither a chemical analysis nor a superficial examination of a corundum ore will determine its cutting qualities, and this can be obtained only by making the corundum into a wheel and testing it.

In estimating the value of an ore it is also necessary to determine to what degree of purity it can be cleaned, or what percentage of the commercial product will be corundum, and also what will be the nature of the foreign minerals. A foreign mineral will always be softer than the corundum, and will to a certain extent reduce its abrasive power. Beyond this, the presence of a small amount of foreign mineral does not materially affect the value of the corundum for making a cement or chemical wheel, but is often the reason for discarding it in manufacturing a vitrified wheel, on account of the low fusibility of the foreign substance. Garnet is perhaps the most objectionable mineral in a corundum ore, it being very difficult to separate it from the corundum, because the specific gravity of the two is nearly the same. Corundum containing even a little of the garnet can not be used in the manufacture of the vitrified wheel.

OTHER USES.

An attempt has been made to use corundum as a source of aluminum, but on account of its refractoriness and the percentage of ferric oxide and silica that it often contains, and on account of the cost of the ore, this use has not been found feasible.

The late Mr. Alfred E. Hunt, of Pittsburg, Pa., made the following statement:[1]

The real difficulty which we find in the use of corundum for this manufacture is the cost of the raw material as compared with that of native bauxites. In this item we include not only the price of the corundum as it has been offered to us, but also the expense of grinding it to an impalpable powder, which must be done before it can be used directly in the manufacture of aluminum, and the cost of preliminary chemical treatment for purification—which latter operation, however, is also required for bauxite.

Corundum has also been used as the source of the aluminum in the manufacture of aluminum-copper and aluminum-iron alloys. In the manufacture of these the corundum, without undergoing any previous treatment, was charged into an electric furnace with a mixture of carbon and copper or carbon and iron, according to whether aluminum oronze or ferro-aluminum was desired. Since 1890, however, when alumina began to be manufactured at a comparatively low price, this artificial oxide has been used in the place of the corundum.

CORUNDUM LOCALITIES IN THE UNITED STATES.

Under this head are included practically all the localities in the United States at which corundum has been found, and if they have been described under the heading "Distribution of corundum" they are simply mentioned here. Regarding the other localities, the mode of occurrence is given in most cases, and also some idea of the extent and character of the corundum.

This list is probably not complete, but it represents all those localities that I have visited and those of which an authenticated record could be obtained. It is taken up alphabetically by States.

ALABAMA.[2]

Dudleyville.—Between this town and Perry Mills, Tallapoosa County, corundum has been picked up at a number of places in the soil, but none has been found in place. Peridotite rocks have been found in the vicinity, and it is not at all improbable that the corundum was derived from these rocks.

Hanover.—Corundum has been found sparingly in Coosa County in the vicinity of this town.

CALIFORNIA.

Plumas County.—An interesting occurrence of corundum has recently been observed in the vicinity of Meadow Valley. Cutting the serpentine rocks of the eastern slope of Spanish Peak at an elevation of about 4,100 feet, and 1½ miles west-northwest of the Meadow Valley post-office, is a series of white coarse-grained dikes that are

[1] Trans. Am. Ins. Min. Eng., Vol. XXVIII, 1898, p. 875.
[2] Geol. Survey Alabama, Report, 1875, p. 85.

composed of 84 per cent of oligoclase and 16 per cent of corundum. The corundum is in crystals up to 2 inches in length and 1 inch in diameter, the general habit being pyramidal, and it is distributed rather irregularly through the groundmass of feldspar. This is a further illustration of the differentiation of a rock magma, supersaturated with alumina which has crystallized out as corundum. It is still uncertain whether these deposits of corundum will prove to be of commercial importance.[1]

COLORADO.

Chaffee County.—Corundum crystals have been found at the Calumet iron mines in the mica-schists at their contact with intrusive dikes of diorite. R. C. Hills, geologist to the Colorado Fuel and Iron Company, writes that the ore occurs in a band of rock 6 inches to 2 feet thick that has been followed for a distance of 500 feet, and that it averages 40 per cent of corundum.

CONNECTICUT.

Litchfield.—Corundum 'was found here associated with talc and pyrite in a mass of blue cyanite. Only surface specimens were found.

Norwich.—In the vicinity of this place corundum was found sparingly with sillimanite.

DELAWARE.

Corundum has been found in this State in the serpentine rocks near the Pennsylvania border. The only locality definitely known is near Chandlers Hollow, in Newcastle County, about 2½ miles south of Concord, Delaware County, Pa. It has been found only in small quantity.

GEORGIA.

Acworth.—Seven miles southwest of Acworth, Cobb County, there is a large peridotite formation which is entirely within Paulding County. From a pit sunk within this formation about 1,000 pounds of corundum were taken out. It is of poor quality, but makes handsome mineral specimens.

Bell Creek mine.—This mine is 4 miles north of Hiwassee, Towns County, and the corundum, mostly of a pink color, occurs in a peridotite. The work done consists of a pit 12 feet square by 12 feet deep. Only a small quantity of corundum was found.

Centralhatchee.—At this place, which is in Heard County, grayish, white, and blue corundum has been found in a matrix of hornblende, which is associated with basic magnesian rocks.

Douglas County.—Blue corundum in a pale greenish cyanite.

Foster mine.—The corundum occurs in quartz-schist. (See p. 60.)

Gainesville—Beautiful specimens of red corundum have been found in the peridotite formation 1 mile east of Gainesville, Hall County.

[1] A. C. Lawson: Am. Geologist, Vol. XXVII, 1901, p. 132; J. A. Edman, letters from.

Habersham County.—Corundum has been found as surface specimens at a number of localities in this county, and at one place in the peridotite formation. There have been no developments and there are no indications of any quantity.

Hamilton mine.—The corundum occurs in a peridotite formation about 5 miles north of Young Harris, Towns County. No large quantity has been found.

Hog Creek mine.—This mine is 2 miles a little south of west of Hiwassee, Towns County, but it lacks development. The corundum is associated with peridotite, and is pink, blue, and white.

Laurel Creek mine.—In peridotite. (See p. 63.)

Monroe.—Four and a half miles from Monroe, Walton County, on the farm of George W. Breedlove, black corundum has been found associated with peridotite rocks. Some little prospecting done here has been within the formation and some near the contact.

Pine Mountain, Rabun County.—In peridotite. (See p. 63.)

Porter Springs.—One mile southeast of this place (in Lumpkin County) corundum has been found in an amphibolite, but there is no quantity.

Powder Springs.—There is a considerable outcrop of peridotite in Cobb County, in the vicinity of Powder Springs, which offers a promising place for prospecting. A small vein has been opened on the W. B. Turner farm.

Rabun Gap.—Several pounds of corundum have been obtained from the Beavett mine; it occurs in a peridotite rock.

Teltonville.—One mile north of this town, in Forsyth County, surface specimens of corundum were found which evidently originated in the quartz-schists of this region.

Stone mine.—This mine, which is in the same general formation as the Track Rock mine (see p. 65), is in Rabun County. Only a little development has been undertaken and the prospect that the deposit may be valuable is not very favorable.

Thomaston.—Seven to 8 miles southwest of Thomaston, Upson County, considerable corundum has been found on the surface at the old Kelly farm. Some of the specimens of the corundum in the matrix indicate that it was derived from a mica-schist.

Track Rock mine.—In peridotite. (See p. 65.)

West Point.—A short distance northeast of this town (in Troup County) corundum has been found sparingly in a narrow strip of peridotite. Apparently no large quantity.

MARYLAND.

Corundum has been reported to occur in the vicinity of Whitehall, but no definite information can be obtained that any has been found here beyond a stray surface specimen.

American Bar.—The lowest bar on the
phires have been found.   (See p. 47.)
Cottonwood Creek.—In the gravels of th
phires have been found.   (See p. 51.)
Dana Bar.—A bar in the Missouri River
phires have been found.   (See p. 47.)
Eldorado Bar.—Sapphires in the gravel.
Emerald Bar.—The highest bar on the
phires have been found.   (See p. 49.)
French Bar.—Sapphires have been found
    (See p. 47.)
Gallatin County.—Corundum in syenite.
Magpie Gulch.—Pale-greenish sapphires
vel.   (See p. 47.)
Metropolitan Bar.—Sapphires occur in th
Missouri River bars.—In the various bars
miles east and northeast of Helena, sapp
gravel.   (See p. 47.)
Rock Creek.—All colors of sapphires are f
ek.   (See p. 50.)
Ruby Bar.—Sapphires occur in an andesi
Spokane Bar.—A bar of the Missouri Riv
been done for sapphires that occur in tl
Yogo Gulch.—Blue sapphires occur in a
)

NEVADA.

Peekskill.—A short distance east of Peekskill emery is found in basic magnesian rocks in some quantity. (See p. 70.)

NORTH CAROLINA.

Acme mine.—This mine is located about three-quarters of a mile west of Statesville, Iredell County. The corundum occurs in crystals in an amphibolite.

Addie.—Crystals of corundum have been found sparingly associated with the peridotite rocks in the vicinity of Addie, Jackson County.

Bad Creek mine.—Corundum associated with peridotite. (See p. 62.)

Bakersville.—Corundum crystals have been found sparingly in the gneiss at William Bowmans, three-fourths of a mile west of Bakersville, Mitchell County.

Behr mine.—This mine is near Elf post-office, on Shooting Creek, Clay County. Pink and white corundum have been found associated with peridotite rocks.

Belts bridge.—Crystals of black corundum occur in an amphibolite 8 miles northwest of Statesville, Iredell County, on the Hunter farm.

Betts Gap.—Corundum in splendid grayish-white crystals that are translucent are found in the gneiss to the south of the gap in Jackson County. Garnet also occurs in the gneiss.

Blue Ridge properties.—Corundum occurs in gneiss. (See p. 59.)

Brockton mine.—Corundum occurs in the peridotite. (See p. 61.)

Buck Creek mine.—Also known as the Cullakeenee. Is in a peridotite formation. (See p. 58.)

Burnt Rock mine.—In a peridotite formation. (See p. 61.)

Caler Fork.—Ruby mine, the crystals being found in the gravels of the creek. (See p. 40.)

Caney Fork.—Two miles above the mouth of this creek, in Jackson County, corundum is found in the chlorite-schist in considerable quantity. At many points along this creek and its tributaries corundum has been found in the chlorite-schists and in gneiss near these schists, as at the mouth of and also 2 miles up Chastains Creek and on Shoal Creek Mountains on the West Fork.

Carpenters Knob.—Along the ridge leading northwest from Carpenters Knob, near the border of Burke, Cleveland, and Catawba counties, corundum in grayish-blue tapering crystals is found associated with garnetiferous gneisses and schists.

Carter mine.—Corundum occurs in a peridotite formation associated with spinel. Considerable work was done here ten years ago, but since then the mine has been idle. This locality offers a somewhat promising prospect.

Celos Ridge.—Corundum crystals 2 to 3 inches long have been found sparingly in the decomposed gneiss on this ridge 8 miles southeast of Burnsville, Yancey County.

Chastains Creek.—See above, under Caney Fork.

Chunky Gal Mountains.—Corundum has been found in the bands of quartz-schists and gneiss of which the Chunky Gal Mountains are composed. Garnet is associated with the corundum, which forms a very small percentage of the rock. This occurrence is described on page 34.

Collins mine.—Pink corundum in cyanite occurs at this mine near Statesville, Iredell County.

Corundum Hill mine.—The corundum at this mine occurs in a peridotite. (See p. 55.)

Cowee Valley.—Ruby and red corundum are found in the alluvial deposits of this valley, many of which are transparent. (See description of ruby mine, pp. 40–44.)

Coweeta.—Pink corundum is found in a greenish cyanite at this place, in Macon County.

Cullakeenee mine.—Same as the Buck Creek mine.

Cullasagee mine.—This is the same as the Corundum Hill mine.

Democrat.—Corundum has been found, sparingly associated with the peridotite rocks, a little to the south of this place, in Buncombe County.

Elf.—Beautiful specimens of pink corundum are found in the green amphibolite. Occasionally there are blue pieces in this rock.

Egypt mine.—This mine is located in Yancey County, 10 miles west of Burnsville, and the corundum is in a peridotite. It is in crystalline masses and distinct crystals of a white color, often mottled with blue. This occurrence is interesting as being the only one where corundum has been found surrounded directly by dunite.

Ellijay Creek.—Corundum has been found at many points in the valley of this creek, associated with peridotite rocks. The more important of these are the Mincey, Haskett, and Higdon mines.

Fairview mine.—At this mine emery occurs in basic magnesian rocks. (See p. 72.)

Fishhawk Mountain.—At an elevation of 4,000 feet on the western slope of this mountain, on Hickory Knoll Creek, in Macon County, corundum has been found sparingly in a small outcrop of dunite.

Foster mine.—Near the summit of Chunky Gal Mountains, near the headwaters of the northern fork of Shooting Creek, in Clay County, corundum occurs in peridotite. (See p. 60.)

Gaston County.—Blue corundum, associated with mica and quartz, has been found at Chubbs, Chrowders, and Kings mountains in this county. Emery also has been found at Chrowders Mountain.

Glenville.—Four miles north of this town, in Macon County, corundum occurs in chlorite-schist similar to that on Caney Fork.

Gray property.—Corundum in peridotite. (See p. 58.)

Grimshaw Gem mine.—Sapphires of various colors have been found at this mine in peridotite. It is near Montvale post-office, Jackson County. (See p. 45.)

Hampton mine.—Same as Mine Fork.

Haskett mine.—This is given under Ellijay Creek.

Herbert mine.—This mine is on Little Buck Creek, Clay County, and is in a long, narrow arm of peridotite extending out from the main mass of the Buck Creek peridotite formation. Some prospecting has been done here, and although corundum has been found, the main mass of it occurs in connection with the main mass of peridotite.

Higdon mine.—This mine was worked for a short time, and there is connected with it a mill for washing and cleaning the ore. (See Ellijay Creek, above.)

Isbel mine.—Corundum occurs sparingly in what may be a decomposed amphibolite. One of the largest washing and cleaning mills in the State is at this mine.

Kings Mountain.—See Gaston County.

Marshall.—Corundum has been found in large gray crystals half mile north of the mouth of Big Ivy River and 3 miles above Marshall, Madison County, on the surface of a large amphibolite outcrop. It is on the property of G. C. Haynie, of Marshall. It has also been found on the property of Hon. J. C. Pritchard near the same town.

McChristians place.—Emery of reddish-brown and grayish colors has been found at this place, which is 7 miles north of Friendship, Guilford County. The property lacks development. Surface specimens of corundum have also been found here.

Mincey mine.—The corundum at this mine is found in peridotite. (See p. 58.)

Mine Fork.—Emery, associated with staurolite.

Montvale.—At many of the peridotite formations in the vicinity of Montvale, Jackson County, corundum has been found. (See p. 45.)

Newfound Gap.—A little to the south of this gap, in Haywood County, red corundum has been found on the surface of a small mass of dunite.

Nona.—Corundum in distinct crystals has been found on the surface, in the vicinity of gneiss, at Nona, Macon County.

Owens Creek.—Crystals and grains of corundum have been found in bowlders of cyanite near the mouth of this creek, in Transylvania County.

Presley mine.—This mine is located 4 miles north of Canton, Haywood County. The corundum, of a blue and bluish-gray color, occurs in a pegmatitic dike.

Reed mine.—The corundum at this mine, which is 6 miles east of Franklin, Macon County, occurs in a saprolitic rock, and is in small prismatic crystals of a bluish color, some of which are nearly transparent.

Retreat.—Near Retreat post-office, in Haywood County, corundum has been found in limited quantity in small pegmatitic dikes in the gneiss.

Sapphire.—The mines in the vicinity of this town are described on page 61.

Sapphire mine.—The corundum occurs in peridotite. (See p. 61.)

Scaly Mountain.—The corundum occurs in quartz-schist. (See p. 60.)

Sheffield mine.—The corundum at this mine is in amphibole-schist. (See p. 58.)

Skeener Gap.—Emery is found here in a basic magnesian rock. (See p. 72.)

Shoups Ford.—At this place, in Burke County, corundum has been found associated with fibrolite.

Socrates mine.—One of the mines in the vicinity of Sapphire. Corundum occurs in peridotite. (See p. 62.)

Swannanoa Gap.—Float corundum has been found near an outcrop of peridotite.

Thumping Creek.—Corundum has been found in rough nodules and flat crystals in gneiss on the property of Curtis Ledford and C. C. Patterson, on this creek, Macon County.

Turkey Knob.—On the summit of this mountain, near the Macon-Jackson county line, corundum has been found sparingly in gneiss.

Waldroop mine.—Emery has been found in a basic magnesian rock. (See p. 72.)

Watayua mine.—Same as the Reed mine.

West Mills.—Red and ruby corundum have been found in the old gravel beds of the streams on the West farm, near West Mills, Macon County.

Whitewater mine.—The corundum is in peridotite. (See p. 63.)

Winston Salem.—Near this place, in Forsyth County, emery has been found similar to that at the McChristian place.

Yellow Mountain.—The gneisses of this section carry a small percentage of corundum. (See p. 60.)

PENNSYLVANIA.

Blackhorse.—Slender grayish crystals of corundum have been found at this place, which is near Media, Delaware County. This has been found inclosed by feldspar.

Fremont.—Near this place, in West Nottingham Township, Chester County, corundum crystals have been found, surrounded by feldspar.

Mineral Hill.—Corundum crystals have been found at this place, which is near Media, in Middletown Township, Delaware County, which were surrounded by feldspar similar to that at Blackhorse.

Newlin.—See under Unionville.

Shimerville.—At this place, in Lehigh County, corundum crystals up to 8 inches in length and $4\frac{1}{2}$ inches in diameter have been found loose in the soil.

Unionville.—In a large mass of serpentine rocks, 1 mile northeast of this village, corundum has been found. (See p. 66.)

Villagegreen.—Large crystals of corundum of a brownish color are found near this village, in Aston Township, Delaware County.

West Chester—Corundum has been found in a serpentine of this township.

SOUTH CAROLINA.

Anderson County.—Corundum has been reported from this county, but none has been found in place.

Energy.—See York County.

Gaffney.—Corundum, usually of a gray color and in irregular masses up to 3 or 4 inches in diameter, has been found about 8 miles north-west of Gaffney, on the Island Ford road, near Maud post-office, on the Turner Phillips farm. It has not been found in situ, but in the gravels of a small stream and as loose fragments in the fields on the adjoining slopes. The fragments and what few crystals have been found are generally free from gangue, but some have been found with mica scales attached to them. It is not at all improbable that this corundum was derived from a mica-schist.

Laurens.—About 1¼ miles northeast of this town, in Laurens County, corundum has been found rather abundantly scattered over the surface. This surface corundum has been found for a number of miles to the southwest of this town. Although no corundum has been found in place, it was probably derived from a mica-schist, for the country rock in this section is largely a schist, and corundum crystals were found with portions of the mica-schist attached to them. The crystals are all rough, and vary from small ones to some that were over 3 inches long and 1 inch in diameter.

Oconee County.—Corundum has been found on the surface in this county, but none has been found in place.

York County.—In the northern part of this county, at Energy, near the North Carolina line, a black corundum has been found quite abundantly. (See p. 66.)

UTAH.

It is reported that a large deposit of corundum was found in this State during the past year, but no accurate information has been thus far obtained regarding location or quantity.

VIRGINIA.

Louisa County.—Deep blue crystals of corundum have been found in the soil in this county, but the exact locality is not known.

Stuart.—Corundum has been found in a mica-schist near this place on Bull Mountain. (See p. 35.) No development of the occurrence has been made to determine the extent of the deposit or the percentage of corundum.

ALASKA.[1]

Copper River.—Asteriated corundum of gray and pink colors is said to occur in a locality on Copper River, Alaska.

CORUNDUM LOCALITIES IN FOREIGN COUNTRIES.

With the exception of the emery deposits of Turkey and the Grecian Archipelago there were no localities outside of the United States where corundum had been mined for abrasive purposes until during the last year or two, when work was begun at the India deposits. As preparations are being made to work both these and the Canadian deposits on a large scale, it has seemed to me that a short description of them would be of interest and of value. I have also added a short description of the emery deposits of Turkey and the Grecian Archipelago.

CANADA.

The Canadian corundum localities that are attracting considerable attention at the present time are in the Province of Ontario, and have been recently described by Prof. W. G. Miller,[2] of the Kingston School of Mines. The corundum occurs as a primary constituent of a rock that is classified as a syenite and has been traced for over 50 miles across Renfrew, Hastings, and Haliburton counties, with smaller belts of the same rock in Peterborough, Lanark, and Frontenac counties to the south, making a total distance of nearly 100 miles in which the corundum-bearing rock has been found.

The rock varies from a normal syenite to a nepheline-syenite and a mica-syenite. Corundum has been found in all three of these varities, but is more abundant in the normal syenite, and this rock has been named corundum-syenite. These rocks, which occur as dikes cutting through the gneisses, are sometimes in large masses that appear to grade into a granite. The width of the dikes varies greatly, but is usually several feet; a few have been observed that were only a few inches wide. These dikes are sometimes thickly studded with corundum crystals. Assays made of this rock from various parts of the dikes indicate that it will average about 12 per cent of corundum. If the corundum can be mined economically, and if tests of the commercial corundum obtained from the ore show that it has the abrasive qualities essential to make it of use in the manufacture of vitrified wheels, these deposits should become of considerable importance.

The Canada Corundum Company, Limited, has been organized and has begun mining operations on the corundum deposits in the extreme northwestern part of Raglan Township, Renfrew County, Ontario, about 7 miles southwest of Combermere. The corundum

[1] Twentieth Ann. Rept. U. S. Geol. Survey, Part VI, 1899. p. 570.
[2] Report Bureau of Mines, Toronto, Can., Vol. VIII. Part II, 1899, pp. 205-240.

here occurs in the normal syenite. A corundum mill has been erected that will have a capacity of 5 tons of cleaned corundum a day.

This company also owns corundum deposits on the York River in Carlow and Dungannon townships, Hastings County. At these localities the corundum occurs in a nepheline-syenite, and while it is apparently of superior quality to that found in Raglan Township, the percentage of corundum is not as high. No mining is being done by the company at these York River localities.

The manager of the company is Mr. B. A. C. Craig, of Toronto, Canada.

Miller[1] has described specimens of corundum from Methuen Township, Peterborough County, that are entirely inclosed by mica. He says: "The corundum is often not observed in the mica until the latter is broken open, when it is found forming the center or core of the mass. The rounded surfaces of the corundum and other characteristics leads to the belief that the masses of light-colored mica are secondary products after corundum." This very closely resembles specimens of corundum surrounded by muscovite mica that have been found at the Presley mine in Haywood County, N. C. (see p. 85), in which the muscovite is undoubtedly a secondary product after the corundum.

In the township of South Sherbrooke, Lanark County,[2] corundum has been found in a rock that is made up of a basic plagioclase feldspar and green hornblende, and has been called anorthosite by Miller. It is more basic in character than the typical varieties of this rock that have been described from other parts of Canada. The width of the belt of rock is nearly three-quarters of a mile and the corundum is found throughout the whole distance. It occurs in crystals of an almost uniform light-gray to white color that are usually about half an inch in diameter, the largest ones being one and a quarter inches long.

INDIA.

The corundum deposits of India have been described by T. H. Holland.[3] He gives the Pararapatti area in the Salem district of the province of Upper Burma as one of the most promising for the mining of corundum for abrasive purposes. He describes the corundum as occuring in a matrix of deep flesh-colored feldspar which is in bands or lenticular masses, and has associated with it often a considerable proportion of sillimanite, rutile, opaque black and green spinel, and biotite. These masses, where they have been actually seen in the rock, are sometimes as much as 15 feet long and 8 feet in diameter. The feldspar rock is composed essentially of anorthite and hornblende,

[1] Report Bureau of Mines, Toronto, Ontario, Vol. VIII, Part II, 1899, p. 210.
[2] Loc cit., p. 25.
[3] Geology of India, Part III, Economic Geology, and Report Bureau of Mines, Vol. VIII, Part II, 1899, p. 230.

and in parts has a gneissoid structure, and these portions carry the corundum. The corundum varies from a deep purplish brown to a dark greenish gray, and is in irregular nodules varying from a quarter of an inch to an inch in diameter and in elongated barrel-shaped crystals sometimes an inch long.

There are two and perhaps more of these corundum-bearing bands that are parallel to each other, making the total length of corundum-bearing rock that is known over 24 miles. The percentage of corundum in the rock is very low, experiments that have been made on samples taken at different points on the band showing the presence of only 3.5 per cent.

Most of the outcrops of the bands of corundum rock have been found in connection with gneiss, and lie in lines that are roughly parallel to the strike of the gneiss. Some of them are, however, in close proximity to a nepheline-syenite.

Specimens of corundum sent by Dr. T. L. Walker from a district about 250 miles north of Calcutta and labeled Pipra, South Rewah, India, are apparently similar to those described by Holland. The corundum is very fine grained in appearance and in nodules up to 2 or more inches long by 1 or more inches broad, with a pinkish to purplish-brown color. These nodules are partially or completely surrounded by a greenish mica, whose folia are small and rather brittle, and which has been referred by Mallet[1] to the euphyllite variety. In the mica there are small rough crystals of tourmaline. Just what the occurrence of this corundum is I do not know, but from the general appearance of the specimens it should make an ore from which the corundum could be readily separated and a very clean product obtained. If the corundum in the rock was 10 to 15 per cent of the amount required to be removed in mining, this should make a very important and profitable corundum deposit. A limited amount of this corundum is now being imported by the Norton Emery Wheel Company, of Worcester, Mass., and is used in the manufacture of their India oilstones.

In other specimens labeled Salbanni, 4 miles east southeast of Barampur, Manbhoorn district, India, there are blue crystals of corundum with a rough hexagonal prism embedded in a mass of interlocking bladed crystals of cyanite.

It is very probable that nearly all of the corundum deposits that are known in India are secondary minerals and the result of metamorphism. Professor Judd, in his paper on the Rubies of Burma and associated Minerals,[2] says that all the corundum-bearing rocks in the districts of Southern Asia appear to be gneisses that sometimes pass into schists and frequently contain masses of limestone and dolomite.

---

[1] Min. India, 1887, p. 191, and Dana's Min., 6th edition, 1892, p. 624.
[2] Trans. Royal Soc., London, 1896, p. 191.

TURKEY.

The Turkish emery is obtained from the province or vilayet of Aidin, in Asia Minor, which embraces nearly the entire basins of the rivers Sarabat and Mender. Smyrna is the principal town of the province, and is the center of trade for all the surrounding district and islands. The deposits that are now being worked are on the Gumush Dagh Mountain and on the slopes of Ak Sivri,[1] which is a mountain about 125 miles to the south. The former of these deposits is about 12 miles east of the ruins of Ephesus, and just north of the river Mender; the latter is in what J. Lawrence Smith[2] describes as the Kulah district, and it is much more inaccessible than the former one. Emery has also been found in small quantities near Adula, a town about 12 or 15 miles east of Kulah, and also at Manser, about 24 miles north, and at Allahinan-Bourgs, about 20 miles south of Smyrna.

The occurrence of the emery at all these localities is very similar, it being embedded in a bluish, coarse-grained to compact marble or limestone, resting upon mica-slates, schists, and gneisses. It always occurs in the limestone or marble; not even a trace has as yet been found in the other rocks. It does not occur in a well-defined vein but in pockets scattered irregularly through the rock that are sometimes up to 200 feet in length and 300 feet in width. The walls of these pockets are very irregular, as the limestone intrudes upon them, and then recedes very suddenly.

GRECIAN ARCHIPELAGO.

In a number of the islands of this archipelago, emery has been found in considerable quantity. The most important of these localities is the island of Naxos, where the emery is found in large blocks more or less mixed with the red soil, and also embedded in white marble. The deposits are located principally on the north and east sides of the island, the best ore being obtained from Vothrie, which is 9 miles from the coast. Another one of the better deposits on this island is at Apperonthos, which is 7 miles from the coast. In the southern part of the island the emery is found near Yasso. It occurs in such abundance on the island, in loose bowlders and in the soil, that there has been little need to mine it in the hard rock.

On the island of Nicaria emery has been found in quality equal to that from Naxos, but the quantity is not so great. A little was also found on the island of Samos. In all these islands the emery occurs in a limestone.

OTHER LOCALITIES.

Corundum has been found sparingly at many other localities, but thus far it has not been found in quantity enough to make the occurrences of economic importance as an abrasive.

---

[1] Trans. Am. Inst. Min. Eng., Vol. XXVIII, 1898, p. 206.
[2] Am. Jour. Sci., 2d series, Vol. X, 1850, p. 357.

The occurrence of sapphire corundum in Burma, Ceylon, and Siam has been mentioned on pages 39 and 46.

Zirkel,[1] mentions the occurrence of corundum as an accessory mineral in the amphibolites of northwestern Austrian Silesia; in the chlorite-schist of Nischne-Issetsk, in the Urals; as a contact product of the diorites of Klausen, in Tyrol; in the andesite and tonalite of the Eifel; in a contact product of quartz-mica-diorite on quartz-phyllite in Val Moja, and similarly in the kersantite of Michaelstein, Harz; also in the graphite of Mühldorf, near Spitz, in Lower Austria.

Pirsson[2] has mentioned the occurrence of corundum in small blue sapphires in the fresh basalt of Unkel on the Rhine and Steinheim near Frankfort on the Main.

Morozewicz[3] has described the occurrences of corundum in Russia, the chief of which is in a rock composed essentially of anorthite and corundum, together with spinel and biotite. He claims that this is a new type of alumino-silicate rock, and calls it "kyschtymit." Other rocks in the Urals that contain corundum are made up almost exclusively of this mineral and orthoclase; some of these are coarse grained, while others are fine. The coarse ones have been called corundum-pegmatite and the finer ones corundum-syenite. These rocks occur as dikes cutting through gneiss.

It may be that when these corundum-bearing rocks of the Urals have been more specially examined as to their economic value they may be found to contain a large enough percentage of corundum to make them of importance as an ore of this mineral.

Dana[4] mentions the occurrence of corundum near Canton, China; in Bohemia, near Petschau; at Saint Gotthard, in dolomite; near Mozzo, in Piedmont, in white compact feldspar; and at Mudgee, New South Wales.

Lacroix, in a paper[5] on the metamorphic and eruptive rocks of Ariège, France, mentions the occurrence of corundum in the marbles of Mercus and Arignac. In a second paper[6] on acid inclusions in the volcanic rocks of the Auvergne, France, corundum is said to occur frequently in the granites and gneisses of this section. He has also described the occurrence of this mineral in the basic magmas (basalts, trachytes, and andesites) in Haute-Loire, France.[7]

Salomon[8] has described the occurrence of corundum in phyllites, epidote-amphibolites, and mica-schists at Mount Aviólo, in the Southern Alps. It occurs but sparingly in these rocks.

[1] Lehrbuch der Petrographie, Leipsic, 1893, p. 461.
[2] Am. Jour. Sci., 4th series, Vol. IV, 1897, p. 422.
[3] Tschermaks Min. und Pet. Mitt., Vol. XVIII, pt. 1; and Rept. Bureau of Mines, Toronto, Vol. VIII, Part II, 1899, p. 285.
[4] Min , 6th edition, 1892, p. 212.
[5] Bull. des Serv. d. l. Carte géol. d. France, No. 11, Vol. II; and Am. Nat., Feb., 1891, pp. 138-139.
[6] Loc. cit.
[7] Bull. Soc. Min, Vol. XIII., 1890, pp 100-106.
[8] Jour. d. d. G. G., Vol. XLII., 1890, p. 450; and Am. Nat., 1891, pp. 571, 572.

In the dune sands on the west coast of Holland, at Sheveningen near the Hague, corundum has been found by Retgers[1] to be one of its constituents.

In describing the geology of the district around Pretoria, South Africa, Molengraaf[2] states that the oldest rocks of the region are granites and crystalline schists. Above these are another series of schist formations, comprising quartzites, clay slates, corundum schists, porphyroids, and chiastolite-schists that are cut by diabase dikes. He states that the corundum porphyroid resembles a feldspar porphyry, and that the corundum occurs in large individuals in a groundmass of quartz and chlorite. From the description given, there is a possibility that there is corundum in quantity in this district.

In many parts of the western Yunnan district, China, as in the prefecture of Shunning Fu, sapphire, ruby, and emerald corundum are said to occur.[3]

[1] Rec. des travaux chimiques des Pays-Bas, Vol. XI, 1892, p. 169; and Am. Nat., 1896, p. 382.
[2] Neues Jahrbuch, Vol. IX, 1894-95, pp. 174-291; and Am. Nat., 1895, p. 470.
[3] U. S. Consular Reports, Jan., 1900, Vol. LXII, No. 232, p. 95; reprinted from Mesny's Chinese Miscellany, published at Shanghai, China.

INDEX.

O

PUBLICATIONS OF UNITED STATES GEOLOGICAL SURVEY.

[Bulletin No. 180.]

The serial publications of the United States Geological Survey consist of (1) Annual Reports, (2) Monographs, (3) Bulletins, (4) Mineral Resources, (5) Water-supply and Irrigation Papers, (6) Topographic Atlas of United States—folios and separate sheets thereof, (7) Geologic Atlas of United States—folios thereof. A circular giving complete lists may be had on application.

The Bulletins treat of a variety of subjects, and the total number issued is large. They have therefore been classified into the following series: A, Economic geology; B, Descriptive geology; C, Systematic geology and paleontology; D, Petrography and mineralogy; E, Chemistry and physics; F, Geography; G, Miscellaneous. This bulletin is the eleventh in Series A, the complete list of which follows:

BULLETINS, SERIES A, ECONOMIC GEOLOGY.

21. Lignites of Great Sioux Reservation: Report on region between Grand and Moreau rivers, Dakota, by Bailey Willis. 1885. 16 pp., 5 pls. Price, 5 cents.

46. Nature and origin of deposits of phosphate of lime, by R. A. F. Penrose, jr., with introduction by N. S. Shaler. 1888. 143 pp. Price, 15 cents.

65. Stratigraphy of the bituminous coal field of Pennsylvania, Ohio, and West Virginia, by Israel C. White. 1891. 212 pp., 11 pls. Price, 20 cents. (Exhausted.)

111. Geology of Big Stone Gap coal field of Virginia and Kentucky, by Marius R. Campbell. 1893. 106 pp., 6 pls. Price, 15 cents.

132. The disseminated lead ores of southeastern Missouri, by Arthur Winslow. 1896. 31 pp. Price, 5 cents.

138. Artesian well prospects in Atlantic Coastal Plain region, by N. H. Darton. 1896. 228 pp., 19 pls. Price, 20 cents.

139. Geology of Castle Mountain mining district, Montana, by W. H. Weed and L. V. Pirsson. 1896. 164 pp., 17 pls. Price, 15 cents.

143. Bibliography of clays and the ceramic arts, by John C. Branner. 1896. 114 pp. Price, 15 cents.

164. Reconnaissance in the Rio Grande coal fields of Texas, by Thomas Wayland Vaughan, including a report on igneous rocks from the San Carlos coal field, by E. C. E. Lord. 1900. 100 pp., 11 pls. and maps. Price, 20 cents.

178. El Paso tin deposits, by Walter Harvey Weed. 1901. 15 pp., 1 pl. Price, 5 cents.

180. Occurrence and distribution of corundum in United States, by J. H. Pratt. 1901. 98 pp., 14 pls. Price, 20 cents.

LOGICAL SUR

No. 181

SERIES F, GEOGRAPHY, 24

Geographic positions between Warrensville triangulation station, United States Lake Survey, and Bedford, via highways.

Stations.	Latitude.	Longitude.
	° ′ ″	° ′ ″
Warrensville triangulation station.............	41 28 39.24	81 30 12.88
Randall station, Erie Rwy., about one-fourth mile west of, road crossing near post-office......	41 25 42.6	81 32 12.0
Bedford station, Cleveland and Pittsburg Rwy.......	41 23 24.1	81 32 09.8

Geographic positions along Cleveland and Pittsburg Railway, between Bedford and Kensington.

Stations.	Latitude.	Longitude.
	° ′ ″	° ′ ″
Macedonia station...............	41 18 48.3	81 30 37.3
Hudson, Western Reserve Academy Observatory..	41 15 37.6	81 26 14.9
Portage and Summit, county line	41 12 45.3	81 23 33.2
Earlville station........................,...............	41 11 21.0	81 20 42.8
Erie Rwy. crossing...........	41 10 18.4	81 18 40.7
Ravenna, Main street crossing......................	41 09 28.0	81 14 52.5
Ravenna, Pittsburg and Western Rwy. crossing.......	41 08 56.4	81 14 44.6
Rootstown station, road crossing 150 feet north of	41 06 18.4	81 12 52.7
Road crossing 15 feet south of milepost 45..	41 04 38.2	81 11 40.5
Road crossing 655 feet north of milepost 48.............	41 02 21.2	81 10 20.6
Atwater station road crossing 295 feet south of........	41 01 25.4	81 09 50.8
Portage and Stark counties, road crossing on county line.....	40 59 17.4	81 08 41.2
Road crossing 1,695 feet south of milepost 55.........	40 56 27.5	81 06 57.0
Alliance, Alliance and Northern Rwy. crossing.......	40 55 33.0	81 06 04.4
Alliance, Pittsburg, Fort Wayne and Chicago crossing.	40 55 18.6	81 05 45.0
Alliance station......................	40 55 17.1	81 05 43.2
Stark and Mahoning counties, road crossing on county line	40 54 44.1	81 05 13.8
Road crossing 1,070 feet north of milepost 61...........	40 52 20.4	81 04 08.3
Homeworth station, road crossing 55 feet south of	40 50 14.8	81 04 04.4
Moultrie station, road crossing 255 feet south of	40 47 47.8	81 04 14.3
Bayard station	40 45 02.7	81 03 58.4
East Rochester station, road crossing 700 feet east of ..	40 44 41.8	81 02 06.3
Hanover-West township line.................	40 44 00.5	80 58 32.2
Kensington station, road crossing 150 feet west of	40 44 05.3	80 57 23.3
Kensington triangulation station	40 43 20.6	80 56 40.5

Geographic positions along Cleveland, Akron and Columbus Railway, Hudson to Akron.

Stations.	Latitude.	Longitude.
	° ′ ″	° ′ ″
Flag station, road crossing at, 1,770 feet south of mile-post 3	41 11 52.4	81 27 53.8
Road crossing 1,370 feet north of milepost 6	41 09 50.3	81 28 10.8
Cuyahoga Falls station	41 08 06.9	81 28 52.0
Road crossing 1,925 feet south of milepost 10	41 06 08.1	81 29 23.0
Cleveland, Terminal and Valley Rwy. crossing, stone arch	41 05 08.5	81 29 24.3
Akron, Union station	41 04 58.7	81 30 34.8
Akron, court-house grounds, south meridian mark	41 04 44.3	81 31 05.0
Akron, court-house grounds, north meridian mark	41 04 47.8	81 31 05.0

Geographic positions along Erie Railway, Akron to Burbank.

Stations.	Latitude.	Longitude.
	° ′ ″	° ′ ″
Akron, Erie station, 2¼ miles west of, old canal crossing	41 02 46.1	81 32 35.7
Road crossing (Baltimore and Ohio Rwy.), 2,200 feet southwest of milepost 18	41 01 56.4	81 34 52.1
Barberton station	41 01 13.2	81 36 36.5
Sherman station	41 00 50.4	81 40 05.0
Wadsworth station	41 01 02.7	81 43 46.6
Road crossing one-half mile west of milepost 217	40 59 46.5	81 44 55.5
Rittman station	40 58 06.4	81 46 55.2
Sterling; Cleveland, Lorain and Wheeling crossing	40 58 10.9	81 50 52.7
Creston station	40 58 56.6	81 53 33.3
Road crossing 370 feet east of water tank	40 59 22.8	81 57 30.2
Burbank station	40 59 24.2	81 59 50.1
Baltimore and Ohio crossing (Lodi and Wooster branch)	40 59 19.4	82 01 33.7

Geographic positions along Cleveland. Lorain and Wheeling Railway, from Sterling to Grafton triangulation station (United States Lake Survey).

Stations.	Latitude.	Longitude.
	° ′ ″	° ′ ″
Sterling, Erie Rwy. crossing	40 58 10.9	81 44 55.5
Seville station	41 00 30.5	81 51 50.5
Road crossing 2.340 feet south of milepost 39	41 02 39.8	81 53 04.0
Flag station 400 feet south of milepost 37	41 04 37.6	81 53 39.8
Road crossing 250 feet north of milepost 34	41 07 16.1	81 53 03.3
Medina station	41 08 18.8	81 52 24.3
Road crossing 2,150 feet south of milepost 29	41 10 01.9	81 55 13.2
Lester station	41 10 48.2	81 56 31.5
Erhart station	41 11 55.2	81 58 21.1
Grafton triangulation station (United States Lake Survey)	41 12 44.21	81 59 37.85

Geographic positions along Lodi and Wooster branch of Baltimore and Ohio Railroad, from Erie crossing to Wooster.

Stations.	Latitude.	Longitude.
	° ′ ″	° ′ ″
Erie crossing	40 59 19.4	82 01 33.7
Road crossing at flag station	40 57 08.3	82 01 27.7
Armstrong flag station	40 54 42.0	82 00 34.0
Overton flag station	40 51 51.0	82 00 32.3
Road crossing 600 feet south of water tank	40 48 38.1	81 58 51.0
Wooster fair grounds, south meridian mark	40 47 50.3	81 57 03.5
Wooster fair grounds, north meridian mark	40 47 55.6	81 57 03.5
Wooster station, Baltimore and Ohio R. R.	40 47 43.6	81 56 55.1

Geographic positions along Pittsburg, Fort Wayne and Chicago Railway, from Millbrook to Orrville.

Stations.	Latitude.	Longitude.
	° ′ ″	° ′ ″
Bridge 121. northwest corner of. copper bolt in bridge abutment	40 43 59.9	81 58 24.6
Road crossing 100 feet east of bridge 121	40 44 00.7	81 58 23.8
Overhead road crossing	40 44 51.8	81 57 41.4
Baltimore and Ohio overhead crossing	40 46 32.6	81 56 47.7
Wooster station	40 47 57.0	81 55 54.8
Stone arch culvert 1,040 feet north of milepost 132	40 49 09.8	81 53 19.6
Smithville station	40 50 25.5	81 51 40.9
Road crossing about one-third mile east of water tank.	40 49 46.0	81 48 35.0
Orrville, Pittsburg. Fort Wayne and Chicago and Cleveland, Akron and Columbus Rwy	40 50 22.1	81 46 05.8

Geographic positions along Wheeling and Lake Erie Railway, between Orrville and Massillon.

Stations.	Latitude.	Longitude.
	° ′ ″	° ′ ″
Burton City station	40 50 36.5	81 42 12.1
Dalton station	40 48 02.0	81 41 15.2
Pocock mine junction	40 48 20.7	81 38 43.9
Sippo station, road crossing 325 feet west of	40 48 56.4	81 36 05.9
Sherwood flag station, road crossing at	40 48 19.8	81 33 17.9
Massillon, crossing of Wheeling and Lake Erie and Cleveland, Lorain and Wheeling Rwys	40 47 43.5	81 31 47.3

Geographic positions along Pittsburg, Fort Wayne and Chicago Railway, between Massillon and Canton.

Stations.	Latitude.	Longitude.
	° ′ ″	° ′ ″
Massillon, East street crossing	40 47 32.4	81 31 01.2
Road crossing 2,150 feet east of milepost 107	40 47 11.6	81 27 57.6
Road crossing 700 feet west of milepost 104	40 46 54.1	81 25 11.8
Canton, Pittsburg, Fort Wayne and Chicago Rwy. and Cleveland Terminal and Valley Rwy. crossing	40 47 24.2	81 23 02.1

Geographic positions along the Cleveland Terminal and Valley Railway, between Canton and Akron.

Stations.	Latitude.	Longitude.
	° ′ ″	° ′ ″
Canton station	40 48 01.5	81 23 16.1
Road crossing 1,525 feet south of milepost 54	40 51 16.8	81 24 49.2
New Berlin station, road crossing 65 feet north of	40 52 54.0	81 25 32.3
Greentown station, road crossing 245 feet north of	40 55 42.5	81 25 10.8
Myersville station, road crossing 215 feet north of	40 58 34.0	81 25 36.7
Road crossing 280 feet north of milepost 44	40 59 41.9	81 26 44.5
Krumroy station, road crossing 225 feet south of	41 00 55.3	81 28 42.8
Overhead road crossing 425 feet south of milepost 39	41 03 07.2	81 28 37.0

Shalersville, 2¼ miles south of, 4 corners. ..
Shalersville, intersection of roads at ....
Mantua station, Erie Railway crossing near
Mantua post-office, road intersection at ....
Julia post-office, county line between Po
    Geauga County ....
Auburn, road intersection at store.... ......
South Newbury post-office, 2,000 feet south
    mile south of creamery, electric railway c
Burton, 2¼ miles southeast of, 4 corners. ...
Burton, street intersection, north side of pa
Burton, about 1⅜ miles north of, 4 corners
Claridon triangulation station (U. S. Lake S

Meridian

CANTON, STARK C

Location of station: On the Stark
    Station mark: A marble post 40 by
the ground, in the center of top of whic
tablet. It is 25 feet north of inside f

Reference mark: Center of judges' stand, 390.6 feet distant; true azimuth, 148° 01' 30".

Distant mark: A marble post 40 by 6 by 8 inches, set 36 inches in the ground, in the center of top of which is a bronze meridian tablet. It is 765 feet north of the station mark and 283 feet south of inside fence at north end of race track.

Center of judges' stand, 480½ feet distant; true azimuth, 25° 30' 00".

Resident referee: Mr. John S. Hoover, county surveyor.

ST. CLAIRSVILLE, BELMONT COUNTY, OHIO.

Location of station: Within the Belmont County Agricultural Society fair grounds.

Station mark: A sandstone post 40 by 12 by 20 inches set 40 inches in the ground, in the center of top of which is cemented a bronze meridian tablet. .

Distant mark: North of station 400 feet, a sandstone post 72 by 12 by 20 inches set 40 inches in the ground, in the center of top of which is cemented a bronze triangulation tablet.

WOOSTER, WAYNE COUNTY, OHIO.

Location of station: On the Wayne County fair grounds.

Station mark: A marble post 36 by 6 by 9 inches set 34 inches in the ground, in the center of top of which is cemented a bronze meridian tablet.

Reference marks: Center of judges' stand, 129 feet distant; true azimuth, 181° 31'; tree, 426 feet distant; azimuth, 104° 00'.

Distant mark: 539.4 feet north of station mark, 40 feet from inside edge of race track, a marble post 36 by 6 by 9 inches set 34 inches in the ground, in the center of top of which is cemented a bronze meridian tablet.

Reference marks: Center of judges' stand, 413 feet distant; true azimuth, 356° 25'; tree, 601 feet distant; azimuth, 43° 25'.

Resident referee: County surveyor.

NORTH CAROLINA.

Primary Traverse.

The following geographic positions were determined by primary railroad traverse by Mr. Oscar Jones, assistant topographer, in September and October, 1900. The line begins at the Episcopal Church spire at Newbern (located by the United States Coast and Geodetic Survey), and follows the Atlantic and North Carolina Railroad to Goldsboro; thence along the Atlantic Coast Line Railroad via Rockymount and Parmele to Washington, connecting with Cedar Grove tri-

angulation station of the United States Coast and Geodetic Survey.
A spur line was run from Parmele to Plymouth.

Geographic positions along Atlantic and North Carolina Railroad between Newbern and Goldsboro.

Stations.	Latitude.	Longitude
	° ′ ″	° ′ ″
Newbern, Episcopal Church spire, United States Coast and Geodetic Survey	35 06 25.04	77 02 21.96
Newbern, national pike crossing	35 07 01.0	77 02 47.7
Road crossing 1,470 feet east of milepost 40	35 07 45.9	77 05 44.1
Clark post-office and sawmill, road crossing at	35 08 44.8	77 09 35.5
Tuscarora station	35 09 34.1	77 12 49.5
Road crossing 2,190 feet east of milepost 51	35 10 34.1	77 16 46.0
Coar Creek station	85 11 11.7	77 19 14.3
Road crossing 2,806 feet east of milepost 56	35 11 50.8	77 21 48.8
Road crossing 1,140 feet west of milepost 58	35 12 31.5	77 24 30.1
Dover station	85 12 57.5	77 26 12.9
Road crossing 1,470 feet west of milepost 64	35 14 00.9	77 30 40.4
Neuse River bridge, east end of	85 14 36.5	77 33 27.0
Kinston, crossing of Atlantic Coast Line Rwy	35 15 31.5	77 34 27.1
Kinston station	35 15 51.4	77 34 53.7
Road crossing 1,480 feet west of milepost 73	85 16 15.8	77 38 13.4
Falling Creek station	85 16 34.8	77 41 22.6
Road crossing 285 feet east of milepost 78	35 17 08.6	77 44 05.8
Lagrange station	35 18 25.7	77 47 17.3
Beston station	35 20 37.0	77 50 49.7
Road crossing 1,080 feet west of milepost 88	85 21 38.6	77 52 59.4
Road crossing 160 feet west of milepost 91	85 22 47.0	77 55 59.6
Goldsboro, junction with Atlantic Coast Line Rwy	35 23 27.9	77 59 34.8
Goldsboro, north meridian mark	35 23 53.4	77 59 37.2
Goldsboro, south meridian mark	35 23 51.7	77 59 37.2

Geographic positions along Atlantic Coast Line Railway, between Goldsboro and Rockymount.

Stations.	Latitude.	Longitude.
	° ′ ″	° ′ ″
Road crossing 160 feet north of milepost 87	35 25 30.0	77 58 58.8
Road crossing 360 feet south of milepost 90	35 28 02.3	77 58 58.2
Pikeville station	35 29 52.6	77 58 57.7
Water tank 580 feet north of milepost 93	35 30 50.5	77 58 57.4
Road crossing 180 feet north of milepost 94	35 31 38.2	77 58 56.4
Fremont station	35 32 41.8	77 58 25.8
Road crossing 1,510 feet south of milepost 99	35 35 24.6	77 57 01.5
Blackcreek station	35 38 14.2	77 55 56.5
Contentnea station, junction main line	35 40 42.8	77 55 51.0
Wilson station	35 43 21.9	77 54 24.5
Road crossing 860 feet north of milepost 110	35 44 47.9	77 53 37.7
Road crossing 20 feet south of milepost 113	35 47 08.2	77 52 24.6
Elm City station	35 48 21.4	77 51 42.4
Road crossing 1,000 feet south of milepost 116	35 49 17.1	77 51 11.8
Sharpsburg	35 52 01.0	77 49 43.8
Road crossing 1,790 feet south of milepost 121	35 53 10.9	77 49 08.4
South Rockymount, main line junction	35 55 51.7	77 48 02.5
Rockymount station	35 56 18.5	77 47 51.7

Geographic positions along Atlantic Coast Line Railway, Rockymount east to Plymouth.

Stations.	Latitude.	Longitude.
	° ′ ″	° ′ ″
Road crossing 15 feet east of milepost 3	35 55 29.1	77 44 58.0
Road crossing 1,495 feet east of milepost 5	35 55 16.8	77 42 30.6
Kinsboro station	35 55 05.6	77 40 14.0
Hartsboro station	35 54 58.3	77 38 44.8
Road crossing 696 feet west of milepost 12	35 54 42.6	77 35 31.8
Tarboro, main-line junction	35 54 28.9	77 32 47.2
Tarboro station	35 54 28.6	77 32 33.0
Tar River bridge, west end of	35 53 35.2	77 32 07.2
Mildred station	35 50 53.8	77 29 29.4
Conetoe station	35 48 56.5	77 27 19.7
Road crossing 340 feet west of milepost 25	35 48 03.7	77 25 15.7
Bethel station	35 48 28.7	77 22 31.7
Parmele, railroad crossing at	35 48 58.4	77 18 50.8
Robersonville station	35 49 27.5	77 15 10.9
Everetts station	35 50 05.6	77 10 23.1
Williamston, junction of spur track to station	35 50 57.1	77 03 51.6
Williamston, road crossing at	35 50 48.0	77 03 35.2

Bull. 181—01——10

Geographic positions along Atlantic Coast Line Railway, Rockymount east to
Plymouth—Continued.

Stations.	Latitude.	Longitude.
	° ′ ″	° ′ ″
Water tank 760 feet west of milepost 48	35 49 18.1	77 02 40.6
Road crossing 990 feet east of milepost 51	35 48 35.8	76 59 14.6
Jamesville, tram road crossing 1 mile west of	35 48 38.6	76 54 41.1
Jamesville station	35 48 21.0	76 53 48.7
Road crossing 510 feet east of milepost 60	35 48 46.6	76 49 40.5
Road crossing 2,610 feet east of milepost 63	35 50 38.0	76 47 25.8
Plymouth, tram road crossing west of	35 51 08.8	76 45 45.0
Plymouth station	35 52 10.0	76 44 52.4
Plymouth, river front, first cross street	35 52 07.2	76 44 54.8
Plymouth, river front, last cross street	35 51 59.0	76 45 14.6
Plymouth, north meridian mark	35 51 41.9	76 45 14.1
Plymouth, south meridian mark	35 51 38.1	76 45 14.1

Geographic positions along the Atlantic Coast Line Railway from Washington to
Parmele.

Stations.	Latitude.	Longitude.
	° ′ ″	° ′ ″
Cedar Grove triangulation station, United States Coast and Geodetic Survey	35 31 52.6	77 02 11.0
Washington station	35 32 43.2	77 03 27.2
Wharton station	35 35 48.9	77 07 19.2
Pactolus station	35 37 41.4	77 13 02.5
Whichard, tramroad crossing east of	35 41 43.3	77 15 13.5
Whichard station	35 41 49.3	77 15 16.6
Williams station	35 45 28.5	77 17 15.1

Geographic positions along Atlantic Coast Line Railway from Parmele to Kinston.

Stations.	Latitude.	Longitude.
	° ′ ″	° ′ ″
Grindool station	35 45 57.0	77 19 57.2
Sawmill, road crossing at	35 41 18.8	77 21 17.2
House station	35 39 15.5	77 21 52.6
Greenville station	35 36 25.2	77 22 48.5
Parksville station	35 33 40.1	77 23 50.8
Winterville station	35 31 44.2	77 24 07.0
Ayden station	35 28 20.4	77 24 58.0
Flag station 1,300 feet north of milepost 72	35 24 25.8	77 25 36.2
Grifton station	35 22 20.5	77 26 17.8
Graingers station	35 19 11.8	77 30 32.0

SOUTH CAROLINA.

Primary Traverse.

A line of primary railroad traverse was run by Mr. S. Tatum, topographer, in 1900 from the Columbia State capitol (located by astronomic methods by the United States Coast and Geodetic Survey) along the Southern Railway to Spartanburg, connecting with the dome of St. Johns College, located by triangulation from the oblique arc of the United States Coast and Geodetic Survey. A circuit was completed by running from Carlisle, of the former line, eastward along the Seaboard Air Line Railway to Chester; thence southward along the Southern Railway to Columbia. Another circuit was completed by running westward from Columbia along the Southern Railway to Leesville; thence northward via highways to Prosperity; thence eastward along the Southern Railway, connecting with the first line at Alston.

Meridian lines were established at Chester, Columbia, Lexington, Union, and Winnsboro.

Geographic positions along Southern Railway from Columbia to Spartanburg.

Station.	Latitude.	Longitude.
	° ′ ″	° ′ ″
Columbia. State capitol dome, United States Coast and Geodetic Survey astronomic position	33 59 56.8	81 02 02.7
Road crossing (near river bridge)	34 01 31.9	81 03 53.6
Milepost 7	34 05 08.1	81 05 36.2
Milepost 11	34 07 50.9	81 07 57.2
Bookman flag station, road crossing at	34 09 44.4	81 09 14.8
Littleton flag station	34 10 42.0	81 10 39.4
Milepost 19	34 12 32.4	81 13 42.3
Wallaceville flag station	34 12 34.4	81 15 05.9
Alston station	34 14 34.7	81 18 59.3
Road crossing 2,885 feet north of milepost 133	34 16 51.9	81 20 17.3
Milepost 131	34 18 04.5	81 20 32.9
Dawkins station	34 21 18.8	81 22 04.8
Road crossing 3,050 feet north of milepost 125	34 22 53.7	81 22 49.0
Strother station	34 23 34.2	81 23 39.8
Blair flag station	34 25 03.6	81 24 10.4
Beaver Creek, center of stream	34 26 25.4	81 24 28.5
Lyles Ford	34 27 06.3	81 25 01.3
Milepost 117	34 28 55.4	81 25 05.3
Shelton station	34 29 48.7	81 25 10.1
Milepost No. 113	34 32 13.5	81 26 07.6
Road crossing 383 feet south of milepost 111	34 33 50.4	81 26 43.4

Geographic positions along Southern Railway from Columbia to Spartanburg—Continued.

Station.	Latitude.	Longitude.
	° ′ ″	° ′ ″
Carlisle station	34 35 31.2	81 27 54.6
Road crossing 1,330 feet north of milepost 107	34 36 52.7	81 29 20.0
Santuck station	34 38 00.8	81 31 07.8
Road crossing 215 feet south of milepost 103	34 39 09.2	81 31 48.7
Road crossing 2,818 feet south of milepost 101	34 40 19.2	81 32 41.8
Road crossing 245 feet south of milepost 100	34 41 11.1	81 33 37.4
Milepost 97	34 42 56.2	81 35 49.0
Union station	34 42 55.8	81 37 12.3
Milepost 94	34 44 10.9	81 37 58.0
Road crossing 2,360 feet south of milepost 93	34 45 20.8	81 37 43.4
Road crossing 1,270 feet south of milepost 90	34 47 08.4	81 38 36.4
Lockhart Junction	34 49 06.5	81 39 01.8
Jonesville station	34 50 07.0	81 40 42.1
Road crossing 4,255 feet south of milepost 83	34 51 14.8	81 42 12.3
Road crossing 200 feet north of milepost 82	34 51 53.9	81 43 44.1
Pacolet station	34 53 53.7	81 45 34.9
Milepost 77	34 54 23.4	81 47 31.0
Rich Hill flag station	34 54 11.8	81 48 59.7
Road crossing 1.265 feet north of milepost 74	34 55 01.5	81 50 34.1
Glendale station	34 55 24.1	81 51 38.5
Spartanburg, dome of St. John's College, United States Coast and Geodetic Survey position	34 57 17.2	81 54 55.6

Geographic positions along Seaboard Air Line Railway from Carlisle to Chester.

Station.	Latitude.	Longitude.
	° ′ ″	° ′ ″
Carlisle, crossing of Seaboard Air Line Rwy. and Southern Rwy	34 35 27.3	81 27 50.8
Broad River, right bank	34 37 21.6	81 25 01.4
Leeds station	34 37 48.8	81 23 40.7
Milepost 54	34 38 41.7	81 20 42.4
Milepost 53	34 39 11.5	81 19 52.4
Milepost 51	34 39 44.6	81 18 05.2
Road crossing 1,955 feet east of milepost 50	34 40 06.4	81 16 46.3
Road crossing	34 42 12.1	81 14 20.3
Chester station, Seaboard Air Line Rwy	34 42 30.2	81 12 57.8

Station.	Latitude.	Longitu
	° ′ ″	° ′
Chester station, Southern Rwy	34 42 16.9	81 12 ?
Road crossing 1,017 feet north of milepost 46	34 41 09.1	81 11 ?
Mi.epost 48	34 39 22.3	81 11 ?
Road crossing (bridge overhead)	34 38 41.9	81 11 ?
Cornwall station	34 36 23.4	81 10 ?
Milepost 54	34 34 40.2	81 10 ?
Blackstock station	34 33 29.3	81 09 ?
Woodward station	34 31 33.7	81 10 ?
Road crossing 270 feet south of milepost 59	34 31 12.0	81 09 ?
Road crossing 700 feet south of milepost 61	34 29 51.1	81 08 ?
Whiteoak station	34 28 19.5	81 07 ?
Milepost 65	34 27 03.7	81 07 ?
Adgers station	34 25 59.0	81 07 ?
Road crossing 550 feet north of milepost 69	34 24 38.3	81 05 ?
Winnsboro station	34 22 33.8	81 05 ?
Milepost 73	34 21 20.8	81 04 ?
Rockton station	34 20 24.7	81 04 4
Milepost 77	34 18 49.6	81 02 ?
Simpson station	34 18 33.9	81 02 4
Milepost 80	34 18 38.4	81 00 ?
Ridgeway station	34 18 18.9	80 57 ?
Milepost 84	34 17 31.5	80 57 0
Campbells flag station	34 16 52.4	80 56 ?
Milepost 87	34 15 13.6	80 57 ?
Blythewood station	34 12 52.7	80 58 2
Milepost 93	34 10 33.5	80 57 1
Killian station	34 08 12.8	80 56 4
Milepost 97	34 07 16.7	80 56 4
Road crossing 815 feet north of milepost 98	34 06 44.2	80 56 ?
Milepost 99	34 05 48.6	80 57 ?
Dents flag station	34 05 08.2	80 58 2
Road crossing 3,475 feet south of milepost 101	34 03 58.6	80 58 ?
Crossing of Seaboard Air Line	34 03 16.2	81 00 1
Milepost 104	34 02 34.2	81 00 3
Columbia, Blanding street station	34 00 39.2	81 01 2
Columbia, East Capitol street crossing	33 59 21.5	81 01 4

Station	°	′	″	°	′	″
Broad River, east bank	33	58	35.0	81	02	48.1
Cayce station	33	58	22.6	81	03	19.8
Road crossing 250 feet west of milepost 114	33	58	33.2	81	07	15.7
Arthur station	33	58	11.2	81	08	48.3
Milepost 119	33	58	17.5	81	12	17.6
Lexington station	33	57	58.3	81	14	05.2
Barrs station	33	56	17.5	81	17	36.4
Shumpert station	33	55	50.6	81	20	05.2
Milepost 129	33	55	25.4	81	21	24.7
Gilbert station	33	55	24.7	81	23	37.6
Summit station	33	55	24.7	81	25	20.6
Fredonia station	33	55	33.6	81	27	44.4
Leesville station	33	54	59.9	81	30	46.5

Geographic positions along highway from Leesville to Prosperity.

Station.	Latitude.			Longitude.		
	°	′	″	°	′	″
Crossing of Hollow Creek	33	56	59.1	81	32	02.4
Delmar post-office, road crossing 2 miles south of	33	59	14.7	81	31	19.8
Delmar post-office	34	00	38.0	81	30	41.3
Delmar post-office, 1½ miles north of, crossing of roads	34	01	29.4	81	29	51.9
Dupler post-office	34	03	00.1	81	29	42.9
Baptist Church	34	03	30.6	81	29	50.0
Saluda River, south bank	34	04	45.1	81	29	07.0
Upwell	34	05	22.6	81	28	48.1
Oneal School	34	07	00.7	81	30	14.6
Prosperity, 3 miles south of, road forks	34	10	27.5	81	32	07.1
Prosperity, 2 miles south of, road crossing (Columbia road)	34	10	48.4	81	31	56.2

Geographic positions along Southern Railway from Prosperity to Alston.

Station.	Latitude.			Longitude.		
	°	′	″	°	′	″
Prosperity, crossing Southern Rwy. and street	34	12	30.8	81	32	57.4
Road crossing 1,025 feet west of milepost 39	34	12	34.3	81	31	27.6
Road crossing 1,992 feet west of milepost 37	34	12	59.2	81	29	38.4
Road crossing 1,920 feet west of milepost 36	34	13	06.9	81	28	36.5
Road crossing, overhead bridge	34	13	49.2	81	26	56.3
Pomaria station	34	15	43.0	81	24	47.8
Road crossing 2,125 feet east of milepost 29	34	15	43.4	81	22	05.2
Road crossing 2,905 feet east of milepost 27	34	14	41.2	81	20	19.4
Road crossing 297 feet west of milepost 26	34	14	39.0	81	20	02.0
Peaks station	34	14	39.2	81	19	22.4
Alston station	34	14	34.7	81	18	59.2

Meridian Marks.

CHESTER, CHESTER COUNTY.

Location of station: In city park, just east of summit house, on top of knoll.

Station mark: A marble post 48 by 8 by 8 inches, set 46 inches in the ground, in the center of top of which is cemented a bronze tablet.

Distant mark: North of station 458 feet, a marble post 48 by 8 by 8 inches, set 46 inches in the ground, in center of top of which is cemented a bronze tablet.

Local reference: James Hamilton, jr., city engineer.

COLUMBIA, RICHLAND COUNTY.

Location of station: In State College park, east of college building and just north of street forming southern boundary of park.

Station mark: A marble post 48 by 6 by 6 inches, set 46 inches in the ground, in the center of top of which is cemented a bronze tablet.

Distant mark: North of station, a marble post 48 by 8 by 8 inches, set 46 inches in the ground, in top of which is cemented a bronze tablet.

Local reference: Professor Colcock.

LEXINGTON, LEXINGTON COUNTY.

Location of station: In city park, near southeast corner, about 10 feet north of south side.

Station mark: A granite post 48 by 10 by 10 inches, set 46 inches in the ground, with bronze tablet cemented in top.

Distant mark: A granite post 48 by 10 by 10 inches, set 46 inches in ground, 360.5 feet distant, in northeast corner of city cemetery.

UNION, UNION COUNTY.

Location of station: In grounds surrounding Union High School, west of high-school building and north of street forming southern boundary of grounds.

Station mark: A marble post 42 by 8 by 8 inches, set 40 inches in the ground, in the center of top of which is cemented a bronze tablet.

Distant mark: North of station 371 feet, near northern boundary of high-school grounds, a marble post 42 by 8 by 8 inches, set 40 inches in the ground, in the center of top of which is cemented a bronze tablet.

Resident referee: Colonel Young.

WINNSBORO, FAIRFIELD COUNTY.

Location of station: In park in front of Winnsboro College, about 200 feet west of east side of park and 5 feet north of south side of park.

Station mark: A granite post 48 by 8 by 8 inches, set 46 inches in the ground, with bronze tablet cemented in top.

Distant mark: North of station 348 feet, a granite post 48 by 8 by 8 inches, set 46 inches in ground.

Local referee: President Winnsboro College.

CENTRAL SECTION OF TOPOGRAPHY.

OHIO.

Primary Traverse.

The following geographic positions were determined from primary traverse in 1900 by Mr. George T. Hawkins, topographer.

Starting from United States Coast and Geodetic Survey astronomic pier at Mount Lookout, Cincinnati, the line follows the Baltimore and Ohio Southwestern and Baltimore and Ohio railroads to Columbus, Ohio; thence along the Hocking Valley Railroad to Toledo, Ohio, where it was tied to St. Mary's Church spire (United States Lake Survey station); thence back to Columbus, following line of Toledo and Ohio Central Railway, and connected with original line. Meridian lines were established at Bowling Green, Delaware, Findlay, Kenton, Marysville, Upper Sandusky, and Washington Court-House.

Geographic positions along Baltimore and Ohio Southwestern and Baltimore and Ohio railroads from Cincinnati to Columbus.

Station.	Latitude.	Longitude.
	° ′ ″	° ′ ″
Cincinnati, Mount Lookout astronomic pier.	39 08 21.93	84 25 21.52
Madisonville station	39 09 26.0	84 23 49.0
East Madisonville station	39 09 35.3	84 23 10.0
Madeira station	39 11 17.0	84 21 45.9
Allandale station.	39 11 49.2	84 20 34.4
Remington station	39 13 35.8	84 19 26.7
Symmes station	39 14 50.0	84 17 45.8
Camp Ground station	39 15 18.2	84 16 47.5
Loveland, crossing of Pennsylvania and Baltimore and Ohio Southwestern railways	39 16 00.6	84 15 31.9
Hills station. crossing 340 feet west of	39 15 18.7	84 11 17.7
Cozaddale station, crossing 80 feet west of	39 16 15.2	84 09 39.9
Pleasant Plain station, crossing 110 feet west of	39 16 47.5	84 06 43.6
Windsor station, crossing 40 feet west of	39 17 04.6	84 02 59.5
Blanchester station. crossing 320 feet east of	39 17 31.4	83 59 14.2
Midland station, crossing 310 feet west of	39 18 13.7	83 54 35.4
Midland station	39 18 14.4	83 54 31.5
Cuba station, crossing under railway 300 feet south of.	39 21 41.0	83 51 58.1

	° ′ ″	° ′ ″
Milepost 52, crossing 450 feet north of	39 23 59.4	83 51 17.8
Wilmington, Baltimore and Ohio station at	39 26 36.6	83 49 25.2
Blind siding, crossing 450 feet west of head block at	39 27 56.2	83 45 05.3
Melvin station, crossing 200 feet east of	39 28 24.8	83 43 01.2
Reesville, crossing at	39 28 57.1	83 40 41.2
Sabina station, crossing 100 feet west of	39 29 33.6	83 38 07.4
Milepost 69, crossing 800 feet west of	39 30 12.2	83 35 19.4
Rattlesnake, crossing over railroad at	39 30 41.8	83 33 09.4
Jasper Mills, crossing at	39 31 08.0	83 31 14.4
Washington Court-House, south azimuth stone 1.400 feet southward from Baltimore and Ohio station, near coal chutes 6 feet east of main track. 11 feet from end of bulkhead leading to elevated tracks. A limestone post, 36 by 8 by 8 inches, set 33 inches in the ground, in the center of top of which is cemented a bronze meridian tablet. Distant mark is a copper bolt cemented in east abutment of wagon bridge. Azimuth 218° 12′ 45″. Distance from south stone 1,093 feet	39 32 04.0	83 26 53.7
Washington Court-House, crossing of Baltimore and Ohio and Cincinnati, Hamilton and Dayton railways.	39 32 13.3	83 26 43.4
Fayette station	39 34 09.9	83 25 13.7
Bloomingburg station, crossing 300 feet east of	39 36 22.7	83 23 17.4
Madison Mills station, crossing 30 feet east of	39 39 13.5	83 20 21.4
Cook station, crossing 200 feet east of	39 40 59.4	83 18 24.3
Mount Sterling station, 300 feet east of Main street crossing	39 43 17.6	83 16 08.7
Era station, crossing 430 feet west of	39 44 23.2	83 14 38.1
Derby station, crossing 350 feet west of	39 46 08.4	83 12 20.5
Morgan station, crossing 100 feet west of	39 48 17.8	83 09 19.5
Pleasant Corners station, crossing 100 feet southwest of	39 50 37.5	83 07 41.1
Grove City station, crossing 100 feet southwest of	39 52 59.7	83 05 44.3
Urbancrest station, crossing 100 feet northeast of	39 53 53.2	83 05 00.4
Briggsdale station, crossing 50 feet northeast of	39 55 36.0	83 03 36.1
United States Geological Survey triangulation station, north base	39 55 57.3	83 03 18.6
Columbus, crossing Baltimore and Ohio Railway and Broad street	39 57 31.9	83 01 54.4

Positions along Hocking Valley Railway from Columbus to Toledo.

Station.	Latitude.	Longitude.
	° ′ ″	° ′ ″
Crossing Hocking Valley Railway and pike road east and west.	39 59 16.8	83 01 37.1
Columbus, Lane avenue station, crossing 150 feet south of	40 00 24.3	83 01 55.5
Olentangy station, crossing under railway 550 feet north of	40 03 48.5	83 02 48.1
Elmwood station, crossing 200 feet south of	40 05 25.2	83 03 09.4
Milepost 113, crossing 850 feet north of	40 07 01.8	83 03 30.7
Powell station, crossing 160 feet south of	40 09 29.6	83 04 42.3
Milepost 107, crossing 170 feet south of	40 11 44.5	83 05 22.7
Hyatts station, crossing 1,200 feet south of	40 12 58.3	83 05 17.6
Milepost 103, crossing 340 feet south of	40 15 12.6	83 05 08.5
Crossing telephone line.	40 17 18.3	83 04 59.5
Delaware, south azimuth stone, 30 feet southeast of "Big Four" and Hocking Valley railways. A limestone post, 28 by 6 by 6 inches, set 28 inches in the ground, in the center of top of which is cemented a bronze meridian tablet. Azimuth 185° 10′.	40 17 34.5	83 04 58.4
Delaware, north azimuth stone, 105 feet north of center of street and 72 feet east of railroad. A limestone post. 36 by 6 by 6 inches, set 30 inches in the ground; in center of top is cemented a copper bolt. Azimuth 5° 10′.	40 17 47.0	83 04 56.9
Delaware station, crossing 50 feet north of	40 17 58.7	83 04 57.4
Siding, crossing 150 feet south of south end of	40 20 00.3	83 06 03.3
Milepost 95, crossing 200 feet north of.	40 21 51.6	83 07 15.9
Radnor station, crossing 160 feet north of	40 23 09.6	83 08 06.0
Mileposts 90 and 91, crossing halfway between	40 25 22.7	83 09 39.1
Prospect station, crossing at	40 27 06.1	83 10 45.7
Crossing, four corners	40 29 28.0	83 09 59.3
Owen station, crossing 600 feet north of	40 31 13.2	83 09 28.6
Mileposts 79 and 80, crossing halfway between	40 34 31.3	83 08 30.8
Marion station, 140 feet south of Main street crossing	40 35 19.2	83 08 28.0
Marion, south azimuth stone, 225 feet north of "Big Four" crossing and 45 feet north of tool house, between Y tracks and main line of Hocking Valley Railway. A limestone post, 40 by 7 by 6 inches, set 40 inches in the ground, in the center of top of which is cemented a bronze meridian tablet. Distant mark is spire of Catholic Church. Azimuth of same is 259° 11′ 30″.	40 35 25.0	83 08 30.1
Crossing under railroad	40 38 01.5	83 10 25.1

Positions along Hocking Valley Railway from Columbus to Toledo—Continued.

Station.	Latitude.	Longitude.
	° ′ ″	° ′ ″
Morral station, crossing 160 feet north of	40 41 12.4	83 12 45.6
T. 3 S., R. 14 E., ¼ corner between secs. 33 and 34.......	40 44 17.6	83 14 44.8
Harpster station	40 44 20.4	83 15 04.2
Milepost 63, crossing 1,180 feet north of	40 47 19.8	83 17 12.1
Upper Sandusky, south azimuth stone, 9 feet east of railway and 1,395 feet distant from north stone. A limestone post, 30 by 5 by 5 inches, set 30 inches in the ground, in the center of top of which is cemented a bronze meridian tablet. Azimuth 180° 18′ 30″.....	40 49 14.8	83 17 31.4
Upper Sandusky, north azimuth stone 55 feet south and 150 feet east of crossing of Pittsburg, Fort Wayne and Chicago Railway and Hocking Valley Railway, 11 feet east of Hocking Valley Railway. A limestone post 38 by 6 by 6 inches, set 34 inches in the ground, in center of top is cemented a copper bolt	40 49 28.6	83 17 31.3
Upper Sandusky station............ ....-......	40 49 30.0	83 17 31.3
T. 2 S., R. 14 E., west corner of secs. 19 and 30	40 50 49.7	83 18 16.6
Crossing at flag station......	40 53 26.8	83 19 54.7
Crawford station, crossing at...................... ..	40 55 05.2	83 21 03.8
Carey station, crossing south of	40 57 04.2	83 22 28.3
Carey, south azimuth stone. A copper bolt sunk and cemented in south abutment of bridge north of station, on second stone and 4 feet east of east rail. Azimuth 151° 40′ 20″ to north mark...........	40 57 10.3	83 22 32.6
Carey, north azimuth stone, 339 feet north of "Big Four" crossing, 8 feet southeast of Northern Ohio crossing and 3½ feet east of east rail on Hocking Valley Railway. A marble post 24 by 8 by 8 inches, set 24 inches in the ground, in center of top is cemented a copper bolt..	40 57 22.9	83 22 41.5
¼ corner north of sec. 5 on base line, range 13 E........	40 59 31.7	83 23 49.1
Milepost 45, crossing 900 feet north of..................	41 01 43.4	83 24 16.0
Alvada station, crossing 100 feet north of	41 03 00.7	83 24 24.1
Siding, crossing 190 feet south of south end of	41 05 38.5	83 24 23.1
Crossing of telephone line	41 07 23.2	83 24 24.0
Fostoria, south azimuth stone, 7 feet east of east rail on Hocking Valley Railway, in arch culvert east of Fostoria Bulb and Bottle Co.'s Works. A bronze meridian tablet cemented in culvert. Azimuth, 179° 35′ 25″ .... ,............-....--	41 08 38.8	83 24 24

Positions along Hocking Valley Railway from Columbus to Toledo—Continued.

Station.	Latitude.	Longitude.
	o ′ ″	o ′ ″
Fostoria, north azimuth stone, 500 feet south of Baltimore and Ohio and Hocking Valley crossing, and 7 feet east of east rail of Hocking Valley Railway. A sandstone post 36 by 8 by 8 inches, set 34 inches in the ground, in the center of top is cemented a copper bolt..	41 09 01.2	83 24 24.8
Fostoria, Hocking Valley Railway, and Toledo and Ohio Central Railway, and street-car crossing. ...	41 09 13.0	83 24 25.6
Fostoria station, Hocking Valley Railway	41 09 40.7	83 24 37.1
Milepost 33, crossing 1,800 feet north of	41 12 11.9	83 25 02.2
Longley station, crossing 320 feet north of	41 13 20.6	83 25 14.3
T. 3 N., Rs. 12 and 13 E., cor. secs. 7, 18, 13, 12	41 13 29.6	83 25 13.7
Risingsun station, crossing 130 feet south of	41 16 06.8	83 25 43.4
T. 4 N., R. 12 E., corner secs. 11, 12, 13, and 14	41 18 43.5	83 26 14.6
Bradner station, crossing 150 feet north of	41 19 22.6	83 26 17.8
Milepost 21, crossing 840 feet south of	41 22 12.1	83.26 47.5
Pemberville station, crossing 80 feet north of..........	41 24 28.6	83 27 11.3
T. 5 N., R. 12 E., corner secs. 2, 3, 10, 11	41 24 49.6	83 27 16.7
Milepost 16, crossing 480 feet south of.................	41 26 33.2	83 27 39.9
Lemoyne station	41 29 39.6	83 28 25.7
Pike crossing..	41 29 45.2	83 28 27.0

Positions along the Toledo and Ohio Central Railway between Toledo and Columbus.

Station.	Latitude.	Longitude.
	o ′ ″	o ′ ″
Lime City, crossing of telephone line road at	41 32 06.2	83 34 01.8
Crossing of telephone line road	41 29 50.4	83 35 15.5
Dowling station, crossing 250 feet north of	41 28 40.4	83 35 53.6
Dowling, 1¼ miles southeast of, corner secs. 20, 21, 28, 29.	41 27 27.8	83 36 35.4
Telephone line road	41 25 13.3	83 37 46.2
Bowling Green station, 200 feet north of, telephone road crossing.......................................	41 23 33.2	83 38 40.8
Corner Ts. 4 and 5 N., Rs. 10 and 11 E	41 20 31.3	83 39 02.4
Portage station, crossing 150 feet south of	41 19 35.9	83 38 44.8
Mermill station, crossing 200 feet north of.............	41 17 51.0	83 38 44.3
Corner Ts. 3 and 4 N., Rs. 10 and 11 E	41 15 14.0	83 39 00.6
Cygnet station, crossing 270 feet north of	41 14 23.5	83 38 43.3
Milepost 32, crossing at	41 12 40.0	83 38 42.8
West corner secs. 30 and 31, T. 3 N., R. 11 E..........	41 10 55.8	83 38 57.6

Positions along the Toledo and Ohio Central Railway between Toledo and Columbus—Continued.

Station.	Latitude.	Longitude.
	° ′ ″	° ′ ″
Galatea, Baltimore and Ohio, and Toledo and Ohio Central crossing	41 10 40.8	83 38 42.8
Vanburen station, crossing 120 feet south of	41 08 17.5	83 38 42.8
Mortimer, crossing 465 feet south of railways	41 06 33.4	83 38 42.9
Mortimer station	41 06 38.0	83 38 42.9
Corner Ts. 1 and 2 N., Rs. 10 and 11 E	41 04 49.9	83 38 58.3
North Findlay, crossing of Lake Erie and Western Railway	41 02 50.7	83 38 42.2
Findlay, north azimuth stone at 790 feet north of "Big Four" crossing, 320 feet north of street, and 5 feet east of east rail of Toledo and Ohio Central Railway. A limestone post 36 by 7 by 5 inches, set 34 inches in the ground. A copper bolt is cemented in top	41 02 23.4	83 38 38.9
Findlay, south azimuth stone, 268 feet south of "Big Four" crossing, 4 feet north of sidewalk on Main street, and 17 feet west of west rail of Toledo and Ohio Central Railway. A limestone post 40 by 7 by 5 inches set 8 ; inches in ground, in center of top of which is cemented a bronze meridian tablet. Azimuth 178° 02′ 30″ to north stone	41 02 15.0	83 38 38.5
Findlay station	41 02 11.0	83 38 37.9
Findlay, crossing of Toledo and Ohio Central Railway and Findlay, Fort Wayne and Western Railway	41 01 20.4	83 38 32.2
Milepost 46, crossing 250 feet south of	41 00 28.2	83 38 28.1
Base line crossing	40 59 36.0	83 38 27.9
Milepost 49, crossing 130 feet south of	40 57 53.4	83 38 33.5
Milepost 51, crossing 200 feet south of	40 56 08.2	83 38 32.4
Corner Ts. 1 and 2 S., Rs. 10 and 11 E	40 54 23.3	83 39 03.7
Northern Ohio Railway crossing	40 53 56.8	83 38 48.7
Arlington station, crossing 180 feet north of	40 53 34.9	83 38 48.9
Milepost 56, crossing 470 feet south of	40 51 46.2	83 38 49.6
Williamstown station, crossing 70 feet south of	40 50 01.6	83 38 49.8
Corner Ts. 2 and 3 S., Rs. 10 and 11 E	40 49 09.7	83 39 04.6
Dunkirk station, crossing 900 feet north of	40 47 24.5	83 38 49.8
Pittsburg, Fort Wayne and Chicago Railway crossing	40 47 17.9	83 38 49.9
Milepost 64, crossing 910 feet south of	40 44 46.5	83 38 34.9
Blanchard station, 150 feet north of; telephone line road crossing	40 43 54.2	83 38 35.6
Milepost 67, crossing 500 feet south of	40 42 14.0	83 38 36.1
Milepost 69, crossing under railway 450 feet south of	40 40 30.3	83 38 35.1

Positions along the Toledo and Ohio Central Railway between Toledo and Columbus—Continued.

Station.	Latitude.	Longitude
	° ′ ″	° ′ ″
Pike crossing	40 39 19.2	83 37 59.9
Kenton, northwest azimuth stone 9 feet south of south rail on Toledo and Ohio Central Railway and 12 feet northwest of switch block. A sandstone post 30 by 6 by 6 inches, set 28 inches in ground, in center of top of which is cemented a bronze meridian tablet. Azimuth 273 48′ 22″ to southeast stone	40 38 40.8	83 36 58.1
Kenton, southeast azimuth stone on middle pier of "Big Four" Railway bridge over Scioto River and Toledo and Ohio Central Railway; 15 feet south of Toledo and Ohio Central Railway and 3½ feet west of west rail of "Big Four" Railway. A copper bolt in top of stonework	40 38 40.0	83 36 42.2
Kenton station, street crossing 140 feet east of	40 38 36.9	83 36 29.2
Erie Railway crossing	40 38 00.6	83 35 47.2
Siding, crossing 70 feet north of north end of	40 34 35.9	83 34 29.9
"Big Four" Railway crossing	40 31 09.6	83 33 47.6
Ridgeway station, crossing 175 feet south of	40 30 57.9	83 33 46.1
Mileposts 83 and 84, crossing halfway between, 1,450 feet north of creek	40 29 21.1	83 33 33.6
Milepost 86, crossing 480 feet north of	40 27 11.0	83 33 16.9
West Mansfield, main road running north from	40 24 34.3	83 32 46.7
Milepost 91, crossing 830 feet south of	40 22 59.3	83 31 24.0
Lunda station, crossing 400 feet south of	41 21 59.2	83 30 31.7
Raymonds station, crossing 180 feet northwest of	40 19 56.2	83 28 11.5
Peoria, Erie Railway crossing at	40 18 39.2	83 27 04.0
Milepost 98, crossing 1.340 feet south of	40 18 05.4	83 26 34.9
Siding, crossing 120 feet north of north end of	40 16 28.9	83 25 11.7
Marysville station, crossing 100 feet east of	40 14 25.7	83 22 13.5
Marysville, north azimuth stone at 940 feet north of "Big Four" crossing. 450 feet north of north end of Y, 200 feet north of east and west road, and 16 feet east of east rail of Toledo and Ohio Central Railway. A sandstone post 30 by 6 by 6 inches, set 26 inches in ground; in center of top is cemented a copper bolt	40 14 12.8	83 21 15.7
Marysville, south azimuth stone at 613 feet south of crossing of "Big Four" Railway, 6 feet east of east rail of Toledo and Ohio Central Railway. A sandstone post 30 by 6 by 6 inches, set 28 inches in ground, in center of top of which is cemented a bronze meridian tablet. Azimuth 139 43′ 20″ to north stone	40 14 01.1	83 21 02.8

Positions along the Toledo and Ohio Central Railway between Toledo and Columbus—Continued.

Station.	Latitude.	Longitude.
	° ′ ″	° ′ ″
Milepost 106, 330 feet south of pike and telephone line crossing...	40 13 36.3	83 20 36.1
Milepost 108, crossing 1,350 feet south of.............	40 12 08.2	83 19 00.5
Blind siding, crossing 20 feet northwest of head block..	40 10 06.4	83 16 48.5
Milepost 113, pike crossing 5:0 feet southeast of........	40 08 54.0	83 15 30.0
Arnold station, 580 feet southeast of pike and telephone line crossing..............................	40 08 27.4	83 15 01.2
Flag station, telephone line 200 feet southeast of......	40 06 15.6	83 12 38.5
Amlin station, crossing 100 feet northwest of.........	40 04 36.4	83 10 51.1
Milepost 122, crossing 300 feet southeast of...........	40 02 54.5	83 09 01.0
Telephone-line crossing....	40 01 56.6	83 07 58.4
Toledo and Ohio Central Railway and Pennsylvania Railway crossing......	40 00 04.5	83 05 57.4
Milepost 127, crossing at..	39 59 36.1	83 05 26.7

Meridian Marks.

BOWLING GREEN, WOOD COUNTY.

Location of station: In southwest corner of court-house grounds.

Station mark: A limestone post 36 by 7 by 5 inches, set 34 inches in the ground, in the center of top of which is countersunk and cemented a bronze tablet.

Reference mark: West line of grounds 21 feet; south line of grounds 12 feet.

Distant mark: North of station 352 feet, a limestone post 36 by 7 by 5 inches, set 36 inches in the ground, having a copper bolt cemented in its top.

Resident referee: County clerk.

DELAWARE, DELAWARE COUNTY.

Location of station: In western part of college grounds.

Station mark: A limestone post 36 by 6 by 6 inches, set 33 inches in the ground, in the center of top of which is countersunk and cemented a bronze tablet.

Reference mark: Fountain bears S. 68° W., distance 69 feet; western line of college grounds 50 feet east.

Distant mark: North of station 480 feet, a limestone post 24 by 6 by 6 inches, set 24 inches in the ground and having a copper bolt cemented in its top.

Resident referee: Custodian of college buildings.

FINDLAY, HANCOCK COUNTY.

Location of station: In southeast part of college grounds.

Station mark: A sandstone post 36 by 6 by 6 inches, set 32 inches in the ground, in the center of top of which is countersunk and cemented a bronze tablet.

Reference mark: Twenty-four feet from south fence, 15 feet from east fence, and 41 feet from water plug at corner.

Distant mark: North of station 525 feet, a sandstone post 36 by 6 by 6 inches, set 36 inches in the ground, having a copper bolt cemented in its top.

Resident referee: President of the school of the Church of God.

KENTON, HARDIN COUNTY.

Location of station: In southeast part of public-school yard.

Station mark: A sandstone post 36 by 7 by 7 inches, set 32 inches in the ground, in the center of top of which is countersunk and cemented a bronze tablet.

Reference marks: Thirty feet north of south fence and 18 feet from east fence and 36 feet from southeast corner of school yard.

Distant mark: North of station 315 feet, a sandstone post 30 by 6 by 6 inches, set 30 inches in the ground, having a copper bolt cemented in its top.

Resident referee: President of school board.

MARYSVILLE, UNION COUNTY.

Location of station: On church lot, 9 feet northeast of the northeast corner of Methodist Church.

Station mark: A sandstone post 36 by 6 by 6 inches, set 34 inches in ground, in center of top of which is countersunk and cemented a bronze tablet.

Reference marks: Twenty-seven feet from corner of street.

Distant mark: In the court-house grounds, north of station 375 feet, a sandstone post 30 by 6 by 6 inches, set 28 inches in the ground, having a copper bolt cemented in its top.

Resident referee: County clerk.

UPPER SANDUSKY, WYANDOT COUNTY.

Location of station: In southeastern part of public-school grounds, 10 feet north of sidewalk.

Station mark: A limestone post 36 by 7 by 7 inches, set 34 inches in the ground, in the center of top of which is countersunk and cemented a bronze tablet.

Reference marks: A white oak tree, 30 inches in diameter, bears N. 30 E., distant 48 feet.

Distant mark: North of station 348 feet, a limestone post 30 by 5 by 5 inches, set 30 inches in the ground, having a copper bolt cemented in its top.

Resident referees: School board.

WASHINGTON COURT-HOUSE, FAYETTE COUNTY.

Location of station: Two feet from curb line on north side of Temple street, in schoolhouse yard.

Station mark: A limestone post 36 by 8 by 8 inches, set 33 inches in the ground, in the center of top of which is countersunk and cemented a bronze tablet.

Reference marks: A locust tree 20 inches in diameter, bears S. 80° W., distant 40 feet; bay window in new schoolhouse, bears N. 40° E., distant 171 feet.

Distant mark: Three hundred feet north of station, a limestone post 30 by 6 by 6 inches, set 30 inches in the ground, having a copper bolt cemented in its top.

Resident referee: County clerk.

KENTUCKY AND INDIANA.

Primary Traverse.

Thirty-eight geographic positions in Kentucky and Indiana were determined from primary traverse by Mr. George T. Hawkins, topographer, in 1900.

This traverse starts from the Coast and Geodetic Survey astronomic pier at Henderson, Ky., and follows line of the Louisville, Henderson and St. Louis Railroad to Hawesville, Ky., crossing the Ohio River by triangulation, thence along the Cannelton branch of Louisville, Evansville and St. Louis Railroad to Lincoln City, Ind., connecting there with point on traverse run in 1899.

A spur line follows the wagon road from Hawesville, Ky., to southern edge of Rockford quadrangle.

Bull. 181 —01——11

Geographic positions along the Louisville, Henderson and St. Louis Railroad.

Station.	Latitude.	Longitude.
KENTUCKY.		
	o ′ ″	o ′ ″
Henderson, astronomic pier	37 50 24.8	87 35 26.1
Baskett, road crossing at	37 52 22.8	87 27 42.7
Spottsville	37 52 16.2	87 24 47.3
Worthington, road crossing at	37 50 18.2	87 17 42.7
Stanley, road crossing west of	37 49 31.3	87 14 42.2
Griffith, road crossing at	37 49 00.9	87 12 44.5
Road crossing near sawmill	37 48 39.6	87 10 04.9
Road crossing at store	37 48 25.2	87 09 15.2
Road crossing	37 47 18.5	87 08 37.8
Owensboro station	37 46 01.5	87 06 40.5
Crossing of Illinois Central and Louisville and Nashville railroads	37 46 11.5	87 05 34.8
Owensboro, road crossing east of	37 46 29.1	87 04 49.3
Thruston or Pates, road crossing at	37 47 56.3	87 03 07.4
Thruston or Pates, road crossing northeast of	37 49 26.1	87 01 52.9
Powers, road crossing at	37 51 57.0	86 59 39.3
Road crossing under railroad	37 53 35.6	86 58 58.9
Waitman, road crossing at	37 54 33.1	86 56 59.8
Lewisport, road crossing at	37 56 02.6	86 53 54.2
Lewisport, road crossing 2 miles east of	37 56 50.8	86 50 51.2
Falcon, road crossing at	37 57 07.5	86 49 33.8
Petri, road crossing at	37 55 44.4	86 48 14.5
Hawesville, crossing of Cross Main street	37 54 13.5	86 44 50.3

Geographic positions along the Louisville, Evansville and St. Louis Railroad.

Station.	Latitude.	Longitude.
INDIANA.		
	o ′ ″	o ′ ″
Cannelton, ferry landing at	37 54 36.6	86 44 40.6
Tell City depot	37 56 38.6	86 46 09.8
Windy Creek road crossing	37 59 06.6	86 47 11.6
Troy station	37 59 47.3	86 48 16.1
Road crossing at east end of big cut	38 02 11.3	86 49 11.2
Evanston, center of section 4, southeast of	38 02 21.5	86 50 18.5
Evanston station	38 02 24.9	86 50 25.0
T. 5 S., Rs. 4 and 5 W., secs. 19 and 24, ¼ corner between	38 04 06.1	86 54 14.0
Kennedy, road crossing at	38 04 46.6	86 55 22.3
T. 5 S., R. 5 W., secs. 9 and 10, ¼ corner between	38 05 55.1	86 57 34.9

Geographic positions along wagon road from Hawesville, Ky., to southern edge of Rockport quadrangle (spur Traverse Line).

Station.	Latitude.	Longitude.
	° ′ ″	° ′ ″
Hawesville, 2¼ miles south of, forks of road	37 52 08.0	86 46 28.4
Chambers, forks of road east of	37 50 19.9	86 46 52.2
Corner of road 500 feet north of Pellville and Knottsville road	37 50 07.9	86 47 26.1
Floral, forks of road, 3 miles northeast of	37 49 26.6	86 47 22.1
Floral, forks of road, 1¼ miles northeast of	37 48 37.5	86 47 51.7
Floral, cross roads at	37 47 16.4	86 48 35.6
Floral, south azimuth mark	37 46 08.9	86 48 39.1

Meridian Marks.

OWENSBORO, DAVIES COUNTY, KY.

Location of station: In southeastern part of court-house grounds.

Station mark: A limestone post 36 by 7 by 7 inches, set 33 inches in the ground, in the center of top of which is countersunk and cemented an aluminum tablet.

Reference marks: Southeastern corner of court-house bears N. 30° W., distance 130 feet. Southeastern corner of grounds bears S. 50° E., distance 70 feet.

Distant mark: North of station 300 feet. A limestone post 36 by 7 by 7 inches, set 36 inches in the ground, having an aluminum tablet countersunk and cemented in its top.

Resident referee: County judge.

HAWESVILLE, HANCOCK COUNTY, KY.; CANNELTON, PERRY COUNTY, IND.

Location of station: In northeastern part of Hawesville, 30 feet north of railway, and on west bank of creek and south bank of Ohio River.

Station mark: A sandstone post 36 by 8 by 7 inches, set 36 inches in the ground, in the center of top of which is countersunk and cemented a bronze tablet.

Reference marks: Northeastern corner of Mr. Carter's yard fence bears S. 45° W., distance 70 feet. Locust tree 24 inches in diameter bears S. 15° W., distance 90 feet.

Distant mark: North of station about 2,700 feet, in Cannelton, Ind., in south part of town, on north bank of Ohio River, and 110 feet from and in front of Sunlight Hotel, a sandstone post 36 by 8 by 6 inches, set 36 inches in the ground, having a copper bolt cemented in its top.

Resident referee: County surveyor.

IOWA.

Primary Traverse.

Thirty-five geographic positions in northeastern Iowa determined from primary railroad traverse by Mr. George T. Hawkins, topographer. in 1899 and 1900.

The traverse begins at the junction of railways at Independence, previously located by primary traverse, and follows the Burlington, Cedar Rapids and Northern Railway to Postville, thence eastward along the Chicago, Milwaukee and St. Paul Railway to McGregor triangulation station of the Mississippi River Commission.

Geographic positions along the Burlington, Cedar Rapids and Northern Railway.

Station.	Latitude.	Longitude.
	° ′ ″	°
Independence, junction of railways at..	42 28 42. 7	91 54 28.9
T. 89 N.. R. 9 W.. corner secs. 21, 22, 27, and 28	42 29 54. 7	91 54 18.9
T. 90 N., R. 9 W., corner secs. 27, 28, 33, and 34	42 34 15. 1	91 54 20.8
T. 90 N., R. 9 W., corner secs. 9, 10, 15, and 16	42 36 52. 6	91 54 18.7
Hazleton station	42 37 06. 8	91 54 21.3
Crossing Chicago Great Western Railway	42 40 18. 8	91 54 42.5
Oelwein station	42 40 44. 9	91 54 42.3
T. 91 N.. R. 9 W.. center section 20	42 40 45. 4	91 54 48.8
T. 91 N., R. 9 W., corner secs. 9, 10, 15, and 16	42 42 04. 6	91 54 15.3
T. 92 N., R. 9 W., corner secs. 22, 23, 26, and 27	42 45 35. 9	91 53 01.0
Maynard station	42 46 28. 8	91 52 59.4
T. 93 N., R. 9 W., corner secs. 14, 15, 22, and 23	42 51 44. 0	91 53 06.7
Randalia station	42 51 49. 4	91 53 06.7
Crossing Chicago, Milwaukee and St. Paul Railway ...	42 53 47. 3	91 52 43.2
T. 94 N., R. 9 W., corner secs. 25, 26, 35, and 36	42 55 16. 6	91 51 54.6
West Union station	42 57 18. 3	91 48 30.4
T. 94 N., R. 8 W., secs. 21 and 22, ¼ corner between	42 56 34. 8	91 47 07.0
Brainard station...............	42 55 52. 1	91 42 26.4
T. 94 N.. R. 7 W., secs. 29 and 30, ¼ corner between	42 55 41. 3	91 42 20.1
Elgin station	42 57 23. 5	91 38 31.3
T. 94 N., R. 7 W., secs. 14 and 15, ¼ corner between	42 57 24. 7	91 38 47.9
T. 94 N.. R. 7 W., secs. 2, 3, 10, and 11, corner of.........	42 58 42. 8	91 38 45.9
Clermont station..........	43 00 14. 2	91 39 11.1
Postville, junction 3 miles west of	43 04 40. 9	91 37.48.0

Geographic positions along the Chicago, Milwaukee and St. Paul Railroad.

Station.	Latitude.	Longitude.
	° ′ ″	° ′ ″
Postville station	43 05 14.8	91 34 17.0
T. 96 N., R. 6 W., secs. 33 and 32, ¼ corner between	43 05 20.75	91 34 08.3
Luana station	43 03 32.66	91 27 09.3
Monona station	43 03 15.8	91 23 32.8
T. 96 N., R. 6 W., secs. 11, 12, 13, and 14, corner of	43 03 06.7	91 23 24.8
Valdora station	43 01 26.7	91 21 03.7
Beulah station	43 01 34.6	91 18 36.8
Giard station	43 02 15.0	91 15 42.4
West McGregor station	43 02 28.9	91 11 57.5
North McGregor, crossing of railroads at	43 02 38.6	91 10 42.3
McGregor, Mississippi River Commission triangulation station	43 03 31.93	91 10 49.35

MISSOURI.

Primary Traverse.

Fifty-seven geographic positions determined by primary railroad traverse by Mr. George T. Hawkins, topographer, in 1900.

Starting from U. S. Mississippi River Commission triangulation station Quincy, the traverse was run along the line of Omaha, Kansas City and Quincy Railroad to Kirksville; thence to Glenwood, via Wabash Railroad; thence eastward to Wayland, via Keokuk and Western Railroad, and there connected with U. S. Mississippi River Commission triangulation station Fox River.

Geographic positions along the Omaha, Kansas City and Quincy Railroad.

Station.	Latitude.	Longitude.
	° ′ ″	° ′ ″
Quincy, Mississippi River Commission triangulation station	39 56 31.00	91 24 51.18
West Quincy station	39 56 07.0	91 26 09.1
Taylor station	39 56 17.5	91 31 18.0
Maywood station	39 57 11.3	91 35 56.1
T. 60 N., Rs. 6 and 7 W., secs. 31 and 36, ¼ corner between	39 57 15.6	91 37 02.3
Durham station	39 58 30.1	91 39 57.4
T. 60 N., R. 7 W., secs. 7, 8, 17, and 18, corner of	40 00 17.3	91 42 39.3
Ewing station	40 00 18.9	91 42 50.8
T. 61 N., R. 8 W., secs. 26 and 27, ¼ corner between	40 03 24.5	91 46 02.5

Geographic positions along the Omaha, Kansas City and Quincy Railroad—
Continued.

Station.	Latitude.	Longitude.
	° ′ ″	° ′ ″
Lewistown station	40 05 08.6	91 48 57.2
T. 61 N., R. 8 W., corner on range line between secs. 7 and 18	40 05 37.4	91 50 16.2
T. 61 N., R. 9 W., secs. 3, 4, 9, and 10, corner of	40 06 30.5	91 53 40.2
Labelle station.......	40 07 02.7	91 54 59.9
Knox station............	40 08 35.1	92 00 38.5
T. 62 N., R. 10 W., secs. 19, 20, 29, and 30, corner of	40 09 11.3	92 02 35.6
T. 62 N., R. 11 W., secs. 20 and 21, ¼, corner between..	40 09 39.7	92 08 00.9
T. 62 N., Rs. 11 and 12 W., secs. 19 and 24, ¼, corner between..	40 09 41.6	92 10 30.8
Edina station	40 09 45.2	92 10 40.5
T. 62 N., R. 13 W.; secs. 24 and 25, ¼, corner between..	40 09 14.8	92 17 55.4
Hurdland station	40 09 06.5	92 18 09.7
Crossing Atchison, Topeka and Santa Fe Railway and Omaha, Kansas City and Quincy Railway..	40 08 46.9	92 20 05.6
Brashear station...	40 08 45.2	92 22 42.3
T. 62 N., R. 14 W., secs. 24 and 25, ¼, corner between .	40 09 12.3	92 24 43.8
T. 62 N., Rs. 14 and 15 W., secs. 13 and 18, ¼, corner between......	40 10 32.1	92 30 56.1
Kirksville, crossing Wabash railroad	40 12 05.0	92 35 10.5

Geographic positions along Wabash Railroad between Kirksville and Glenwood.

Station.	Latitude.	Longitude
	° ′ ″	° ′ ″
T. 63 N., R. 15 W., secs. 20 and 21, ¼, corner between.	40 14 59.7	92 35 31.5
T. 65 N., R. 15 W., secs. 33 and 34, corner on township line between	40 18 03.1	92 34 22.6
Sublett station	40 18 09.8	92 34 13.0
Greentop station................................... .	40 20 47.6	92 34 03.3
Queen City station.....................................	40 24 28.7	92 34 09.6
T. 65 N., R. 15 W., corner secs. 21, 22, 27, and 28.......	40 25 27.8	92 34 41.4
Julesburg station	40 27 54.5	92 36 21.5

Geographic positions along or near Keokuk and Western railroad, between Glenwood and Wayland.

Station.	Latitude.	Longitude.
	° ′ ″	° ′ ″
T. 66 N., R. 15 W.. secs. 14, 15, 22, and 23, corner of....	40 31 07.4	92 33 29.9
T. 66 N., R. 14 W., secs. 13 and 24, corner on range line between	40 31 09.3	92 31 14.3
Crossing of railroad and range line between Rs. 13 and 14, T. 66 N ...., ...	40 30 13.9	92 24 57.6
T. 66 N., R. 13 W., secs. 28. 29, 32, and 33, corner of...	40 29 29.8	92 22 16.6
Downing station	40 29 13.6	92 22 07.7
T. 65 N., R. 14 W., secs. 5 and 6, corner on township line between	40 28 39.3	92 16 29.3
Crawford station................................	40 28 28.4	92 16 29.0
Memphis station	40 27 13.8	92 09 56.9
T. 65 N., R. 11 W., secs. 8 and 9. ¼ corner b tween .	40 27 22.4	92 08 04.2
T.65 N., R. 11 W., secs. 10 and 11, ¼ corner between...	40 27 20.1	92 05 47.3
Arbela station...............	40 24 49.6	92 00 58.8
Granger station	40 28 00.0	91 58 31.9
T. 65 N., R. 10 W., sec. 2, center of	40 28 05.7	91 58 31.4
T. 65 N., Rs. 9 and 10 W., crossing of railroad and range line between	40 27 41.4	91 56 43.6
Luray station	40 27 03.0	91 52 29.1
T. 65 N., R. 9 W., secs. 11 and 14, ¼ corner between ...	40 26 41.3	91 51 46.7
Ashton station .... -	40 26 46.6	91 48 26.4
T. 65 N., R. 8 W.. secs. 8, 9, 16, and 17, corner of.....	40 26 41.7	91 48 00.4
Crossing of Atchison, Topeka and Santa Fe Railroad .	40 26 17.9	91 46 32.4
Kahoka station.................	40 25 22.1	91 43 02.4
Clark City	40 25 11.0	91 40 53.5
T. 65 N., R. 7 W.. sec. 21, center of	40 25 09.5	91 40 23.9
T. 65 N., R. 6 W., secs. 29, 30, 31, and 32, corner of.. .	40 23 41.8	91 35 16.1
Wayland station	40 23 42.2	91 35 07.4
Fox River. Mississippi River Commission triangulation station	40 21 34.82	91 35 20.87

MISSOURI-KANSAS.

Primary Traverse.

Forty geographic positions along or near the Kansas City, Fort Scott and Memphis Railway between the astronomic pier at Fort Scott, Kans., and the astronomic pier at Springfield, Mo., located from primary railroad traverse by Mr. George T. Hawkins, topographer, in 1900.

Geographic positions along the Kansas City, Fort Scott and Memphis Railway.

Station.	Latitude.	Longitude.
KANSAS.		
	° ′ ″	° ′ ″
Fort Scott astronomic pier	37 50 25.76	94 42 26.75
Washburn station	37 47 10.2	94 41 51.2
Clarksburg station	37 45 36.2	94 39 23.1
T. 26 S., R. 25 E., secs. 26, 27, 34, and 35, corner of	37 45 16.7	94 38 58.0
T. 26 S., R. 25 E., sec. 36, southeast corner of	37 44 49.4	94 38 24.4
Garland station	37 43 56.2	94 37 19.2
T. 27 S., R. 25 E., secs. 23, 24, 25, and 26, corner of	37 40 27.5	94 37 50.0
Arcadia, section corner ¼ mile west of	37 38 42.1	94 37 50.0
Arcadia station	37 38 38.7	94 37 40.0
Crossing of railway and Kansas-Missouri State line	37 37 47.8	94 37 03.6
MISSOURI.		
Last Chance station	37 36 18.5	94 35 29.2
Ts. 32 and 33 N., R. 33 W., secs. 2, 3, 34, and 35, corner of	37 38 58.8	94 31 59.0
Liberal, crossing of railroads	37 33 37.9	94 31 27.5
Liberal station	37 33 28.9	94 31 13.9
T. 32 N., R. 32 W., secs. 13, 14, 23, and 24, corner of	37 31 08.9	94 24 24.0
Iantha station	37 31 02.1	94 23 57.0
T. 32 N., Rs. 31 and 32 W., crossing of railway and range line between	37 30 59.1	94 23 18.4
Lamar station	37 29 13.8	94 16 44.9
T. 32 N., R. 30 W., sec. 32, ¼ corner, south side of	37 28 16.6	94 15 13.1
Kenoma station	37 26 17.9	94 11 58.3
T. 31 N., Rs. 29 and 30 W., secs. 18, 19, 24, and 13, corner of	37 25 31.2	94 10 18.0
Golden City station	37 24 01.3	94 05 28.7
T. 31 N., R. 29 W., sec. 26, center of	37 24 04.1	94 05 24.1
T. 31 N., R. 28 W., secs. 17, 18, 19, and 20, corner of	37 23 32.7	94 02 40.5
Lockwood station	37 23 16.0	93 57 17.4
T. 31 N., Rs. 27 and 28 W., crossing of railway and range line between	37 23 09.5	93 56 05.6
Fletcher station	37 22 46.4	93 53 44.8
T. 30 N., R. 26 W., sec. 6, ¼ corner north of	37 22 29.9	93 50 25.1
South Greenfield station	37 22 34.3	93 50 23.7
Pilgrim station	37 21 29.6	93 46 34.2
T. 30 N., R. 25 W., secs. 8 and 17, ¼ corner between	37 20 36.3	93 42 26.5
Everton station	37 20 28.3	93 42 19.8
Emmet station	37 19 32.0	93 39 35.8
T. 30 N., R. 24 W., secs. 20 and 21, ¼ corner between	37 19 04.5	93 35 19.3
Ash Grove station	37 19 01.9	93 35 16.2

Geographic positions along the Kansas City, Fort Scott and Memphis Railway—
Continued.

Station.	Latitude.	Longitude.
MISSOURI—continued.	° ′ ″	° ′ ″
T. 30 N., R. 24 W., secs. 34 and 35, south corner of	37 16 52.9	93 33 12.1
T. 29 N., R. 24 W., secs. 1 and 1, 2 and 2, corner of	37 15 33.5	93 30 48.5
Bois D'Arc station	37 15 30.3	93 30 28.1
T. 29 N., R. 23 W., secs 9, 10, 15, and 16, corner of	37 18 43.2	93 26 28.1
Elwood station	37 18 35.3	93 25 55.9
Nichols Junction	37 13 10.2	93 21 52.9

The following positions were obtained by Mr. George T. Hawkins, topographer, in 1900, from primary traverse, which starts from Springfield, Mo., astronomic pier and follows the St. Louis and San Francisco Railroad to Oswego, Kans., where it was connected with the courthouse spire, located by astronomic methods in 1884.

Geographic positions along the St. Louis and San Francisco Railroad.

Station.	Latitude.	Longitude.
MISSOURI.	° ′ ″	° ′ ″
Springfield astronomic pier	37 13 15.96	93 17 17.58
Dorchester station	37 12 36.4	93 23 13.3
T. 28 N., R. 23 W., sec. 2, ¼ corner north of	37 10 12.0	93 24 56.7
Brookline station	37 09 50.2	93 25 12.7
Republic station	37 07 11.1	93 28 53.2
T. 28 N., R. 23 W., secs. 19 and 20, ¼ corner between	37 07 09.9	93 28 52.6
T. 27 N., R. 24 W., secs. 4, 5, 8, 9, corner of	37 04 10.1	93 33 18.3
Billings station	37 04 03.4	93 33 19.9
Logan, section corner just east of	37 01 07.0	93 36 37.7
Logan station	37 00 51.8	93 37 00.6
Marionville station	36 59 59.9	93 37 53.0
Aurora station	36 58 37.5	93 43 16.2
T. 26 N., R. 26 W., secs. 11 and 12, ¼ corner between	36 58 38.1	93 44 11.8
Verona station	36 57 54.0	93 47 52.4
T. 26 N., R. 26 W., secs. 17 and 20, ¼ corner between	36 57 24.6	93 47 59.5
T. 26 N., R. 27 W., secs. 25 and 30, ¼ corner between	36 56 07.7	93 49 39.1
Globe station	36 55 53.6	93 51 09.4
Monett station	36 55 14.6	93 55 19.8
Pierce City, secs. 21 and 28, ¼ corner between	36 56 46.5	94 00 00.2
Pierce City station	36 56 41.8	94 00 10.9
Snyder station	36 58 01.7	94 01 10.6
T. 26 N., R. 28 W., secs. 17 and 18, ¼ corner between	36 58 07.1	94 01 31.9

Geographic positions along the St. Louis and San Francisco Railroad—Continued.

Station.	Latitude.	Longitude.
	° ′ ″	° ′ ″
MISSOURI—continued.		
Wentworth station	36 59 43.6	94 04 23.5
Talmage station	37 00 58.1	94 05 36.2
Talmage, section corner at	37 01 15.7	94 05 46.3
T. 27 N., R. 29 W., secs. 20 and 21, ¼ corner between	37 02 35.6	94 06 48.4
Sarcoxie station...........	37 04 03.0	94 07 01.1
T. 28 N., R. 30 W., secs. 25 and 36, corner on range line between	37 06 34.4	94 08 51.4
Reeds station..........	37 07 06.1	94 10 04.5
T. 28 N., R. 30 W., secs. 17, 18, 19, 20, corner of	37 08 27.1	94 14 14.8
Knights station	37 08 35.2	94 14 59.6
T. 28 N., R. 31 W., secs. 11, 12, 13, 14, corner of......	37 09 20.4	94 16 26.0
Carthage station	37 11 06.1	94 18 35.7
T. 28 N., R. 31 W., sec. 6, one-fourth corner west of (elevation 960 feet)..	37 10 39.2	94 20 42.7
Crossing, north and south (elevation 998 feet).	37 10 44.1	94 21 53.8
Macy station	37 11 11.6	94 23 48.0
Mansur station .. ..,	37 11 40.6	94 25 07.2
Boysur, road crossing	37 11 46.1	94 26 44.8
Joplin Junction, head block	37 11 43.6	94 27 44.3
T. 29 N., R. 33 W., secs. 25, 26, 35, and 36, corner of .	37 12 03.0	94 29 24.6
T. 28 N., R. 33 W.. secs. 4 and 5, corner on township line between	37 11 17.0	94 32 40.1
Crossing, Missouri Pacific Railway	37 11 08.3	94 32 49.5
Carl Junction......... . ...'	37 10 46.5	94 33 50.5
Smithfield station .. ..,	37 10 10.6	94 36 09.1
Missouri-Kansas State Line and "Frisco" Railway, crossing of	37 10 01.6	94 37 02.9
KANSAS.		
T. 33 S., R. 25 E., secs. 17 and 18, ¼ corner between..	37 10 17.4	94 42 13.3
Crestline station . . .., ...	37 10 17.4	94 42 17.1
T. 33 S., R. 24 E., secs. 13 and 14, ¼ corner between..	37 10 17.6	94 44 34.6
T. 33 S., R. 24 E., secs. 16 and 17, ¼ corner between..	37 10 18.1	94 47 41.3
Kansas City, Pittsburg and Gulf Rwy., crossing of....	37 10 35.4	94 50 12.1
Columbus station.........	37 10 34.2	94 50 32.4
Sherwin, crossing of Missouri Pacific R. R	37 10 48.6	94 56 51.5
T. 33 S., Rs. 22 and 23 E., secs. 7, 18, 12, 13, corner of..	37 10 47.9	94 57 29.0
Oswego, section corner 3 miles east of............	37 09 56.3	95 02 56.5
Oswego, court-house spire.......	37 09 58.9	95 06 34.0

Meridian Marks.

EDINA, KNOX COUNTY, MO.

Location of station: In court-house square.

Station mark: A granite post 36 by 6 by 6 inches, set 34 inches in the ground, 15 feet north of east and west walk and 78 feet from fence on east side of grounds. In center of top of the post is countersunk and cemented a bronze tablet.

Distant mark: Four hundred feet north of station, a marble post 20 by 6 by 6 inches, set 20 inches in the ground, in center of top of which is cemented a copper bolt. Stone is 10 feet south of east and west fence on north side of square and 80 feet from fence on east side of grounds.

Resident referee: County clerk.

CARTHAGE, JASPER COUNTY, MO.

Location of station: In west part of Central Park.

Station mark: A limestone post 42 by 8 by 6 inches, set 40 inches in the ground, in the center of top of which is countersunk and cemented a bronze tablet.

Reference marks: Forty-eight feet from southwest corner of park and 1 foot from line of fence.

Distant mark: North of station 252 feet, a limestone post 30 by 8 by 6 inches, set 28 inches in ground and with a copper bolt cemented in its top.

Resident referee: County clerk.

KAHOKA, CLARK COUNTY, MO.

Location of station: In eastern part of court-house grounds.

Station mark: A marble post 36 by 6 by 6 inches, set 32 inches in the ground, in the center of top of which is countersunk and cemented a bronze tablet.

Reference marks: An ash tree 10 inches in diameter N. 73° W., distant 24 feet. An ash tree 14 inches in diameter N. 60° E., distant 15 feet.

Distant mark: North of station 300 feet, on inside line of sidewalk on north side of grounds, a marble post 30 by 6 by 6 inches, set 30 inches in the ground; has a copper bolt cemented in its top.

Resident referee: County clerk.

KIRKSVILLE, ADAIR COUNTY, MO.

Location of station: In northwest part of Normal School grounds.

Station mark: A limestone post 36 by 6 by 6 inches, set 34 inches in the ground, in the center of top of which is countersunk and cemented a bronze tablet.

Reference marks: A maple tree 10 inches in diameter bears N. 46°
E., distant 63 feet. A maple tree 24 inches in diameter bears S. 80°
W., distant 72 feet.

Distant mark: A limestone post 24 by 6 by 6 inches, set 24 inches
in the ground, 360 feet north of station, 28 feet southwest of large
maple tree, and 120 feet from northwest corner of grounds. Stone
post has a copper bolt cemented in center of its top.

Residence referee: County clerk.

LAMAR, BARTON COUNTY, MO.

Location of station: In western part of court-house grounds.

Station mark: A limestone post 36 by 8 by 8 inches, set 34 inches
in the ground, in the center of top of which is countersunk and
cemented a bronze tablet.

Reference marks: Southwest corner of court-house N. 35° E., distant 132 feet. Southwest corner of grounds bears S. 50° W., distant
63 feet.

Distant mark: North of station 322 feet, a limestone post 24 by 9
by 9 inches, set 24 inches in the ground, with copper bolt in its top.

Resident referee: County clerk.

LANCASTER, SCHUYLER COUNTY, MO.

Location of station: In east part of public-school yard.

Station mark: A limestone post 40 by 8 by 6 inches, set 30 inches
in the ground, in the center of top of which is countersunk and
cemented a bronze tablet.

Reference marks: Southeast corner of schoolhouse N. 10° 30' W.,
distant 123 feet; 3 feet from south line and 45 feet from east line of
grounds.

Distant mark: North of station 276 feet, on line of sidewalk on north
side of street, 36 feet west of street corner, a limestone post 30 by 8
by 8 inches, set 30 inches in ground, having a copper bolt cemented
in its top.

Resident referee: County clerk.

MEMPHIS, SCOTLAND COUNTY, MO.

Location of station: In eastern part of high-school grounds.

Station mark: A limestone post 40 by 8 by 6 inches, set 36 inches
in the ground, in the center of top of which is countersunk and
cemented a bronze tablet.

Reference marks: Southeast corner of schoolhouse N. 16° W., distant 123 feet. Maple tree 8 inches in diameter bears N. 74° E., distant 30 feet.

Distant mark: North of station 290 feet and 4 feet south of north

fence. A limestone post 30 by 8 by 8 inches, set 30 inches in the ground, with copper bolt cemented in the top.
Resident referee: County clerk.

COLUMBUS, CHEROKEE COUNTY, KANS.

Location of station: In eastern part of court-house grounds.

Station mark: A limestone post 36 by 6 by 6 inches, set 34 inches in the ground, in the center of top of which is countersunk and cemented a bronze tablet.

Reference marks: Southeastern corner of court-house N. 50° W., distant, 84 feet. It is 21 feet from south line and 30 feet from east line of grounds.

Distant mark: North of station 270 feet. A limestone post 24 by 6 by 6 inches, set 24 inches in the ground, in the center of top of which is set a copper bolt.

Resident referee: County clerk.

ARKANSAS.

Primary Traverse.

Twenty-two geographic positions, determined by Mr. Geo. T. Hawkins, topographer, from primary traverse in Arkansas, in 1900. The line starts from a position in front of station at Gurdon, established by primary traverse in 1898, and follows the St. Louis, Iron Mountain and Southern Railway to Camden; thence along the St. Louis and Texas Railway to Harlow.

Geographic positions in Arkansas.

Station.	Latitude.	Longitude.
	° ′ ″	° ′ ″
Gurdon station	33 55 08.0	93 09 12.1
Whelan station	33 49 47.1	93 07 36.3
Sayre, road crossing at	33 45 04.3	93 05 32.3
T. 11 S., R. 19 W.. secs. 29 and 30, ¼ corner between	33 45 02.7	93 05 15.2
Basham station	33 43 21.7	93 03 14.0
Chidester station	33 42 07.9	93 01 14.1
T. 12 S., R. 19 W., secs. 11, 12, 13, 14, corner of	33 41 55.1	93 01 10.4
Van Wagoner station	33 41 00.9	92 59 15.1
Wise station	33 39 30.9	92 56 02.5
Lester, crossing ¼ mile north of	33 38 56.0	92 55 06.8
Camden, at road crossing 1 mile northwest of, iron bench-mark post, elevation 143 feet	33 35 44.9	92 51 10.5
Camden, crossing of telephone line	33 34 55.8	92 50 00.6

Geographic positions in Arkansas—Continued.

Station.	Latitude.	Longitude.
	° ′ ″	° ′ ″
Camden, crossing, street to Iron Mountain station at south end of bridge	33 34 51.0	92 49 41.4
Camden, road crossing at post-office 4 miles northeast of	33 39 02.9	92 46 34.7
Lilley station	33 40 09.3	92 44 25.2
Onalaska station	33 40 19.8	92 43 57.6
Eagle Mill station	33 40 53.2	92 42 30.5
Millville station	33 42 22.7	92 39 19.1
T. 11 S., R. 15 W., secs. 34 and 35, ¼ corner between	33 43 30.6	92 37 14.5
Bearden station	33 43 22.1	92 36 58.6
Best station	33 43 40.9	92 36 18.3
Harlow station	33 44 45.3	92 33 59.8

Meridian Marks.

CAMDEN, OUACHITA COUNTY, ARK.

Location of station: In western part of court-house grounds.

Station mark: A limestone post 42 by 8 by 8 inches, set 38 inches in the ground, in the center of top of which is countersunk and cemented a bronze tablet.

Reference marks: 27 feet from west gate, 39 feet from west door of court-house, and 6 feet south of walk.

Distant mark: 260 feet north of station, in northern part of Methodist churchyard, across street from court-house, 2 feet from north line of churchyard and 10 feet from north wall of church, a limestone post 30 by 8 by 8 inches, set 30 inches in the ground, having a copper bolt set in center of its top.

Resident referee: County clerk.

ROCKY MOUNTAIN SECTION OF TOPOGRAPHY.

SOUTH DAKOTA-WYOMING.

Triangulation Stations.

In 1900 Mr. A. F. Dunnington, topographer, executed control for the Edgemont quadrangle by reoccupying Fossil, Bradley, Sullivan, and Alkali, and establishing two new stations—Provo and Cottonwood. He also extended triangulation northward from Terry Peak, Bear Butte, and Crow Peak, occupying eight new stations, controling three 30-minute quadrangles.

PROVO, FALL RIVER COUNTY, S. DAK.

On highest point of knob on west end of bald ridge 2 miles southeast of Provo station, Burlington and Missouri River Railroad, and about 10 miles south of Edgemont.

Station mark: A bronze bench-mark tablet cemented in sandstone, 9 by 13 by 6 inches, set flush with surface of ground.

[Latitude 43° 10' 18.03". Longitude 103° 48' 12.52".]

To station—	Azimuth.	Back azimuth.	Log. distance.
	° ' "	° ' "	Meters.
Cottonwood	111 22 38.98	291 10 41.84	4.4043384
Sullivan	161 40 02.55	341 32 07.30	4.6932508
Bradley	208 34 01.20	28 41 37.58	4.4956729
Fossil	261 06 55.77	81 19 23.45	4.3973066

COTTONWOOD, CONVERSE COUNTY, WYO.

This station is on the highest point of the bald divide, about 2½ miles west of the Dakota-Wyoming State line. It is 6 miles northwest of the junction of Alum and Cottonwood creeks and about 2½ miles southwest of south end of hay road, which bears southwest, and leaves the Edgemont and Lance Creek wagon road about 8 miles west of Edgemont.

Station mark: A bronze bench-mark tablet set in sandstone, 10 by 10 by 6 inches, 3 inches below surface of ground; a mound of small stones was erected over tablet.

[Latitude 43° 15' 16.38". Longitude 104° 05' 39.88".]

To station—	Azimuth.	Back azimuth.	Log. distance.
	° ' "	° ' "	Meters.
Alkali Butte	143 49 32.85	323 33 37.12	4.7222453
Sullivan	191 57 58.51	12 02 02.85	4.5849751
Provo	291 10 41.84	111 22 38.98	4.4043384

OWL BUTTE, BUTTE COUNTY, S. DAK.

A lone, bare butte in open prairie about 35 miles northeast of Sturgis, on divide east of Willow Creek. Station is near the center of summit.

Station mark: A bronze triangulation tablet cemented in rock in place.

[Latitude 44° 48′ 50.27″.   Longitude 103° 13′ 05.18″.]

To station—	Azimuth.	Back azimuth.	Log. distance
	° ′ ″	° ′ ″	Meters.
Bear Butte	23 36 51.15	208 28 22.65	4.6012777
Susie Peak	79 32 16.68	259 10 20.70	4.6312654
Castle Rock	141 36 30.14	321 26 47.25	4.4640921

CASTLE ROCK, BUTTE COUNTY, S. DAK.

A prominent peak in T. 12 N., R. 5 E., Black Hills meridian, 28 miles air line northeast of Belle Fourche, 12 miles southwest of junction of Sand Creek and South Fork of Moreau River. The summit is a narrow ridge about 150 yards in length, the station being on a knob at northern end, which is about 10 feet lower than south end. Road from Belle Fourche to Slim Buttes passes from southwest to northeast about 2 miles east of the peak.

Station mark: A bronze triangulation tablet cemented in a flat rock buried in the ground flush with surface.

[Latitude 45° 00′ 38.65″.   Longitude 103° 26′ 50.82″.]

To station	Azimuth.	Back azimuth.	Log. distance
	° ′ ″	° ′ ″	Meters.
Susie Peak	36 58 45.39	216 46 29.57	4.5814773
Wymonkota	90 11 12.42	269 44 24.24	4.6971830
Owl Butte	321 26 47.25	141 36 30.14	4.4640921
Bear Butte	357 49 38.82	177 50 48.88	4.7740756

SUSIE PEAK, BUTTE COUNTY, S. DAK.

A small conical peak near the center of T. 9 N., R. 3 E., Black Hills meridian, situated on east end of a high ridge bearing southeast and northwest, being the divide between Crow and Owl creeks, about 6 miles northeast of the town of Belle Fourche and about 2 miles north of Belle Fourche River.

Station mark: A bronze triangulation tablet cemented in stone sunk flush with surface of ground.

[Latitude 44° 44′ 10.08″.   Longitude 103° 44′ 13.75″.]

To station—	Azimuth.	Back azimuth.	Log. distance.
	° ′ ″	° ′ ″	Meters.
Terry	8 09 49.51	189 05 58.21	4.6616893
Crow Peak	30 34 32.16	210 25 19.14	4.5342997
Warren Peak	63 20 21.79	242 50 33.50	4.7991448
Wymonkota	138 34 02.37	318 19 33.87	4.6099751
Castle Rock	216 46 29.57	36 58 45.39	4.5814773
Owl Butte	259 10 20.70	79 32 16.68	4.6212654
Bear Butte	318 43 45.57	138 57 09.55	4.5838871

WYMONKOTA, CUSTER COUNTY, MONT.

A small conical peak situated in southeastern corner of State, on bare divide between Owl and Lone Tree creeks, about one-half mile southeast of head of the latter, about 2 miles west of Watson's sheep ranch, and about 1½ miles west of the "Hash Knife" road from Belle Fourche.

Station mark: A bronze triangulation tablet cemented in large rock set in ground.

[Latitude 45° 00' 37.62". Longitude 104° 04' 44.71".]

To station—	Azimuth.	Back azimuth.	Log. distance.
	° ' "	° ' "	Meters.
Warren	26 15 49.71	206 00 23.64	4.8175736
Alzada	70 47 36.29	250 30 27.84	4.5290474
Castle Rock	269 44 24.24	90 11 12.42	4.6971830
Susie Peak	318 19 33.87	138 34 02.37	4.6099751
Crow Peak	350 43 02.11	170 48 14.23	4.7836118

ALZADA, CROOK COUNTY, WYO.

A bald peak, most southerly of group of bare hills, about 8 miles southwest from Alzada post-office, Mont., on the divide between the Little Missouri and Belle Fourche rivers, about 6 miles southwest from the big bend of the latter, and about 5 miles south of the Wyoming-Montana line.

Station mark: A bronze triangulation tablet cemented in stone sunk below surface of ground between two large rocks bearing southeast and northwest about 3½ feet apart, the southeast rock 30 by 18 inches, 5 inches above ground, and the northwest rock 24 by 8 inches, 12 inches above ground.

[Latitude 44° 54' 34.73". Longitude 104° 29' 00.17".]

To station—	Azimuth.	Back azimuth.	Log. distance.
	° ' "	° ' "	Meters.
Wymonkota	250 30 27.84	70 47 36.29	4.5290474
Crow Peak	319 12 17.68	139 34 33.11	4.8078017
Warren Peak	356 17 47.66	176 19 26.09	4.6801626

WARREN PEAK, CROOK COUNTY, WYOMING.

The most easterly of the two high bare summits of the Bear Lodge Mountains, about 6 miles northwest of the town of Sundance, Wyoming, at the head of Bear and Miller creeks. Richardson's ranch lies

Bull. 181—01——12

about 6 miles north, on Beaver Creek. Road from ranch to Sundance
passes about three-fourths of a mile northeast of station.

Station mark: A bronze triangulation tablet cemented in stone in
place on highest point, 6 feet southeast of a mining claim stake in
cairn of rocks.

[Latitude 44° 28' 46.79''. Longitude 104° 26' 40.23''.]

To station—	Azimuth.	Back azimuth.	Log. distance
	° ' ''	° ' ''	Meters
Alzada	176 19 26.09	356 17 47.66	4.6801626
Wymonkota	206 00 23.64	26 15 49.71	4.8175736
Susie Peak	242 50 33.50	63 20 21.79	4.7991148
Belle Fourche	244 47 34.89	65 12 58.96	4.7230777
Crow Peak	271 16 58.99	91 37 31.29	4.5898094

BELLE FOURCHE, BUTTE COUNTY, SOUTH DAKOTA.

A three-point station on summit of a sandy hill north of Belle
Fourche River, a meridian mark distant 1,570 feet north of south
meridian station, which is in the grounds of the county court-house
in Belle Fourche.

Station mark: A sandstone post, 36 by 12 by 12 inches, set 25 inches
in the ground, in the top of which is cemented a bronze meridian
tablet.

[Latitude 44° 40' 50.31''. Longitude 103° 50' 28.93''.]

To station—	Azimuth.	Back azimuth.	Log. distance
	° ' ''	° ' ''	Meters
Crow Peak	21 21 15	201 16 25	4.3984959
Warren Peak	65 12 59	244 47 35	4.7230707
Susie Peak	233 12 58	53 17 22	4.0131451

DEER EARS, BUTTE COUNTY, SOUTH DAKOTA.

(Not occupied.)

The south summit of a double-topped hill known as "Deer Ears,"
near the line between T. 12 N., Rs. 7 and 8 E., Black Hills meridian.

[Latitude 44° 59' 57.09''. Longitude 103° 10' 41.88''.]

STATE CORNER—WYOMING, MONTANA, AND SOUTH DAKOTA.

The stone post marking the corner common to Wyoming, Montana,
and South Dakota, being the northeast corner of Wyoming.

Station mark: A white sandstone, 18 by 22 inches, 20 inches above ground, bearing no marks; against this rests a triangular sandstone column, 50 inches long, which has fallen from its original position above the other, one side 16 inches wide marked "Dak. 45 N. L.," underneath "27 W. L.;" one side 12 inches wide marked "N. W. Mont.," and the other 12 inches wide marked "S. W. Wyo." Three pits, each 4 feet square, lie north, west, and south of mark.

[Latitude 44° 59' 54.0". Longitude 104° 03' 02.4".]

STATE CORNER, MONTANA AND SOUTH DAKOTA.

(Not occupied.)

The stone post marking the southeast corner of Montana.

Station mark: A stone, 20 by 8 inches, 33 inches above ground. Among a lot of large loose stones on ground, one is marked on one side " Wyo.," on another side " Mon. 45 N. L.," and another stone is marked "Dak. 27 W. L."

Reference marks: Three stones set in ground 6 feet distant east, northwest, and southwest from station are marked on top " D.," "M.," and " W.," respectively.

[Latitude 44° 59' 55.7". Longitude 104° 01' 57.3".]

Meridian Mark.

BELLE FOURCHE, BUTTE COUNTY, SOUTH DAKOTA.

Location of station: In grounds of county court-house.

Station mark: Red sandstone post, 60 by 10 by 10 inches, set 56 inches in the ground, in center of top of which is cemented a bronze bench-mark tablet.

Reference mark: Southeast corner of court-house, distant 47.75 feet. True azimuth to same is 167° 10'.

Distant mark: North of station 1,570 feet, on summit of sand hill north of Belle Fourche River, a sandstone post, about 30 by 12 by 12 inches, set 25 inches in the ground, in top of which is cemented a meridian tablet.

TEXAS.

Triangulation Stations.

In March, April, and May, 1900, triangulation control was extended from stations County Line, Dexter, Tex., and Marietta, Ind. T., westward over the Gainesville and Montague quadrangles, by Mr. R. H. Chapman, topographer.

In addition to the occupation of the three old stations, nine new stations were selected and occupied, and four points were located by intersections.

180   PRIMARY TRIANGULATION AND PRIMARY TRAVERSE. [BULL. 19

HENSON, COOKE COUNTY.

On a rocky, thinly timbered hill, about 6 miles northeast of Gainesville, about 150 yards northeast of Henson's house, about 6 miles southwest from Callisburg, and one-half mile east of Gainesville-Whitesboro road.

Theodolite elevated 18 feet.

Station mark: A bronze tablet cemented in rock in place level with surface.

Reference marks: Nail in base blaze on post oak, azimuth 129° 13', distance 42 feet; nail in base blaze on post oak, azimuth 243° 54', distance 18.9 feet; nail in base blaze on post oak, azimuth 12° 54', distance 14.2 feet.

[Latitude 33° 38' 45.87".   Longitude 97° 03' 24.41".]

To station—	Azimuth.	Back azimuth.	Log. distance.
	° ′ ″	° ′ ″	Meters.
Hood	70 11 31.76	250 02 27.00	4.4311207
Hemphill	107 57 58.85	287 51 01.20	4.3094543
Huneycutt	173 35 18.33	353 34 54.10	4.0030462
County Line	227 02 59.91	47 06 06.66	4.0737968

HUNEYCUTT, COOKE COUNTY.

On a flat, timbered ridge, about 12 miles northeast of Gainesville, about one-eighth mile west of Gainesville-Horseshoe Bend road, and one-half mile northwest of the widow Huneycutt's house, from which a wood road passes station. Due east from station is a very sandy field.

Theodolite elevated 18 feet.

Station mark: A bronze tablet cemented in rock in place about inches under surface of ground.

Reference marks: Nail in blaze on black-oak tree, azimuth 302° 13', distance 36.65 feet; nail in blaze on post-oak tree, azimuth 44° 32', distance 24.10 feet; nail in blaze on post-oak tree, azimuth 142° 31', distance 33.70 feet.

[Latitude 33° 44' 10.69".   Longitude 97° 04' 08.10".]

To station—	Azimuth.	Back azimuth.	Log. distance
	° ′ ″	° ′ ″	Meters.
Hood	51 41 32.10	231 33 50.90	4.4901191
Hemphill	78 29 38.85	258 23 04.96	4.2706120
Marietta	175 10 59.88	355 10 22.26	4.3153285
Dexter	229 01 55.28	49 05 48.81	4.1555001
County Line	281 08 41.03	101 12 12.24	3.9994935
Henson	353 34 54.10	173 35 18.33	4.0030462

GAINESVILLE, THIRD WARD SCHOOL, COOKE COUNTY.

(Not occupied.)

Station mark: Middle of statue on cupola of Third Ward school building.

[Latitude 33° 38′ 04.48″.   Longitude 97° 08′ 51.86″.]

To station —	Azimuth.	Back azimuth.	Log. distance.
	° ′ ″	° ′ ″	*Meters.*
Hemphill	124 33 22.25	304 29 26.20	4.1243076
Henson	261 22 52.45	81 25 53.85	3.9311680

HEMPHILL, COOKE COUNTY.

On a high, rolling prairie, about 11 miles northwest from Gainesville, in pasture owned by J. C. Hemphill, just east of line of posts (no wire) running north and south and on highest point in vicinity. It is one-half mile northeast from Hemphill homestead, one-fourth mile north of house occupied by J. R. Bice, and about 1 mile northeast of Van Slack church.

Station mark: A bronze tablet in sandstone post 36 by 8 by 10 inches, set 32 inches in the ground.

[Latitude 33° 42′ 09.39″.   Longitude 97° 15′ 57.65″.]

To station—	Azimuth.	Back azimuth.	Log. distance.
	° ′ ″	° ′ ″	*Meters.*
Hood	21 05 53.53	201 03 45.56	4.2189604
Muenster	63 36 24.98	242 32 46.93	4.0573381
Meador	92 24 21.45	272 17 30.02	4.2812156
Marietta	214 06 33.63	34 12 30.88	4.4684405
Dexter	245 38 15.59	65 48 43.34	4.5036342
Huneycutt	258 23 04.96	78 29 38.85	4.2706120
Henson	287 51 01.20	107 57 58.85	4.3094543

HOOD, COOKE COUNTY.

On a high, rolling prairie ridge, about 12 miles southwest from Gainesville, 2 miles northeast from Hood post-office, and 5 miles southwest from Myra post-office. In pasture owned by W. P. Gregory, 57 yards northeast from J. F. Hood's house, one-half mile south of W. P. Gregory's house, and 6 feet west of fence on west side of road from Myra to Hood. It is 52 feet 4 inches north (6 feet west) of corner post on line of Gregory and Hood property, between Gainesville-Rosston and Gainesville-Forrestburg roads.

Station mark: A bronze tablet in sandstone post 30 by 8 by 8 inches, set 30 inches in the ground.

[Latitude 33° 33' 47.98″.   Longitude 97° 19' 48.70′.]

To station—	Azimuth.	Back azimuth.	Log. distance.
	° ′ ″	° ′ ″	*Meters.*
Jackson	102 32 46.31	282 29 16.77	4.0004447
Meador	141 01 13.31	320 56 30.61	4.3199664
Muenster	157 42 37.58	337 41 07.82	4.0420488
Hemphill	201 03 45.56	21 05 53.53	4.2186604
Huneycutt	231 33 50.90	51 42 32.10	4.4901191
Henson	250 02 27.00	70 11 31.76	4.4311207

MUENSTER, COOKE COUNTY.

The belfry on the Roman Catholic Church at Muenster was occupied at a point about 45 feet above ground.
Station mark: Gilt cross on spire of church.

[Latitude 33° 39' 18.81′.   Longitude 87° 22' 30.87″.]

To station—	Azimuth	Back azimuth.	Log. distance.
	° ′ ″	° ′ ″	*Meters.*
Jackson	34 52 06.74	214 50 06.74	3.9901891
Jim Ned	78 57 58.34	258 49 28.52	4.3833586
Meador	123 58 48.57	303 55 35.45	4.0339101
Hemphill	242 32 46.93	62 36 24.98	4.0573381
Hood	337 41 07.82	157 42 37.58	4.0420488

JACKSON, COOKE COUNTY.

On a high rolling prairie, about 7 miles southwest of Muenster and 7 miles northwest from Hood (post-office), one-half mile north of Gainesville-Forrestburg road, in pasture owned by J. S. Jackson, one-half mile northward from his house. Higher ground under cultivation lies one-fourth mile northward of station.

Station mark: A bronze tablet set in fossiliferous limestone post, 24 by 8 by 8 inches, set 24 inches in ground.

[Latitude 33° 34' 58.40″.   Longitude 97° 26' 07.61″.]

To station—	Azimuth.	Back azimuth.	Log. distance.
	° ′ ″	° ′ ″	*Meters.*
Jim Ned	100 34 01.41	280 27 32.01	4.2660753
Muenster	214 50 06.74	34 52 06.74	3.9901891
Hood	282 29 16.77	102 32 46.31	4.0004447

MEADOR, MONTAGUE COUNTY.

On a prairie knoll, with few small trees, about 4 miles northeast of Saint Jo and 1 mile north of Missouri, Kansas and Texas Railway track, in "stack" yard owned by Meador Bros. (Saint Jo). The Saint Jo-Marysville road passes about 400 yards west of station. Theodolite elevated 18 feet.

Station mark: A bronze tablet cemented in a stone post, about 36 by 8 by 10 inches, set 36 inches in ground.

[Latitude 33° 42′ 34.81″.   Longitude 97° 28′ 19.05″.]

To station—	Azimuth.	Back azimuth.	Log. distance.
	° ′ ″	° ′ ″	*Meters.*
Jim Ned	54 05 15.87	232 59 58.68	4.2604098
Saint Jo	76 48 55.23	256 42 19.02	3.6615794
Mosley	94 54 05.67	274 50 04.80	4.0497723
Hemphill	272 17 30.02	92 24 21.45	4.2812156
Muenster	303 55 35.45	123 58 48.57	4.0339101
Hood	320 56 30.61	141 01 13.31	4.3199664

SAINT JO (SCHOOLHOUSE), MONTAGUE COUNTY.

(Not occupied.)

Station mark: Point of cupola on brick schoolhouse at Saint Jo.

[Latitude 33° 42 00.60″.   Longitude 97 31′ 12.44″.]

To station—	Azimuth.	Back azimuth.	Log. distance.
	° ′ ″	° ′ ″	*Meters.*
Jim Ned	46 51 37.99	226 47 56.93	4.1489547
Mosley	106 39 41.46	286 37 17.02	3.8452950
Meador	256 42 19.02	76 43 55.23	3.6615794

MOSLEY, MONTAGUE COUNTY.

On northern point of prairie ridge, about 5 miles west of Saint Jo, 3 miles south of Bonita and one-half mile south of Saint Jo-Nocona road, in pasture owned by Luke Mosley, who lives about one-half mile northeast from station.

Station mark: A bronze tablet set in a stone post, 30 by 10 by 8 inches, set 23 inches in the ground.

Reference mark: Nail in blaze on north side of tree 4 inches in diameter. Azimuth, 333° 32′; distance, 55 feet.

[Latitude 33° 43′ 05.70″.   Longitude 97° 35′ 33.01″.]

To station—	Azimuth.	Back azimuth.	Log. distance.
	° ′ ″	° ′ ″	*Meters.*
Jim Ned	17 01 14.61	196 59 57.95	4.0856216
Bowie	55 00 48.97	234 52 13.30	4.4669171
Montague	63 16 22.11	243 12 06.91	4.1194725
Meador	274 50 04.80	94 54 05.67	4.0497723
Saint Jo	286 37 17.02	106 39 41.46	3.8452950

JIM NED, MONTAGUE COUNTY.

On highest point of a bare, flat hill known as "Jim Ned Lookout," about 8 miles southwest from Saint Jo, 8 miles southeast from Montague Court-House, and 1 mile south of Dye post-office, in pasture owned by B. R. Raymond, who lives one-half mile southwest from station. The Dye-Bowie road passes one-eighth mile west of station. Theodolite elevated 18 feet.

Station mark: A bronze tablet cemented in sandstone post, 30 by 10 by 8 inches, set 28 inches in ground.

[Latitude 33° 36′ 47.68′.   Longitude 97° 37′ 51.31″.]

To station—	Azimuth.	Back azimuth.	Log. distance.
	° ′ ″	° ′ ″	*Meters.*
Bowie	75 49 20.60	255 42 02.15	4.3239329
Montague	124 54 50.57	304 51 54.33	3.9998274
Mosley	196 59 57.95	17 01 14.61	4.0856216
Meador	233 59 58.68	54 05 15.87	4.2604098
Muenster	258 49 28.52	78 57 58.34	4.3333586
Jackson	280 27 32.01	100 34 01.41	4.2660752
Saint Jo	226 47 56.93	46 51 37.99	4.1489547

MONTAGUE COURT-HOUSE, MONTAGUE COUNTY.

(Not occupied.)

Station mark: Figure of Justice on tower of court-house at Montague.

[Latitude 33° 39′ 53.27″.   Longitude 97° 43′ 09.46′.]

To station—	Azimuth.	Back azimuth.	Log. distance.
	° ′ ″	° ′ ″	*Meters.*
Mosley	243 12 08.91	63 16 22.11	4.1194725
Jim Ned	304 51 54.33	124 54 50.57	3.9998274

BOWIE, MONTAGUE COUNTY.

(Not occupied.)

Station mark: Middle of top of standpipe in town of Bowie.

[Latitude 33° 33′ 59.37″.   Longitude 97° 51′ 03.82″.]

To station—	Azimuth.	Back azimuth.	Log. distance.
	° ′ ″	° ′ ″	Meters.
Mosley	234 52 13.30	55 00 48.97	4.4669171
Jim Ned	255 42 02.15	75 49 20.60	4.3239329

Primary Traverse.

In April and May, 1901, Mr. W. M. Beaman, topographer, ran a line of primary traverse southward from Bell Mountain triangulation station across the Fredericksburg and Boerne quadrangles, and connecting with the Boerne triangulation station, a linear distance of 61 miles. Three hundred and seventy transit stations were occupied, from which the following 29 geographic positions were computed:

Geographic positions along highways between Bell Mountain triangulation station and Waring.

Station.	Latitude.	Longitude.
	° ′ ″	° ′ ″
Bell Mountain triangulation station	30 26 47.45	98 43 00.12
Fredericksburg. 14¼ miles northeast of, at forks of Bell Mountain-Fredericksburg and Bell Mountain-Willow City roads; bench-mark post, elevation 1,749 feet.	30 24 40.4	98 43 44.9
Fredericksburg, 12¼ miles northeast of, at forks of Bell Mountain-Fredericksburg and Willow City-Fredericksburg roads; bench-mark post, elevation 1,826 feet.	30 22 58.1	98 44 03.2
Fredericksburg, 9¼ miles northeast of, north side of road near bend in fence; bench-mark post, elevation 1,953 feet	30 21 37.2	98 46 10.8
Fredericksburg, 8 miles northeast of, center of road opposite a galvanized stock tank	30 21 23.0	98 46 34.6
Fredericksburg, 6¼ miles northeast of, 60 feet east of gate to Grobes's ranch; bench-mark post, elevation 1,724 feet.	30 19 45.7	98 47 57.0
Fredericksburg, 4¼ miles northeast of, north side of road 650 feet northeast of Palo Alto Creek; bench-mark post, elevation 1,649 feet	30 18 28.8	98 48 55.2

Geographic positions along highways between Bell Mountain triangulation station and Waring—Continued.

Station.	Latitude.	Longitude.
	° ′ ″	
Fredericksburg, 2¼ miles northeast of, at forks with a settlement road running northward; bench-mark post, elevation 1,824 feet	30 17 34.6	98 50 01.1
Fredericksburg, county court-house, southeast front of; bronze tablet, elevation 1,708 feet	30 16 30.2	98 52 17.1
Fredericksburg, forks of Fredericksburg-Burnet and Fredericksburg - Comfort lower roads; temporary bench mark on telephone pole, elevation 1,665 feet	30 16 08.7	98 51 23.9
Fredericksburg, 2¼ miles southeast of, on Comfort lower road; temporary bench mark, east side of road and 3 feet from fence, elevation 1,635 feet	30 14 14.9	98 50 49.9
Fredericksburg, 3 miles southeast of; milestone at forks of Fredericksburg-Austin, and lower Fredericksburg-Comfort roads, elevation 1,618 feet	30 14 31.4	98 50 28.6
Fredericksburg, 5 miles southeast of; gate southwest forks of settlement and Comfort lower road	30 12 39.1	98 50 25.8
Fredericksburg, 5¼ miles southeast of; culvert between fences	30 12 19.4	98.50 08.2
Pedernales and South Grape creeks, summit of Fredericksburg and Comfort lower road between	30 10 07.1	98 49 17.3
Comfort-Luckenback and Comfort-Fredericksburg lower roads, at forks of; iron bench-mark post, elevation 1,784 feet	30 09 02.5	98 49 04.4
Gillespie and Kendall County line, stone post west side of road	30 08 33.8	98 49 03.6
Block and South Grape creeks, summit of Fredericksburg-Comfort lower road between	30 06 05.0	98 49 10.7
Forks of Comfort lower road and lane westward to Giles ranch; bench-mark post, elevation 1,611 feet	30 04 04.5	98 49 42.6
Comfort and Waring road forks, at bend in road, 1¼ miles north of; bench-mark post, elevation 1,453 feet	30 01 53.0	98 49 58.6
Comfort and Waring road forks; temporary bench mark at milestone, elevation 1,415 feet	30 00 42.0	98 50 02.6
Fredericksburg-Waring and Fredericksburg-Sisterdale road forks; iron bench-mark post, elevation 1,553 feet	29 59 41.0	98 40 04.5

Geographic positions along San Antonio and Aransas Pass Railroad.

Station.	Latitude.	Longitude.
	° ′ ″	° ′ ″
Waring, road crossing 300 feet north of	29 57 01.2	98 48 16.0
Road crossing, 60 feet north of milepost 281	29 56 22.5	98 47 18.3
Welfare, water tank	29 54 27.2	98 47 08.9
Public road crossing, 1,135 feet north of milepost 278	29 53 57.4	98 47 06.0
Road under railroad, one-third mile north of mile post 276	29 52 31.1	98 46 18.3
Milepost 273	29 49 45.2	98 45 42.2

Geographic positions between Boerne City and Boerne triangulation station.

Station.	Latitude.	Longitude.
	° ′ ″	° ′ ″
Boerne, intersection of Main street and street to Boerne Hotel	29 47 30.9	98 43 54.2
Boerne, 1 mile southwest of; middle of lane, roads to Boerne, Bandera, and Balcones ranch	29 46 45.3	98 44 14.6
Boerne, triangulation station	29 45 27.24	98 45 30.75

MONTANA.

Secondary Triangulation Stations.

In the fall of 1900 Mr. R. H. Chapman added two new stations—Hospital and Columbia—to the local scheme at Butte, and a new station was established at Walkerville within a few feet of the site of the former one.

From these and other stations, including many "three-point" locations, numerous mines, shaft houses, tunnel mouths, and gallows frames, 100 points in all, were located in the vicinity of Butte in order to give accurate control for underground-mine maps.

The positions given are from preliminary computations only, no figure or station adjustment having been made.

HOSPITAL, SILVERBOW COUNTY.

On long smooth western slope of East Ridge, about one-fourth mile nearly due south from Boston and Montana Hospital, and 923 feet from northwest corner of collar of Atlantic shaft, which bears N. 118° 34′ 30″ E.

Station mark: An aluminum tablet cemented in granite block 30 by 8 by 8 inches, set 24 inches in the ground.

[Latitude 46° 01′ 38.36″.   Longitude 112° 29′ 41.96″.]

To station—	Azimuth.	Back azimuth.	Log. distance
	° ′ ″	° ′ ″	Meters.
Three (Roadway)	22 02 11	202 01 24	3.59033
Walkerville	119 04 42	299 03 05	3.52146
Columbia	298 35 58	118 36 12	3.30127
Southeast Base	346 34 52	166 35 16	3.48214

COLUMBIA, SILVERBOW COUNTY.

On rocky hill about 1 mile north of Columbia Garden, on first ridge south of Horse Canyon.   It is the highest point on ridge west of road from Homestake mine to Columbia Garden, and about three-fourths mile west from mine.

Station mark: An aluminum tablet cemented in rock in place.

[Latitude 46° 01′ 07.36″.   Longitude 112° 28′ 20.29″.]

To station—	Azimuth.	Back azimuth.	Log. distance.
	° ′ ″	° ′ ″	Meters.
Three (Roadway)	50 31 01	230 29 13	3.63009
Big Butte	92 46 56	272 43 12	3.83855
Walkerville	118 55 19	298 52 43	3.73625
Hospital	118 36 12	298 35 53	3.30127

WALKERVILLE, SILVERBOW COUNTY.

On low summit covered with granite bowlders, one-fourth mile north of brick schoolhouse at Walkerville, and one-half mile northeast of shaft house at Alice mine.   Elevation 6,463.

Station mark: An aluminum tablet cemented in granite bowlder just north (25 feet approximate) of prospect hole on "First Stake" claim and about 250 feet east of Butte-Stringtown road.

[Latitude 46° 02′ 30.66″.   Longitude 112° 31′ 57.02″.]

To station—	Azimuth.	Back azimuth.	Log. distance
	° ′ ″	° ′ ″	Meters
Big Butte	42 36 51	222 35 32	3.48500
Columbia	298 52 43	118 55 19	3.73625
Hospital	299 03 05	119 04 42	3.52146
Southeast Base	321 39 35	141 41 36	3.76493

"TUNNEL 10" PROSPECT, SILVERBOW COUNTY.

Prospect hole on highest point of hill southwest from Tunnel 10, Montana Central Railway. The ridge is a spur from "East Ridge" and is cut through by the railway tunnel. Center of prospect hole is 4.5 feet east from position given.

[Latitude 46° 01′ 28.06″. Longitude 112° 28′ 40.08″.]

Mines located near Butte.

Name of mine.	Point located.	Latitude.	Longitude.
		o ′ ″	o ′ ″
Gopher	West post of gallows frame..	46 00 51.77	112 31 05.04
Nora	West post of gallows frame.	46 00 53.63	112 31 03.01
Iduna	West post of gallows frame..	46 00 47.73	112 31 09.02
Shaft at northeast corner of South Gaylord and East Mercury streets.	Middle of gallows frame	46 00 51.16	112 31 12.88
Westlake	North post of gallows frame.	46 00 51.38	112 31 09.37
Shaft on lot east of No. 432 East Park street.	East post of gallows frame	46 00 54.72	112 31 37.62
Oneida	East post of gallows frame ..	46 00 50.06	112 30 47.04
Pat Wall & Co	West post of gallows frame..	46 00 47.76	112 30 45.99
Neva	West post of gallows frame..	46 00 47.25	112 30 42.75
Bell	Center of gallows frame	46 01 35.96	112 31 22.80
Shaft at northeast corner of North Atlantic and East Galena streets.	West post of gallows frame..	46 00 53.55	112 31 24.36
Monita	West post of gallows frame.	46 00 48.07	112 30 53.07
West Stewart	West post of gallows frame..	46 01 12.88	112 32 07.27
Anaconda	Middle of gallows frame.....	46 01 11.08	112 31 24.71
Diamond	Flagstaff over shaft	46 01 36.96	112 31 27.63
Neversweat	Middle of gallows frame.....	46 01 08.84	112 31 34.02
J. I. C	Middle of gallows frame.....	46 00 43.71	112 31 00.32
Little Rosa	Middle of gallows frame. ...	46 01 01.45	112 31 25.52
Widow Reed (owner).	Middle of gallows frame....	46 01 00.06	112 31 02.65
St. Lawrence	Middle of gallows frame. ..	46 01 08.75	112 31 11.26
St. Lawrence	Middle of big ventilator . ..	46 01 11.94	112 31 11.40
Mine south of Mountain View.	Middle of gallows frame.....	46 01 11.58	112 31 06.06
Boston and Montana No. 7.	Middle of gallows frame.....	46 01 05.74	112 29 14.63
Belmont	Ventilator shaft	46 00 48.23	112 31 20.42

Mines located near Butte—Continued.

Name of mine.	Point located.	Latitude.	Longitude.
		° ′ ″	° ′ ″
Modoc	Middle of hood on shaft house.	46 01 31.27	112 30 49.92
West Colusa	Middle of gallows frame	46 01 23.74	112 30 43.04
Minnie Healy	Middle frame over southeast shaft.	46 01 18.13	112 30 32.50
Minnie Healy	Middle frame over northwest shaft.	46 01 18.85	112 30 33.51
Leonard	Flagstaff	46 01 22.21	112 30 30 92
East Colusa	Middle comb on shaft house.	46 01 26.49	112 30 25.27
Bordeaux	Middle of gallows frame	46 01 28.93	112 30 02.80
Speculator	Middle of gallows frame.	46 01 39.52	112 31 09.61
L. E. R	Middle of gallows frame.	46 01 17.20	112 31 26.07
Humboldt	Ventilator	46 01 23.94	112 32 19.19
Buffalo	Middle comb on shaft house.	46 01 29.64	112 32 12.50
Mountain Con No. 2	Flagstaff	46 01 30.70	112 31 56.48
West Grayrock	Intersection of gables on shaft house.	46 01 42.14	112 31 44.21
Green Mountain	Flagstaff	46 01 33.37	112 31 41.90
Wake-up-Jim	Middle comb on shaft house.	46 01 33.20	112 31 35.52
Nipper	Middle frame of vertical shaft.	46 01 14.22	112 31 44.07
Nipper	Middle frame at top of incline shaft.	46 01 14.98	112 31 46.74
Little Mina	South ventilator	46 01 17.96	112 31 50.78
Gagnon	Flagstaff	46 01 08.84	112 32 19.53
Josephine	Middle of west gallows frame	46 01 49.00	112 31 58.99
Magna Charta	Flagstaff	46 02 07.02	112 31 56.26
Lilly	Middle of gallows frame	46 01 07.98	112 28 58.70
"Doc" Wierhurst (owner).	Stack, tunnel south of Columbia garden.	46 00 17.40	112 27 29.06
Valdemere	Flagstaff	46 02 06.02	112 31 44.25
Moose	Flagstaff	46 02 01.46	112 31 40.46
East Grayrock	Flagstaff	46 01 38.32	112 31 30.76
Poulin	Flagstaff	46 01 26.93	112 32 23.94
Highore No. 2	Middle of gallows frame	46 01 26.22	112 31 09.52
Ramsdell Parrot	Peak of gallows frame	46 01 06.36	112 31 37.67
Colusa Parrot	Flagstaff	46 01 06.31	112 31 40.02
Sirius	Middle of gallows frame	46 01 32.12	112 30 30.34
Balaklava	Middle of gallows frame	46 01 34.30	112 30 38.54
Mountain Chief	Middle of gallows frame	46 01 36.50	112 30 39.83
Sioux Chief	Middle of gallows frame	46 01 39.36	112 30 51.90
Old Joe (fraction)	Ventilator	46 01 39.02	112 31 00.96
Adirondack	Middle of gallows frame	46 01 41.20	112 31 09.14

Mines located near Butte—Continued.

Name of mine.	Point located.	Latitude.	Longitude.
		° ′ ″	° ′ ″
Tycoon	Middle of gallows frame	46 01 42.74	112 31 17.12
Speculator No. 6	Middle of gallows frame	46 01 41.92	112 31 25.40
Gem	Ventilator	46 01 48.44	112 30 54.71
Wild Bill	Middle of gallows frame	46 01 42.94	112 31 27.50
Cora (east)	Ventilator	46 01 47.46	112 31 38.14
Atlantic	Northwest corner of shaft collar.	46 01 33.87	112 29 30.57
Star	Middle comb of shaft house	46 01 28.29	112 32 18.08
Tramway	Ventilator	46 01 11.82	112 30 32.70
Mountain View	Middle of gallows frame	46 01 16.55	112 31 05.76
Parnell	Middle of gallows frame	46 01 20.67	112 31 19.92
Stewart	Middle of gallows frame	46 01 13.00	112 31 53.56
Original	Flagstaff	46 01 08.66	112 32 16.68
Parrot	Middle of gallows frame	46 01 06.98	112 31 35.85
Washoe	Middle of cupola	46 01 04.95	112 31 57.58
Bluejay	Middle of gallows frame	46 01 02.65	112 31 48.52
Moonlight	Middle of gallows frame	46 01 01.31	112 31 32.74
Sarsfield	Middle of gallows frame	46 01 00.82	112 28 53.00
Bellona	Middle of gallows frame	46 01 01.92	112 31 36.96
Amazon	Middle of gallows frame	46 00 22.36	112 28 51.40
Altona	Middle of gallows frame	46 00 21.02	112 28 46.04
Homestake	Ventilator	46 01 25.38	112 27 57.53
Clinton	Boiler stack at tunnel	46 01 29.32	112 27 50.12
B. & M. No. 4	Middle of gallows frame	46 01 38.29	112 30 06.54
Sinbad	Middle of gallows frame	46 01 23.28	112 29 16.30
Bill Moran (owner)	Middle of gallows frame	46 00 11.22	112 28 39.60
Glass Bros	Middle frame of shaft	46 00 43.48	112 30 09.48
Rarus	Vertical bolt in middle of stay frame east of shaft.	46 01 07.24	112 30 43.41
Glengary	Middle of gallows frame	46 00 44.60	112 30 44.80
Shaft west of south of Anaconda mine.	Middle of ventilator	46 01 04.28	112 31 28.25
Mine southeast of Neversweat shaft.	Middle of gallows frame	46 01 06.03	112 31 31.01
Silverbow	Ventilator	46 00 53.90	112 30 42.20
Silverbow No. 3	Flagstaff	46 00 44.59	112 30 36.28
Berkeley	Flagstaff	46 01 02.12	112 30 37.10
Pennsylvania	Middle of gallows frame	46 00 59.28	112 30 53.77

UTAH-WYOMING.

Triangulation Stations.

The following stations form a belt of quadrilaterals which starts from a line of the United States Coast and Geodetic Survey station Deseret-Nebo, and extends northeasterly and then easterly along the forty-first parallel of latitude through the Uinta Forest Reserve. Nine of these stations were published in the Nineteenth and the remainder in the Twentieth Annual Report of the United States Geological Survey. All the positions have been recomputed and based on the "U. S. Standard" datum, and are now republished with corrected values.

NEBO, JUAB COUNTY, UTAH.

[Latitude 39° 48′ 39.11″.   Longitude 111° 45′ 56.92″.]

To station—	Azimuth.	Back azimuth.	Log. distance.
	° ′ ″	° ′ ″	*Meters.*
Deseret	134 47 27.68	314 14 12.20	5.0118874
Timpanogos	189 49 32.25	9 54 33.61	4.8107167
Spanish Fork Peak	213 26 56.70	33 36 08.50	4.5674464

DESERET, TOOELE COUNTY, UTAH.

[Latitude 40° 27′ 35.30″.   Longitude 112° 37′ 32.55″.]

To station—	Azimuth.	Back azimuth.	Log. distance.
	° ′ ″	° ′ ″	*Meters.*
Timpanogos	275 20 54.42	95 59 25.06	4.9264460
Spanish Fork Peak	293 28 17.08	114 10 51.86	5.0092198
Nebo	314 14 12.20	134 47 27.68	5.0118874

TIMPANOGOS, UTAH COUNTY, UTAH.

[Latitude 40° 23′ 04.92″.   Longitude 111° 38′ 09.04″.]

To station—	Azimuth.	Back azimuth.	Log. distance.
	° ′ ″	° ′ ″	*Meters.*
Nebo	9 54 33.61	189 49 32.25	4.8107167
Deseret	95 59 25.06	275 20 54.42	4.9264460
Clayton	195 47 43.75	15 50 42.67	4.3756781
Kamas	227 15 07.05	47 32 13.42	4.7082109
Currant Creek Peak	270 51 37.53	91 09 34.01	4.5983849
Spanish Fork Peak	344 15 55.66	164 20 08.53	4.5840982

SPANISH FORK PEAK, UTAH COUNTY, UTAH.

[Latitude, 40° 05' 17.46".   Longitude, 111° 31' 37.56".]

To station—	Azimuth.	Back azimuth.	Log. distance.
	° ' "	° ' "	Meters.
Nebo	33 36 08.50	213 26 56.70	4.5674464
Deseret	114 10 51.86	293 28 17.08	5.0092198
Timpanogos	164 20 08.53	344 15 55.66	4.5340282
Kamas	202 33 01.42	22 45 51.01	4.8616269
Currant Creek Peak	222 51 16.76	43 04 57.11	4.6489550
Strawberry	275 25 26.49	95 46 24.82	4.6678909
Grey Head	280 38 47.28	101 10 20.60	4.8518116
Indian Head	293 26 04.72	113 50 13.17	4.7662870

CURRANT CREEK PEAK, WASATCH COUNTY, UTAH.

[Latitude, 40' 22' 42.51".   Longitude, 111° 10' 27.48".]

To station—	Azimuth.	Back azimuth.	Log. distance.
	° ' "	° ' "	Meters.
Spanish Fork Peak	43 04 57.11	222 51 16.76	4.6489550
Timpanogos	91 09 34.01	270 51 37.53	4.5932849
Clayton Peak	125 59 02.55	305 44 02.70	4.6050691
Wanship	154 05 43.90	333 53 53.12	4.7704972
Kamas	176 49 22.38	356 48 28.80	4.5431299
Grey Head	318 55 39.11	139 13 38.95	4.7815030
Peak	323 24 40.00	143 40 47.00	4.7763501
Strawberry	336 10 21.58	156 17 4:..70	4.6040241

CLAYTON PEAK, AT CORNER OF SUMMIT, SALT LAKE, AND WASATCH COUNTIES, UTAH.

[Latitude 40' 35' 27.46".   Longitude 111' 33' 33.48".]

To station—	Azimuth.	Back azimuth.	Log. distance.
	° ' "	° ' "	Meters.
Timpanogos	15 50 42.67	195 47 43.75	4.3766781
Wanship	192 51 38.26	12 54 45.17	4.4792754
Porcupine	218 28 39.76	38 46 17.17	4.7836351
Kamas	249 40 20.57	69 54 29.61	4.5137508
Currant Creek Peak	305 44 02.70	125 59 02.55	4.6050691

KAMAS, SUMMIT COUNTY, UTAH.

[Latitude 40° 41′ 33.01″. Longitude 111° 11′ 49.91″.]

To station—	Azimuth.	Back azimuth.	Log. distance.
	° ′ ″	° ′ ″	*Meters.*
Spanish Fork Peak	22 45 51.01	202 33 01.42	4.8516269
Timpanogos	47 32 13.42	227 15 07.05	4.7032109
Clayton Peak	69 54 29.61	249 40 20.57	4.5137508
Wanship	127 18 26.73	307 07 22.51	4.4763953
Porcupine	191 28 34.44	11 32 00.20	4.5674671
Medicine Butte	198 17 51.24	18 29 16.19	4.8880062
La Motte Peak	256 19 48.60	76 37 15.85	4.5880839
Currant Creek Peak	356 48 28.80	176 49 22.38	4.5431299

WANSHIP, ON BOUNDARY LINE BETWEEN SUMMIT AND MORGAN COUNTIES.

[Latitude 40′ 51′ 20.24″. Longitude 111° 28′ 46.97″.]

To station—	Azimuth.	Back azimuth.	Log. distance.
	° ′ ″	° ′ ″	*Meters.*
Clayton Peak	12 54 45.17	192 51 38.26	4.4792754
Medicine Butte	220 51 58.21	41 14 32.92	4.8645769
Porcupine	239 44 46.60	59 59 19.11	4.5565221
Elizabeth Mountain	257 40 58.82	78 10 26.43	4.8101140
La Motte Peak	278 08 42.73	98 37 16.48	4.7931848
Kamas	307 07 22.51	127 18 26.73	4.4763953
Currant Creek Peak	333 53 53.12	154 05 48.90	4.7704972

PORCUPINE, SUMMIT COUNTY, UTAH.

[Latitude 40° 01′ 06.39″. Longitude 111° 06′ 35.38″.]

To station—	Azimuth.	Back azimuth.	Log. distance.
	° ′ ″	° ′ ″	*Meters.*
Kamas	11 32 00.20	191 28 34.44	4.5674671
Clayton Peak	38 46 17.17	218 28 39.76	4.7836351
Wanship	59 59 19.11	239 44 46.60	4.5565221
Medicine Butte	204 31 22.58	24 39 22.57	4.6109744
Elizabeth Mountain	278 01 22.26	98 16 19.18	4.5069383
La Motte Peak	311 49 13.98	132 03 18.71	4.6085751

LA MOTTE PEAK, SUMMIT COUNTY, UTAH.

[Latitude 40° 46′ 26.67″.   Longitude 110° 45′ 05.04″.]

To station—	Azimuth.	Back azimuth.	Log. distance.
	° ′ ″	° ′ ″	*Meters.*
Kamas	76 37 15.85	256 19 48.60	4.5880839
Wanship	98 37 16.48	278 08 42.73	4.7931848
Porcupine	132 03 18.71	311 49 13.93	4.6085751
Medicine Butte	168 31 24.33	348 25 15.56	4.8168173
Elizabeth Mountain	184 33 11.98	4 34 02.28	4.3547610
Bridger Butte	202 30 52.24	22 42 12.37	4.7989716
Gilbert Peak	260 50 54.64	81 07 03.28	4.5463910

ELIZABETH MOUNTAIN, SUMMIT COUNTY, UTAH.

[Latitude 40° 58′ 38.09″.   Longitude 110° 43′ 48.18″.]

To station—	Azimuth.	Back azimuth.	Log. distance.
	° ′ ″	° ′ ″	*Meters.*
La Motte Peak	4 34 02.28	184 33 11.98	4.3547610
Wanship	78 10 26.43	257 40 58.82	4.8101140
Porcupine	98 16 19.18	278 01 22.26	4.5089383
Medicine Butte	160 25 21.23	340 18 21.14	4.6461719
Bridger Butte	212 05 39.46	32 16 10.43	4.6232448
Sage Creek	248 57 50.75	69 21 36.84	4.7341364
Gilbert Peak	297 15 45.93	117 31 06.26	4.5688482

MEDICINE BUTTE, UINTA COUNTY, WYO.

[Latitude 41° 21′ 09.90″.   Longitude 110° 54′ 26.39″.]

To station—	Azimuth.	Back azimuth.	Log. distance.
	° ′ ″	° ′ ″	*Meters.*
Kamas	18 29 16.19	198 17 51.24	4.8880052
Porcupine	24 39 22.57	204 31 22.53	4.6109744
Wanship	41 14 32.92	220 51 58.21	4.8645769
Bridger Butte	279 15 39.85	99 33 14.11	4.5758129
Gilbert Peak	320 44 12.65	141 06 35.92	4.8789648
Elizabeth Mountain	340 18 21.14	160 25 21.23	4.6461719
La Motte Peak	348 25 15.56	168 31 24.33	4.8168173

BRIDGER BUTTE, UINTA COUNTY, WYO.

[Latitude 41° 17′ 50.40″.   Longitude 110° 27′ 49.07″.]

To station—	Azimuth.	Back azimuth.	Log. distance.
	° ′ ″	° ′ ″	*Meters.*
La Motte Peak	22 42 12.37	202 30 52.24	4.7989716
Elizabeth Mountain	32 16 10.43	212 05 39.46	4.6232448
Medicine Butte	99 33 14.11	279 15 39.35	4.5758129
Sage Creek	299 51 00.03	120 04 18.12	4.5126707
Gilbert Peak	348 44 47.41	168 49 40.71	4.7293086

GILBERT PEAK, ON LINE BETWEEN WASATCH AND SUMMIT COUNTIES, UTAH.

[Latitude 40° 49′ 25.45″.   Longitude 110° 20′ 22.56″.]

To station—	Azimuth.	Back azimuth.	Log. distance.
	° ′ ″	° ′ ″	*Meters.*
La Motte Peak	81 07 03.28	260 50 54.64	4.5463910
Elizabeth Mountain	117 31 06.26	297 15 45.93	4.5688482
Medicine Butte	141 06 35.92	320 44 12.65	4.8789648
Bridger Butte	168 49 40.71	348 44 47.41	4.7293086
Sage Creek	206 07 18.94	26 15 40.40	4.6073643
Turtle Bluff	218 40 53.40	38 51 45.65	4.5701299
Widdop	235 56 47.98	56 07 25.77	4.4393071
Phil Pico	244 49 20.32	65 05 47.90	4.5907433
North Burro	260 49 03.06	80 55 32.98	4.1507944
Leidy Peak	278 00 01.68	98 19 51.90	4.6349144
Marsh Peak	285 57 57.66	106 18 00.22	4.6528536

SAGE CREEK, UINTA COUNTY, WYO.

[Latitude 41° 09′ 03.30″.   Longitude 110° 07′ 38.02″.]

To station—	Azimuth.	Back azimuth.	Log. distance.
	° ′ ″	° ′ ″	*Meters.*
North Burro	6 35 39.39	186 33 49.02	4.5354837
Gilbert Peak	26 15 40.40	206 07 18.94	4.6073643
Elizabeth Mountain	69 21 36.34	248 57 50.75	4.7341364
Bridger Butte	120 04 18.12	299 51 00.03	4.5126707
Phil Pico	318 43 47.07	138 51 55.70	4.4210797
Turtle Bluff	323 48 45.24	143 51 16.87	3.9597700
Widdop	346 50 12.14	166 52 29.89	4.3331520

TURTLE BLUFF, UINTA COUNTY, WYO.

[Latitude 41° 05′ 04.76″. Longitude 110° 03′ 47.44″.]

To station—	Azimuth.	Back azimuth.	Log. distance.
	° ′ ″	° ′ ″	Meters.
Widdop	2 03 07.42	182 02 53.73	4.1342101
Gilbert Peak	38 51 45.65	218 40 53.40	4.5701299
Sage Creek	143 51 16.87	323 48 45.24	3.9597700
Phil Pico	316 05 50.87	136 11 27.82	4.2382357
Milepost 314	344 06 02.80	164 07 20.11	4.0021400
Milepost 315	353 18 40.62	173 19 12.48	3.9683851

WIDDOP, SUMMIT COUNTY, UTAH.

[Latitude 40° 57′ 43.48″. Longitude 110° 04′ 08.30″.]

To station—	Azimuth.	Back azimuth.	Log. distance.
	° ′ ″	° ′ ″	Meters.
North Burro	34 01 37.55	213 57 30.09	4.1992517
Gilbert Peak	56 07 25.77	235 56 47.98	4.4398071
Sage Creek	166 52 29.87	346 50 12.14	4.3331520
Turtle Bluff	182 02 53.73	2 03 07.42	4.1342101
Milepost 314	219 22 54.67	39 24 25.56	3.7081856
Phil Pico	264 46 20.88	84 52 11.10	4.0983480
Leidy Peak	317 12 06.38	137 21 22.82	4.4661622

NORTH BURRO, SUMMIT COUNTY, UTAH.

[Latitude 40° 50′ 38.23″. Longitude 110° 10′ 26.23″.]

To station—	Azimuth.	Back azimuth.	Log. distance.
	° ′ ″	° ′ ″	Meters.
Gilbert Peak	80 55 32.98	260 49 03.06	4.1507944
Sage Creek	186 33 49.02	6 35 39.39	4.5354837
Widdop	213 57 30.09	34 01 37.55	4.1992517
Phil Pico	236 11 30.26	56 21 27.54	4.4093534
Leidy Peak	286 08 29.01	106 21 49.80	4.4759231

MILEPOST 315, UTAH-WYOMING.

[Latitude 40° 59' 51.29''. Longitude 110° 02' 58.92''.]

To station—	Azimuth.	Back azimuth.	Log. distance.
	° ' ''	° ' ''	Meters.
Turtle Bluff	173 19 12.48	353 18 40.62	3.9883851
Milepost 314	269 50 10.40	89 50 55.84	3.2092432
Phil Pico	284 27 35.04	104 32 39.87	4.0500968

UINTA, SWEETWATER COUNTY LINE, INITIAL POINT, WYOMING.

[Latitude 40° 59' 51.30''. Longitude 110° 02' 54.85''.]

MILEPOST 314, UTAH-WYOMING.

[Latitude 40° 59' 51.43''. Longitude 110° 01' 49.65''.]

To station—	Azimuth.	Back azimuth.	Log. distance.
	° ' ''	° ' ''	Meters.
Widdop	39 24 25.56	219 22 54.67	3.7081856
Milepost 315	89 50 55.84	269 50 10.40	3.2092432
Turtle Bluff	164 07 20.11	344 06 02.80	4.0021400
Phil Pico	286 53 46.33	106 58 05.74	3.9851925

PHIL PICO, UINTA COUNTY, UTAH.

[Latitude 40° 58' 20.18''. Longitude 109° 55' 14.14''.]

To station—	Azimuth.	Back azimuth.	Log. distance.
	° ' ''	° ' ''	Meters.
North Burro	56 21 27.54	236 11 30.26	4.4093534
Gilbert Peak	65 05 47.90	244 49 20.32	4.5907433
Widdop	84 52 11.10	207 28 30.66	4.0963480
Milepost 315	104 32 39.87	284 27 35.04	4.0500968
Milepost 314	106 58 05.74	286 53 46.33	3.9851925
Turtle Bluff	136 11 27.82	316 05 50.87	4.2382357
Sage Creek	138 51 55.70	318 43 47.07	4.4210797
Twin Buttes	218 14 15.28	38 22 46.53	4.4668992
Richards Butte	264 33 43.08	84 57 58.50	4.7166557
Lena	295 34 16.88	115 54 08.97	4.6754428
Trout Creek Peak	318 53 50.69	139 02 11.33	4.4358754
Leidy Peak	342 00 22.18	162 03 47.16	4.3762588
Marsh Peak	344 53 55.73	164 57 33.64	4.4774312

LEIDY PEAK, UINTA COUNTY, UTAH.

[Latitude 40° 46′ 06.79″.   Longitude 109° 50′ 00.89″.]

To station—	Azimuth.	Back azimuth.	Log. distance.
	° ′ ″	° ′ ″	*Meters.*
Gilbert Peak	98 19 51.90	278 00 01.68	4.6849144
North Burro	106 21 49.80	286 08 29.01	4.4759231
Widdop	137 21 23.82	317 12 08.38	4.4661622
Phil Pico	162 03 47.16	342 00 22.18	4.3762588
Trout Creek Peak	259 02 24.06	79 07 19.08	4.0329170
Lena	266 32 16.83	86 48 42.36	4.5495441
Marsh Peak	355 47 36.34	175 47 49.36	3.8050251

MARSH PEAK, UINTA COUNTY, UTAH.

[Latitude 40° 42′ 40.42″.   Longitude 109° 49′ 40.94″.]

To station—	Azimuth.	Back azimuth.	Log. distance.
	° ′ ″	° ′ ″	*Meters.*
Gilbert Peak	106 18 00.23	285 57 57.66	4.6528536
Phil Pico	164 57 33.64	344 53 55.73	4.4774312
Leidy Peak	175 47 49.36	355 47 36.34	3.8050251
Twin Buttes	191 16 48.14	11 21 39.70	4.7243835
Trout Creek Peak	230 15 37.15	50 20 18.97	4.1194058
Richards Butte	232 26 46.63	52 47 20.28	4.7448761
Lena	256 18 37.30	76 34 49.24	4.5554878
Little Mountain	330 16 33.05	150 21 36.00	4.3440832

TROUT CREEK PEAK, UINTA COUNTY, UTAH.

[Latitude 40° 47′ 13.03″.   Longitude 109° 42′ 29.19″.]

To station—	Azimuth.	Back azimuth.	Log. distance.
	° ′ ″	° ′ ″	*Meters.*
Marsh Peak	50 20 18.97	230 15 37.15	4.1194058
Leidy Peak	79 07 19.08	259 02 24.06	4.0329170
Phil Pico	139 02 11.33	318 53 50.69	4.4358754
Little Mountain	358 21 41.82	178 22 03.68	4.4410184

TWIN BUTTES, SWEETWATER COUNTY, WYO.

[Latitude 41° 10′ 45.54″.   Longitude 109° 42′ 16.05″.]

To station—	Azimuth.	Back azimuth.	Log. distance.
	° ′ ″	° ′ ″	Meters.
Marsh Peak	11 21 39.70	191 16 48.14	4.7243875
Pail Pico	38 22 46.53	218 14 15.28	4.466399?
Richards Butte	298 20 57.24	118 36 44.26	4.5826379
Lena	330 38 27.97	150 49 52.43	4.6983833

RICHARDS BUTTE, SWEETWATER COUNTY, WYO.

[Latitude 41° 00′ 54.25″.   Longitude 109° 18′ 15.37″.]

To station—	Azimuth	Back azimuth.	Log. distance.
	° ′ ″	° ′ ″	Meters.
Lena	20 10 09.52	200 05 49.86	4.4306414
Marsh Peak	52 47 20.28	232 26 46.63	4.7448761
Phil Pico	84 57 58.50	264 38 43.03	4.7166557
Twin Buttes	118 36 44.26	298 20 57.24	4.5826379

LENA, UINTA COUNTY, UTAH.

[Latitude 40° 47′ 13.44″.   Longitude 109° 24′ 51.94″.]

To station—	Azimuth.	Back azimuth.	Log. distance.
	° ′ ″	° ′ ″	Meters.
Little Mountain	41 08 57.10	220 57 50.04	4.5636299
Marsh Peak	76 34 49.24	256 18 37.30	4.5554878
Leidy Peak	86 48 42.36	266 32 16.83	4.5495441
Phil Pico	115 54 08.97	295 34 16.38	4.6754428
Twin Buttes	150 49 52.43	330 38 27.97	4.6983833
Richards Butte	200 05 49.86	20 10 09.52	4.4306414

LITTLE MOUNTAIN, UINTA COUNTY, UTAH.

[Latitude 40° 32′ 18.40″.   Longitude 109° 41′ 55.65″.]

To station—	Azimuth.	Back azimuth.	Log. distance.
	° ′ ″	° ′ ″	Meters.
Marsh Peak	150 21 36.00	330 16 33.05	4.3440832
Trout Creek Peak	178 22 03.68	358 21 41.82	4.4410184
Lena	220 57 50.04	41 08 57.10	4.5636299

STRAWBERRY, WASATCH COUNTY, UTAH.

[Latitude 40° 02′ 50.21″.　Longitude 110 59′ 02.69″.]

To station—	Azimuth.	Back azimuth.	Log. distance.
	° ′ ″	° ′ ″	*Meters.*
Spanish Fork Peak	95 46 24.82	275 25 26.49	4.6678909
Currant Creek Peak	156 17 43.70	336 10 21.58	4.6040241
Grey Head	290 42 49.22	110 53 25.10	4.3996083
Peak	300 11 14.91	120 19 59.04	4.3501804
Indian Head	339 20 18.91	159 23 31.16	4.3044758

INDIAN HEAD, NEAR THE COUNTY LINE BETWEEN UTAH AND WASATCH COUNTIES, UTAH.

[Latitude 39° 52′ 38.52″.　Longitude 110° 54′ 03.36″.]

To station—	Azimuth.	Back azimuth.	Log. distance.
	° ′ ″	° ′ ″	*Meters.*
Spanish Fork Peak	113 50 13.17	293 26 04.72	4.7662870
Strawberry	159 23 31.16	339 20 18.91	4.3044758
Peak	238 13 36.16	58 19 07.32	4.1587604
Grey Head	238 39 17.42	58 46 40.08	4.2825707

GREY HEAD, WASATCH COUNTY, UTAH.

[Latitude 39° 58′ 01.24″.　Longitude 110° 42′ 33.58″.]

To station—	Azimuth.	Back azimuth.	Log. distance.
	° ′ ″	° ′ ″	*Meters.*
Indian Head	58 46 40.08	238 39 17.42	4.2825707
Peak	60 04 27.00	240 02 36.00	3.6772294
Spanish Fork Peak	101 10 20.60	280 38 47.23	4.8518116
Strawberry	110 53 25.10	290 42 49.22	4.3996083
Currant Creek Peak	139 13 38.95	318 55 39.11	4.7815030

PEAK (SECONDARY POINT), WASATCH COUNTY, UTAH.

[Latitude 39° 56′ 44.28″.　Longitude 110° 45′ 27.22″.]

To station—	Azimuth.	Back azimuth.	Log. distance.
	° ′ ″	° ′ ″	*Meters.*
Indian Head	58 19 07.3	238 13 36.1	4.1587604
Strawberry	120 19 59.0	300 11 14.9	4.3501804
Currant Creek Peak	143 40 47.0	323 24 40.0	4.7763501
Grey Head	240 02 36.0	60 04 27.0	3.6772294

WYOMING, SOUTHWEST CORNER STONE.

[Latitude 40° 59′ 53.48″.   Longitude 111° 02′ 56.67″.]

To station—	Azimuth.	Back azimuth.	Log. distance.
	° ′ ″	° ′ ″	*Meters.*
Porcupine	112 50 36	292 48 06	3.7638576

PACIFIC SECTION OF TOPOGRAPHY.

IDAHO.

Triangulation Stations.

In order to control the Coeur d'Alene mining district triangulation was extended eastward from Chilco and Skalan in June, 1900, by Mr. C. F. Urquhart, topographer.   Five new stations were occupied.

STEVENS, SHOSHONE COUNTY.

On line between Shoshone County, Idaho, and Missoula County, Mont., on a well-known mountain about 5 miles south of Mullan, Idaho.   There is a good trail from Mullan to the station.

Station mark: The lone signal tree, about 45 feet south of highest point of mountain.

Reference mark: A copper bolt marked "U. S. G. S." set in solid rock 45 feet from signal tree.   Azimuth from signal to bolt 167° 45′.

[Latitude 47° 25′ 29.89″.   Longitude 115° 46′ 26.26″.]

To station—	Azimuth.	Back azimuth.	Log. distance.
	° ′ ″	° ′ ″	*Meters.*
Latour	91 27 22.97	271 01 20.43	4.6481838
Kellogg	104 51 23.76	284 35 39.87	4.4432141
Chilco	132 37 45.67	312 04 10.16	4.8864328
Rocky	143 44 46.29	323 30 47.10	4.6029676
Murray	170 37 01.65	350 34 28.86	4.4233965

MURRAY, SHOSHONE COUNTY.

(Not occupied.)

On highest point of mountain 3 miles north of Murray and reached by a trail from that town.

Station mark: A copper bolt set in solid rock, over which is a rock monument.

[Latitude 47° 39′ 36.10″.   Longitude 115° 49′ 53.86″.]

To station—	Azimuth.	Back azimuth.	Log. distance.
	° ′ ″	° ′ ″	*Meters.*
Kellogg	49 43 18.52	229 30 05.72	4.4693979
Latour	58 01 20.20	237 37 47.52	4.6748654
Rocky	107 36 27.05	287 24 59.43	4.3082328
Chilco	116 22 22.58	295 51 16.67	4.7665873

ROCKY, SHOSHONE COUNTY.

(Not occupied.)

The highest point of a high, rocky mountain, on north fork of
Coeur d'Alene River.

Station mark: Summit of peak.

[Latitude 47° 42′ 54.21″.   Longitude 116° 05′ 23.22″.]

To station—	Azimuth.	Back azimuth.	Log. distance.
	° ′ ″	° ′ ″	*Meters.*
Kellogg	6 49 33.70	186 47 47.28	4.4047370
Latour	33 25 24.87	213 13 17.95	4.5736341
Skalan	81 37 53.23	260 57 58.06	4.8849247
Chilco	120 48 15.23	300 28 37.39	4.5849139
Murray	287 24 59.48	107 36 27.05	4.3082328
Stevens	323 30 47.10	143 44 46.29	4.6028676

KELLOGG, SHOSHONE COUNTY.

A well-known mountain about 3 miles south from Wardner, reached
by a good trail from that town.

Station mark: The lone fir signal tree on northeast end of summit.

Reference mark: A copper bolt marked "U. S. G. S." set in rock
20.1 feet from signal tree.   Azimuth from tree to bolt is 89° 25′.

[Latitude 47° 29′ 17.77″.   Longitude 116° 07′ 47.40″.]

To station—	Azimuth.	Back azimuth.	Log. distance.
	° ′ ″	° ′ ″	*Meters.*
Latour	71 00 10.77	250 49 51.40	4.2702192
Skalan	103 15 21.92	282 37 17.47	4.8222362
Chilco	146 13 00.71	325 55 11.60	4.7324703
Rocky	186 47 47.28	6 49 33.70	4.4047370
Murray	229 30 05.72	49 43 18.52	4.4693979
Stevens	284 35 39.87	104 51 23.76	4.4432141

LATOUR, KOOTENAI COUNTY.

On the highest peak of the high mountain near the head of Latour Creek, about 3 miles south of the well-known point called "Baldy." There is a trail up Latour Creek to mouth of Rocky Creek, thence up ridge on north side of Rocky Creek, around the head of same to station.

Station mark: A copper bolt marked "U. S. G. S." set in solid rock, surmounted by a rock monument 7 feet in height.

[Latitude 47° 26′ 00.54″.   Longitude 116° 21′ 48.00″.]

To station—	Azimuth.	Back azimuth.	Log. distance.
	° ′ ″	° ′ ″	Meters.
Skalan	114 11 17.60	293 43 34.19	4.7128985
Chilco	166 07 57.68	346 00 30.41	4.7197069
Rocky	213 13 17.95	33 25 24.87	4.5736341
Murray	237 37 47.52	58 01 20.20	4.6748654
Kellogg	250 49 51.40	71 00 10.77	4.2702192
Stevens	271 01 20.43	91 27 22.97	4.6481338

WASHINGTON.

Triangulation Stations.

Triangulation in north-central Washington was extended westward from the 119th meridian to the 120th meridian, controlling four 30-minute quadrangles and connecting the work based upon the Spokane astronomic station and base with that based upon Ellensburg. Six new and five old stations were occupied during the season of 1900 by Mr. C. F. Urquhart, topographer.

KELLER, FERRY COUNTY.

On the highest point on range of mountains about 7 miles (air line) west from Keller post-office. To reach station take trail from Keller to Nespalem, and at 7 miles from former take trail running northwest up small dry creek, thence up the ridge.

Station mark: A fir tree about 50 feet high, trimmed up.

Reference mark: A copper bolt set in large rock (18 or 20 feet high) 33.6 feet north of tree.

[Latitude 48° 03′ 39.93″.   Longitude 118° 47′ 48.89″.]

To station—	Azimuth.	Back azimuth.	Log. distance.
	° ′ ″	° ′ ″	Meters.
Salt Lake	108 05 26.64	287 31 18.60	4.7760009
Omach	138 42 51.92	318 19 52.78	4.7601759
Moses	150 19 12.87	330 07 19.51	4.5994835
Paint Rock	208 13 28.45	28 26 41.31	4.6646004
Whitestone	281 30 34.12	101 43 20.40	4.3380503

TONK, OKANOGAN COUNTY.

On the highest point of mountain on the north side of Tonk Creek, a small stream that empties into the Okanogan River, a little south from Riverside post-office. The station can be easily reached from the south side, which is covered with bunch grass nearly to the summit.

Station mark: A lone fir tree 18 feet high about 20 feet north of highest point.

Reference mark: A copper bolt marked "U. S. G. S." set in large rock 17.6 feet S. 3° E. from tree.

[Latitude 48 32' 43.23''.   Longitude 119 14' 15.36.'']

To station—	Azimuth.	Back azimuth.	Log. distance.
	o ′ ″	o ′ ″	*Meters.*
Omach	26 40 32.95	206 37 16.77	4.0787940
Bonaparte	197 27 31.35	17 32 39.77	4.4663412
Fir	238 59 51.86	59 13 24.89	4.4128438
Moses	326 08 28.00	146 16 19.39	4.3666952

OMACH, OKANOGAN COUNTY.

On the highest peak on ridge between Tonk and Omach creeks, at the head of Similkin Creek, a small stream flowing into the Okanogan River parallel to Omach Creek. The peak is about 6 miles east of the Okanogan River and can best be ascended from the south and west sides. All timber has been cut from the summit of mountain.

Station mark: A copper bolt marked "U. S. G. S." set in solid rock, above which a rock monument was erected.

[Latitude 48° 26' 56.31''.   Longitude 119° 18' 37.30''.]

To station—	Azimuth.	Back azimuth.	Log. distance.
	o ′ ″	o ′ ″	*Meters.*
Salt Lake	36 49 35.99	216 38 22.64	4.4918667
Buck	88 04 23.29	267 41 20.68	4.5811673
Lemanasky	144 50 59.09	324 36 59.53	4.6022378
Bonaparte	200 10 04.43	20 18 29.15	4.6001909
Tonk	206 37 16.77	26 40 32.95	4.0787940
Fir	228 50 52.45	49 07 41.26	4.5631331
Moses	295 04 43.11	115 15 50.06	4.3066980
Keller	318 19 52.78	138 42 51.92	4.7601759

SALT LAKE, OKANOGAN COUNTY.

On a low timbered hill 5 or 6 miles east from Molett, on west side of Okanogan River and 13 miles southeast from Alma post-office and ferry. The hill is the highest point in the immediate vicinity and has salt lakes on every side of it.

Station mark: A pine tree trimmed up for signal.
Reference mark: A copper bolt marked "U. S. G. S." set in solid rock 21 feet west from tree.

[Latitude 48° 13' 31.03". Longitude 119° 33' 38.62".]

To station—	Azimuth.	Back azimuth.	Log. distance.
	° ' "	° ' "	Meters.
Buck	140 12 34.31	320 00 28.29	4.4854816
Omach	216 38 22.64	36 49 35.99	4.4918667
Moses	246 04 17.57	66 26 36.30	4.6060605
Keller	287 31 18.60	108 05 26.64	4.7760002

LEMANASKY, OKANOGAN COUNTY.

On the highest point on ridge between the Okanogan River and Sinlohegan Creek, about 17 miles from Conconully and 8 miles south from Loomis. The road from Conconully to Lemanasky Lake goes within 2 miles of mountain. All timber has been cut from summit except on north side.

Station mark: A bronze tablet cemented in solid rock, above which was erected a rock cairn 7 feet high.

[Latitude 48° 44' 34.06". Longitude 119° 37' 24.94".]

To station—	Azimuth.	Back azimuth.	Log. distance.
	° ' "	° ' "	Meters.
Buck	23 39 30.89	203 30 26.39	4.5703951
Tiffany	70 24 16.66	250 10 17.61	4.3847799
Chapaca (2)	156 58 50.42	336 53 14.31	4.3661596
Bonaparte	262 31 57.97	82 54 31.81	4.5689617
Fir	279 28 30.68	99 59 28.98	4.7102014
Moses	314 42 29.04	135 07 42.81	4.7669900
Omach	324 36 59.53	144 50 59.09	4.6022378

CHAPACA (2), OKANOGAN COUNTY.

(Not occupied.)

A sharp rocky peak 8 or 10 miles a little north of west from Loomis; the flat ridge about 2 miles west is higher.

Station mark: Summit of peak.

[Latitude 48° 56′ 06.12″.   Longitude 119° 44′ 51.88″.]

To station—	Azimuth.	Back azimuth.	Log. distance.
	° ′ ″	° ′ ″	Meters.
Lemanasky	336 53 14.31	156 58 50.42	4.3661596
Tiffany	24 54 10.88	204 45 46.51	4.5128241

BUCK, OKANOGAN COUNTY.

A round, timbered mountain, locally known as Buck Mountain, on the divide between Okanogan and Methow rivers. It is the most southeastern high point on ridge and is at the head of Johnson and Sweat creeks. The road between Twisp and Conconully passes about 4 miles south from station at the point where it crosses Sweat Creek, 17 miles from Twisp. From this point horses can be ridden to station. It is difficult to reach from north and west sides.

Station mark: The lone pine signal tree, 20 feet high.

Reference mark: An aluminum bolt, marked "U. S. G. S.," set in rock. Azimuth from tree 134° 09′, distance 5.9 feet.

[Latitude 48° 26′ 10.72″.   Longitude 119° 49′ 30.94″.]

To station—	Azimuth.	Back azimuth.	Log. distance.
	° ′ ″	° ′ ″	Meters.
Lookout	63 07 29.09	242 51 10.72	4.4804841
Tiffany	162 50 58.70	342 46 05.81	4.4831645
Lemanasky	203 30 26.89	23 39 30.89	4.5703951
Bonaparte	232 53 29.34	53 25 04.68	4.8106748
Fir	248 30 00.29	69 09 58.40	4.8473307
Omach	267 41 20.68	88 04 23.29	4.5811673
Moses	276 59 28.07	97 33 41.19	4.7552967
Salt Lake	320 00 28.29	140 12 24.31	4.4854816

TIFFANY, OKANOGAN COUNTY.

A round, bare, double-topped mountain, lying in the main range between the Okanogan and Methow rivers at the head of Boulder Creek, which is the first tributary of any size of the Chewach River above Winthrop. The station is on the higher and more southerly summit of mountain.

Station mark: A hole drilled 6 inches deep in solid rock on highest point, over which was erected a rock cairn 8 feet high.

[Latitude 48° 40' 09.23''.   Longitude 119° 56' 01.69''.]

To station—	Azimuth.	Back azimuth.	Log. distance.
	° ' ''	° ' ''	Meters.
Lookout	25 32 01.12	205 20 33.59	4.6423317
Chapaca (2)	204 45 46.51	24 54 10.88	4.5128241
Lemanasky	250 10 17.61	70 24 16.66	4.3847799
Moses	296 53 56.32	117 33 05.90	4.8595761
Buck	342 46 05.81	162 50 58.70	4.4331645

LOOKOUT, OKANOGAN COUNTY.

A round-topped, bunch-grass hill, partly timbered on northwest slope, lying on west side of Methow River between Twisp and Lydle creeks, about 10 miles, by trail, from Twisp post-office.

Station mark: An aluminum bolt, stamped "U. S. G. S.," set in drill hole in solid rock, surmounted by a small rock monument.

[Latitude 48° 18' 46.18''.   Longitude 120° 11' 19.79''.]

To station—	Azimuth.	Back azimuth.	Log. distance.
	° ' ''	° ' ''	Meters.
Tiffany	205 20 33.59	25 32 01.12	4.6423317
Buck	242 51 10.72	63 07 29.09	4.4804841

CENTRAL CALIFORNIA (SIERRA FOREST RESERVE).

Triangulation Stations.

Three 30-minute quadrangles in the high Sierras were controlled during the summer of 1900 by Mr. E. T. Perkins, jr., topographer, who extended triangulation southward from Mounts Conness, Lyell, Hoffman, and Devil. In addition to reoccupying these, 10 new stations were occupied and numerous prominent peaks located by intersection.

Positions published herewith are based upon the 1901 United States standard datum of the Coast and Geodetic Survey.

CONNESS, MONO COUNTY.

A primary station of the Coast and Geodetic Survey 10 miles north of Soda Springs. In shape, an irregular parallelogram of granite, from northwest portion of which rises the top of peak with precipitous side of 1,000 feet or more. It can be ascended from Soda Springs in four hours by a trail built by the Coast and Geodetic Survey. Grass and water can be found within 1 mile of summit.

Station mark: Concrete pier with five-eighths-inch copper bolt in center.

[Latitude 37° 58′ 02.59″.　Longitude 119° 19′ 14.23″.]

To station—	Azimuth.	Back azimuth.	Log. distance.
	° ′ ″	° ′ ″	*Meters.*
Red	12 36 41.02	192 33 26.59	4.5515767
Clarks Peak	17 29 05.74	197 25 09.01	4.4979644
Devil	37 22 32.54	217 07 08.88	4.7855483
Hoffman	31 21 09.23	231 14 10.79	4.3288340
Cottonwood Peak	83 06 44.80	262 51 29.07	4.5639041
Dana	310 11 57.93	130 15 39.67	4.0621370
Lyell	350 09 07.63	170 10 57.54	4.4088947

DANA, TUOLUMNE COUNTY.

A large, bare, somewhat irregular peak, with cone-shaped top, covered with broken sandstone and granite.

Station mark: Stone monument about 6 feet high.

[Latitude 37° 54′ 00.88″.　Longitude 119° 13′ 13.53″.]

To station—	Azimuth.	Back azimuth.	Log. distance.
	° ′ ″	° ′ ″	*Meters.*
Lyell	14 01 13.38	193 59 22.02	4.2637680
Clarks Peak	39 02 46.85	218 55 09.22	4.4680003
Hoffman	77 04 59.75	256 54 20.18	4.4171931
Conness	130 15 39.67	310 11 57.93	4.0621370

HOFFMAN, TUOLUMNE COUNTY.

About 2 miles west of Lake Tenaya and 39 miles from Sequoia, on the west of Tioga road. The mountain has three sharp ridges of granite and the point occupied is the highest and farthest west. On this ridge is Chimney Rock, a cylinder of granite rising from main ledge to height of 60 feet, and it is north of this that station occupied is situated.

Station mark: A cross cut in rock, over which was erected a monument 5 feet high.

Bull. 181—01——14

[Latitude 37° 50′ 50.13″.   Longitude 119° 30′ 35.94″.]

To station—	Azimuth.	Back azimuth.	Log. distance.
	° ′ ″	° ′ ″	Meters.
Devil	29 59 03.70	209 50 37.68	4.6092431
Pilot	76 06 02.86	255 50 24.41	4.5866541
Cottonwood	114 13 51.81	294 05 35.56	4.3353253
Conness	231 14 10.79	51 21 09.23	4.3283340
Dana	256 54 20.18	77 04 59.75	4.4171931
Lyell	299 28 12.89	119 37 00.01	4.3836744
Clarks Peak	336 34 41.61	156 37 42.36	4.2597926
Red	337 23 09.91	157 26 52.71	4.2654986

DEVIL, MARIPOSA COUNTY.

At the southeast end of short, sharp ridge, 9 miles southwest of Wawona Park, bare on top and covered with loose rock. Ascended by wagon road from Wawona. Nearest camping place is 1¼ miles northeast of summit.

Station mark: A cairn of stones, 4 feet base, 4½ feet high, on site of old monument, 5.6 feet west of "U. S. G. S." chiseled on rock.

[Latitude 37° 31′ 46.80″.   Longitude 119° 44′ 23.06″.]

To station—	Azimuth.	Back azimuth.	Log. distance.
	° ′ ″	° ′ ″	Meters.
Pilot	146 23 49.18	326 16 39.63	4.4928478
Cottonwood	180 37 19.76	00 37 31.81	4.6445464
Hoffman	209 50 37.68	29 59 03.70	4.6092431
Conness	217 07 08.88	37 22 32.54	4.7855484
Clarks Peak	235 55 55.04	56 07 20.30	4.5212361
Red	244 35 09.78	64 47 16.70	4.5097490
Kaiser	297 47 02.53	118 07 16.04	4.7451616
Big Shuteye	305 41 47.10	125 53 10.71	4.5325137

LYELL, MONO COUNTY.

Situated 14 miles southeast of Soda Springs, at end of Tuolomne Meadows. In shape very irregular. The south side is a nearly perpendicular wall, the north a series of meadows until the glacier is reached; the east and west sides are rather steep. The highest point is a short, sharp ridge, about 200 yards long, running northwest and southeast, the northwest end being lower. Ascended from head of Lyell Fork and northeast side of peak.

Station mark: Small stone monument; "U. S. G. S." chiseled on rock east of it.

[Latitude 37° 44' 23.22".   Longitude 119° 16' 15.15".]

To station—	Azimuth.	Back azimuth.	Log. distance.
	° ' "	° ' "	*Meters.*
Big Shuteye	17 46 48.27	197 41 04.96	4.6571504
Red	52 03 35.82	231 58 32.37	4.1882294
Clarks Peak	71 03 13.41	250 57 27.71	4.1654618
Hoffman	119 37 00.01	299 28 12.89	4.3836744
Conness	170 10 57.54	350 09 07.63	4.4068947
Dana	193 59 23.02	14 01 13.38	4.2637680
Silver	323 29 17.71	143 38 27.25	4.5704988
Kaiser	351 13 21.55	171 16 30.07	4.6987072

RED, MADERA COUNTY.

Ascended from camp at large meadows south of Merced Peak, on trail from Wawona to Soda Springs (or "77" corral), five hours by trail. Could camp much nearer at head of Illilouette River and climb the mountain in three hours. Approached mountain from west, apparently the best way. Can take mules to within 2,000 feet of top.

Station mark: A bronze triangulation tablet set between two large rocks, over which is erected a cairn of rocks 5 feet at base, 7 feet high.

[Latitude 37° 39' 15.31."   Longitude 119° 24' 31.41".]

To station—	Azimuth.	Back azimuth.	Log. distance.
	° ' "	° ' "	*Meters.*
Big Shuteye	2 48 05.05	182 47 24.19	4.5289143
Devil	64 47 16.70	244 35 09.78	4.5097490
Hoffman	157 26 52.71	337 23 09.91	4.3654986
Conness	192 33 26.59	12 36 41.02	4.5515767
Lyell	231 58 32.37	52 03 35.82	4.1882294
Silver	300 40 31.80	120 54 43.33	4.6010921
Kaiser	333 32 06.49	153 40 16.75	4.6487389

BIG SHUTEYE, MADERA COUNTY.

On the bare granite summit of Big Shuteye Peak (Chiquito Peak), the highest point on Chiquito Range, at southeast end of the ridge. Follow trail from Jackass Meadows to where it crosses ridge, then turn to south.

Station mark: A bronze triangulation tablet cemented in solid granite, above which is erected a cairn of rocks 4 feet base and 4 feet high.

[Latitude 37° 21′ 00.26″. Longitude 119° 25′ 38.53″.]

To station—	Azimuth.	Back azimuth.	Log. distance.
	° ′ ″	° ′ ″	Meters.
Devil	125 53 10.71	305 41 47.10	4.5325137
Red	182 47 24.19	2 48 05.05	4.5289143
Lyell	197 41 04.96	17 46 48.27	4.6571504
Silver	249 38 51.80	69 48 41.16	4.5842369
Hilgard	268 29 47.16	88 51 40.06	4.7264787
Kaiser	285 51 29.47	106 00 18.72	4.3493243
Three Sisters	305 14 15.24	125 27 35.30	4.6014723

SILVER, FRESNO COUNTY.

On the highest peak between Fish Creek and Mono Creek, at head of Silver Creek. Summit is flat, running north-northeast and south-southwest. Highest point is at southwest end. Can camp at meadows below Margaret Lakes; thence it is three and one-half hours' travel to station. Can take mules within 700 feet of summit on east. There is grass and water for one night within 1,200 feet of summit.

Station mark: A bronze triangulation tablet set in solid rock, on which was erected a cairn of rocks 5 feet base and 5 feet high.

[Latitude 37° 28′ 12.56″. Longitude 119° 01′ 14.54″.]

To station—	Azimuth.	Back azimuth.	Log. distance.
	° ′ ″	° ′ ″	Meters.
Three Sisters	5 29 45.00	185 28 18.92	4.5635462
Kaiser	36 48 49.60	216 42 50.78	4.3855104
Big Shuteye	69 48 41.16	249 33 51.80	4.5842369
Red	120 54 43.33	300 40 31.80	4.6010921
Lyell	143 38 27.25	323 29 17.71	4.5704983
Hilgard	305 02 47.29	125 09 52.52	4.3230108

KAISER, FRESNO COUNTY.

On a bald peak at the head of Kaiser and Pittman creeks. It is easily ascended from south side. There are numerous lakes and small meadows in the neighborhood.

Station mark: A bronze triangulation tablet set in loose earth, there being no solid rock, above which was erected a cairn of rocks 5 feet base and 5 feet high.

[Latitude 37° 17' 41.24".   Longitude 119° 11' 05.57".]

To station—	Azimuth.	Back azimuth.	Log. distance.
	° ' "	° ' "	*Meters.*
Big Shuteye	106 00 18.72	285 51 29.47	4.3493243
Red	153 40 16.75	333 32 06.49	4.6487389
Lyell	171 16 30.07	351 13 21.55	4.6987072
Silver	216 42 50.78	36 48 49.60	4.3855104
Hilgard	256 50 47.29	77 03 50.04	4.5135451
Goddard	237 01 21.12	117 18 14.22	4.6669912
Three Sisters	326 51 09.06	146 55 40.62	4.3067670

HILGARD, FRESNO COUNTY.

Ascended peak from camp on Bear Creek; five and one-half hours' travel. Could camp an hour closer by going to summit of ridge between Bear Creek and Mono Creek. This mountain is best approached along the ridge between Bear and Mono creeks, finally dropping down into northeast fork of Bear Creek and climbing peak from east. On summit of this peak are three small high points of rock. The point occupied is the one to north, or center one.

Station mark: A large flat rock, on which is set a bronze triangulation tablet surmounted by a cairn of rocks 3 feet base and 3 feet high.

[Latitude 37° 21' 40.11".   Longitude 118° 49' 34.65".]

To station—	Azimuth.	Back azimuth.	Log. distance.
	° ' "	° ' "	*Meters.*
Three Sisters	40 31 08.67	220 22 39.06	4.5049242
Kaiser	77 03 50.04	256 50 47.29	4.5135451
Big Shuteye	88 51 40.06	268 29 47.16	4.7264787
Silver	125 09 52.52	305 02 47.29	4.3230108
Goddard	341 35 56.51	161 39 49.84	4.4786204

THREE SISTERS, FRESNO COUNTY.

On the south end of summit of the Three Sisters. Can be reached by trail between Shaver and Blaney Meadow (or Hot Springs). Leave trail at large meadow between Red Mountain and Potato Hill, traveling southeast. At foot of mountain on northeast side is a small meadow with running water. Animals can be taken nearly to summit from south to southeast.

Station mark: A bronze triangulation tablet set in loose rock, with a cairn of rocks built over it 3 feet at base and 3 feet high.

[Latitude 37° 08′ 30.59″.   Longitude 119° 03′ 36.59″.]

To station—	Azimuth.	Back azimuth.	Log. distance.
	° ′ ″	° ′ ″	*Meters.*
Big Shuteye	125 27 35.30	305 14 15.24	4.6014723
Kaiser	146 55 40.62	326 51 09.06	4.3067670
Silver	185 28 18.92	5 29 45.00	4.5635462
Hilgard	220 22 39.06	40 31 08.67	4.5049242
Goddard	277 50 59.53	98 03 19.88	4.4854257
Silliman	329 28 41.38	149 41 47.00	4.8062703
Big Baldy	342 58 38.44	163 05 03.75	4.7358215

GODDARD, FRESNO COUNTY.

Ascended peak by ridge running from the southwest up from camp on south fork of San Joaquin, at pasture 1½ miles above the camp of the Mount Goddard Copper Mining Company. Can take animals within 1,500 feet of summit. The south end of the mountain was occupied, although the north end is slightly higher. The south end seems to be the recognized summit and is much easier of access.

Station mark: A bronze triangulation tablet set in loose shale rock, over which is erected a cairn of rocks 4 feet base and 4 feet high.

[Latitude 37° 06′ 13.35″.   Longitude 118° 43′ 09.82″.]

To station—	Azimuth.	Back azimuth.	Log. distance.
	° ′ ″	° ′ ″	*Meters.*
Big Baldy	16 54 10.44	196 48 19.23	4.6967440
Three Sisters	98 03 19.88	277 50 59.53	4.4854257
Kaiser	117 18 14.22	297 01 21.12	4.6669912
Hilgard	161 39 49.34	341 35 56.51	4.4786204
Silliman	357 42 48.51	177 43 37.67	4.7076974

SILLIMAN, TULARE COUNTY.

Highest point in group on west end of ridge. Best reached from camp at Wet Meadows; cross low divide east, follow up creek to first lake, then climb on south side of ridge. Can take mules to top of first point; then one and one-half hours' climb to summit. Good camp at Wet Meadows, from which it is four hours' climb to summit.

Station mark: A bronze triangulation tablet set in solid rock, over which is a cairn of rocks 6 feet base and 6 feet high.

[Latitude 36° 38' 39.71".   Longitude 118° 41' 47.89".]

To station—	Azimuth.	Back azimuth.	Log. distance.
	° ′ ″	° ′ ″	*Meters.*
Big Baldy	100 48 39.50	280 42 01.26	4.2269529
Three Sisters	149 41 47.00	329 28 41.38	4.8062703
Goddard	177 43 37.67	357 42 48.51	4.7076974

SPANISH, FRESNO COUNTY.

Spanish Mountain can be easily ascended either from Statum or Collins Meadows by riding about two hours.

Station mark: A bronze triangulation tablet set in top of granite rock, over which is erected a cairn of rocks 3 feet base and 3 feet high.

[Latitude 36° 54' 35.21".   Longitude 118° 53' 27.21".]

To station—	Azimuth.	Back azimuth.	Log. distance.
	° ′ ″	° ′ ″	*Meters.*
Three Sisters	149 43 36.33	329 37 29.89	4.4747072
Goddard	215 17 45.76	35 23 57.36	4.4213575

BIG BALDY, TULARE COUNTY.

Ascended from camp at Woodard's cabin by trail.   Time of ascension one hour.   Top of mountain is a bare ridge about 200 yards long. Tops of trees growing on the side of hill interfere somewhat with view. South end of hill occupied.

Station mark: A bronze triangulation tablet set in solid rock, and a rock cairn erected over it 7 feet base and 10 feet high.   A tree about 15 feet high placed in monument.

[Latitude 36° 40' 21.81".   Longitude 118° 52' 54.94".]

To station—	Azimuth.	Back azimuth.	Log. distance.
	° ′ ″	° ′ ″	*Meters.*
Three Sisters	163 05 03.75	342 58 38.44	4.7358215
Goddard	196 48 19.23	16 54 10.44	4.6987440
Silliman	280 42 01.26	100 48 39.50	4.2269529

SOUTHERN CALIFORNIA.

Triangulation Stations.

Triangulation in southern California was extended northward and westward from Santa Clara and San Fernando stations of the United

States Coast and Geodetic Survey and connected with two other stations of the same organization—Gaviota and Tepusquet—all based on Yolo base data. Nine new primary stations were occupied and 7 secondary points located by intersections, controlling three 30-minute quadrangles between latitudes 34° 30′ and 35° 00′ and longitudes 118° 30′ and 120° 00′.

The field work was done by Mr. C. F. Urquhart, topographer, during portions of May, June, November, and December, 1900.

LIEBRE, LOS ANGELES COUNTY.

On the highest point of a high, round mountain, sometimes known as Sawmill Mountain, near the east end of the Liebre Range. The mountain is covered with brush about 5 feet high. The new road from Elizabeth Lake to Gorman station passes about 4 miles north from the station at a point 9 miles from former. A trail leaves the road about 1 mile west from Joe Kirby's shack and goes south to summit of an open ridge, from which signal can be seen.

Station mark: An oak tree wired up and used as signal.

Reference mark: A copper bolt marked "U. S. G. S." set in solid rock. Azimuth from reference mark to signal tree 13° 42′; distance 6 feet.

[Latitude 34° 40′ 53.35″. Longitude 118° 34′ 38.63″.]

To station—	Azimuth	Back azimuth.	Log. distance.
	° ′ ″	° ′ ″	*Meters.*
San Fernando	3 13 38.57	183 12 49.60	4.5938706
Hines	67 27 48.01	247 10 48.77	4.6952879
Frazier	105 59 53.39	285 46 28.84	4.5723919
Alamo	72 59 13.47	252 49 16.46	4.4457065

SAN FERNANDO, LOS ANGELES COUNTY.

A station of the United States Coast and Geodetic Survey, on the highest or western crest of San Fernando Mountain, about 5 miles from the long tunnel of the Southern Pacific Railroad.

Station mark: A terra-cotta pipe 24 by 4 inches filled with concrete and set in a triangle of concrete.

[Latitude 34° 19′ 41.47″. Longitude 118° 36′ 05.08″.]

To station—	Azimuth.	Back azimuth.	Log. distance.
	° ′ ″	° ′ ″	*Meters.*
Santa Clara	89 28 35.36	269 13 45.80	4.6056340
Hines	114 50 26.99	294 34 21.17	4.6815183
Frazier	145 48 47.71	325 31 15.76	4.7772296
Liebre	183 12 49.60	3 13 38.57	4.5938706

ALAMO, LOS ANGELES COUNTY.

(Not occupied.)

A high, rocky mountain near the eastern end of the Alamo Range, sometimes known as Bowlder Peak. It can be reached by trail from the Alamo ranch around by Mr. Bailey's ranch, which is about 6 miles south from the road between Elizabeth Lake and Gorman station, at a point 5 miles from the latter.

Station mark: A small tree on highest point of the mountain.

[Latitude 34° 36' 27.04''.   Longitude 118° 52' 05.92''.]

To station—	Azimuth.	Back azimuth.	Log. distance.
	° ′ ″	° ′ ″	*Meters.*
Santa Clara	26 38 24.17	206 32 35.20	4.5460392
Frazier	153 16 34.07	333 13 12.39	4.3146687
Liebre	252 49 16.46	72 59 13.47	4.4457065
San Fernando	321 33 54.87	141 42 58.66	4.5967546

FRAZIER, VENTURA COUNTY.

On the highest point of a mountain locally known as Frazier Mountain, in the northeastern corner of Ventura County, about 2 miles from the Los Angeles County line. The wagon road from Gorman station to Bakersfield passes about 4 miles from the station, at a point 4 miles from the former. There is a good trail from Gorman station to Frazier mine, which is near the triangulation station. Another trail from Cuddy's ranch to Frazier mine passes 100 yards north from station.

Station mark: A lone pine tree 100 feet north from the summit of the mountain.

[Latitude 34° 46' 25.21''.   Longitude 118° 58' 10.93''.]

To station—	Azimuth.	Back azimuth.	Log. distance.
	° ′ ″	° ′ ″	*Meters.*
Hines	18 24 44.23	198 21 06.61	4.4902268
Reyes	60 50 55.17	240 40 15.20	4.5157054
Pine	103 13 38.72	283 06 51.20	4.2706034
Liebre	285 46 28.84	105 59 53.39	4.5723919
San Fernando	325 31 15.76	145 43 47.71	4.7772296
Alamo	333 13 12.39	153 16 34.07	4.3146687

SANTA CLARA, VENTURA COUNTY.

A station of the United States Coast and Geodetic Survey, on the highest part of the mountain on the south side of Santa Clara River, about 2 miles in an air line from the town of Santa Paula.

Station mark: A terra-cotta pipe 24 by 4 inches filled with concrete and set in a triangle of concrete.

[Latitude 34° 19′ 26.69″. Longitude 119° 02′ 22.57″.]

To station—	Azimuth.	Back azimuth.	Log. distance.
	° ′ ″	° ′ ″	Meters.
Hines	170 44 32.36	350 43 18.21	4.3181190
San Fernando	269 13 45.80	89 28 35.36	4.6056340

HINES, VENTURA COUNTY.

On the highest point of a mountain locally known as Hines Peak, near the source of Santa Paula Creek and on the divide between Santa Paula and Sespe creeks. The point is rather difficult to reach, though there is a trail up Santa Paula Creek to foot of mountain. It may be reached from the Hot Springs on Sespe Creek. The summit is cleared of brush.

Station mark: A bunch of brush about 7 feet high wired together and used as a signal.

Reference mark: A copper bolt marked "U. △ S." $\begin{smallmatrix} \text{U.} \\ \text{G.} \end{smallmatrix} \triangle \begin{smallmatrix} \text{S.} \\ \text{S.} \end{smallmatrix}$ set in solid rock 8.33 feet southwest from signal and station mark.

[Latitude 34° 30′ 33.01″. Longitude 119° 04′ 33.77″.]

To station—	Azimuth.	Back azimuth.	Log. distance.
	° ′ ″	° ′ ″	Meters.
Reyes	125 15 00.85	305 08 00.24	4.3640299
Pine	165 55 35.48	345 52 27.04	4.5394977
Frazier	198 21 06.61	18 24 44.23	4.4902268
Liebre	247 10 48.77	67 27 48.01	4.6952879
San Fernando	294 34 21.17	114 50 26.99	4.6815183
Santa Clara	350 43 18.21	170 44 32.36	4.3181190

PINE, VENTURA COUNTY.

On the highest point on western end of Pine Mountain, more generally known as San Amedia Mountain, which is the highest point in the county. There is an old signal, used by the Wheeler survey, on the east end of mountain about 1 mile from the station. There is a good trail from Mr. Cuddy's ranch to summit.

Station mark: A copper bolt marked "U. △ S." $\begin{smallmatrix} \text{U.} \\ \text{G.} \end{smallmatrix} \triangle \begin{smallmatrix} \text{S.} \\ \text{S.} \end{smallmatrix}$ set in loose rock, above which is a flat rock marked "U. + S." $\begin{smallmatrix} \text{U.} \\ \text{G.} \end{smallmatrix} + \begin{smallmatrix} \text{S.} \\ \text{S.} \end{smallmatrix}$

[Latitude 34° 48′ 43.09″. Longitude 119° 10′ 05.12″.]

To station—	Azimuth.	Back azimuth.	Log. distance.
	° ′ ″	° ′ ″	*Meters.*
Reyes	27 16 08.13	207 12 14.63	4.3577728
Santa Ynez	67 04 40.56	246 37 00.23	4.9075345
San Rafael	79 18 24.52	258 56 17.86	4.7800219
McPherson	98 13 30.47	277 51 22.50	4.7754341
Frazier	283 06 51.20	103 13 38.72	4.2706034
Hines	345 52 27.04	165 55 35.48	4.5394977

REYES, VENTURA COUNTY.

On the highest point of the divide between Sespe Creek and Cuyama River, about 8 miles northwest from Rafael Reyes's residence. A wagon road down Cuyama River goes to Mr. Reyes's residence, thence go by good trail to station. Another hill 100 yards north has timber on it and a line was cut through it in line with Pine station.

Station mark: A lone fir tree used as a signal.

Reference mark: A copper bolt marked "U. S." / "G. △ S." set in a large rock 4.5 feet south from signal tree.

[Latitude 34° 37′ 45.47″. Longitude 119° 16′ 55.01″.]

To station—	Azimuth.	Back azimuth.	Log. distance.
	° ′ ″	° ′ ″	*Meters.*
Santa Ynez	79 59 25.73	259 35 41.90	4.8127423
San Rafael	100 28 41.94	280 10 31.52	4.6955497
McPherson	120 35 27.28	300 17 16.07	4.7517482
Pine	207 12 14.63	27 16 08.13	4.3577728
Frazier	240 40 15.20	60 50 55.17	4.5157054
Hines	305 08 00.24	125 15 00.85	4.3640299

MONTECITO, SANTA BARBARA COUNTY.

(Not occupied.)

The highest point in range of mountains, about 15 miles northeast from Santa Barbara and 12 miles west from Nordoff.

Station mark: A small tree on summit of mountain.

[Latitude 34° 32′ 16.09″. Longitude 119° 28′ 02.44″.]

To station—	Azimuth.	Back azimuth.	Log. distance.
	° ′ ″	° ′ ″	*Meters.*
Santa Ynez	88 28 44.70	268 11 26.42	4.6719106
Pine	221 57 31.18	42 07 44.09	4.6122972
Reyes	239 07 20.27	59 13 39.08	4.2968168

CUYAMA, VENTURA COUNTY.

(Not occupied.)

A prominent mountain on the south side of the Cuyama River, about 10 miles below Rafael Reyes's ranch.

Station mark: Highest point of mountain.

[Latitude 34° 45' 09.39". Longitude 119° 28' 33.68".]

To station—	Azimuth.	Back azimuth.	Log. distance.
	° ' ''	° ' ''	Meters.
McPherson	115 53 33.34	295 42 03.73	4.5352838
Pine	256 45 41.17	76 56 13.56	4.4615707
Reyes	307 30 51.89	127 37 29.51	4.3509242

CALIENTE, SANTA BARBARA COUNTY.

(Not occupied.)

About 8 miles northwest from the Cuyama ranch, on the highest point of the white, barren mountains, on the north side of the Cuyama River.

Station mark: Highest point of mountain.

[Latitude 35° 02' 05.42". Longitude 119° 45' 38.11".]

To station—	Azimuth.	Back azimuth.	Log distance.
	° ' ''	° ' ''	Meters.
McPherson	16 29 20.48	196 27 31.05	4.2326250
Pine	294 22 31.13	114 42 52.23	4.7746474
Reyes	315 38 33.94	135 54 53.05	4.7977730

M'PHERSON, SANTA BARBARA COUNTY.

About 14 miles from the Cuyama ranch, on a high round mountain covered with brush about 4 feet high. A road goes from this ranch to Bart McPherson's house, from which there is a trail to foot of mountain. A long ridge leads to summit, which may be ascended on horseback. Station called "Peak," distant 2¾ miles a little north of east, is about 50 feet higher.

Station mark: The oak signal tree.

Reference mark: A copper bolt marked "U. $\triangle$ S." set in loose rock, with a rock marked "U. + S." placed over it. Azimuth from signal tree to reference mark 286° 41'; distance 9.5 feet.

[Latitude 34° 53' 13.75".　Longitude 119° 48' 49.08".]

To station—	Azimuth.	Back azimuth.	Log. distance.
	° ′ ″	° ′ ″	Meters.
San Rafael	0 12 48.02	180 12 46.38	4.2947312
Santa Ynez	20 43 12.35	200 37 33.66	4.6822557
Tepusquet	94 05 47.00	273 52 58.05	4.5341310
Pine	277 51 22.50	98 18 30.47	4.7754341
Reyes	300 17 16.07	120 35 27.28	4.7517482

SAN RAFAEL, SANTA BARBARA COUNTY.

On the northernmost of two rather flat mountains, the highest of the San Rafael Range. The point is rather difficult to reach. The best route is probably up Santa Cruz Creek from Santa Ynez Valley.

Station mark: A bronze triangulation tablet set in loose rock with a rock marked "U. S. G. △ S." above it, surmounted by a rock monument 7 feet high.

[Latitude 34° 42' 34.06".　Longitude 119° 48' 51.97".]

To station—	Azimuth.	Back azimuth.	Log. distance.
	° ′ ″	° ′ ″	Meters.
Santa Ynez	36 30 39.52	216 25 03.23	4.4044042
Tepusquet	123 03 08.37	302 50 22.77	4.6087544
McPherson	180 12 46.38	0 12 48.02	4.2947312
Pine	258 56 17.86	79 18 24.52	4.7800219
Reyes	280 10 31.52	100 28 41.94	4.6955497

M'KINLEY, SANTA BARBARA COUNTY.

(Not occupied.)

A sharp, rocky peak, sometimes called McKinley Mountain. It can be reached from Los Olivos, from which point it shows as the highest point of the San Rafael Mountains.

Station mark: Highest point of mountain.

[Latitude 34° 42' 03.28".　Longitude 119° 50' 44.58".]

To station—	Azimuth.	Back azimuth.	Log. distance.
	° ′ ″	° ′ ″	Meters.
Santa Ynez	32 09 03.51	212 04 27.73	4.3612394
Gaviota	55 37 39.82	235 25 34.91	4.5946496
Tepusquet	126 31 04.31	306 19 23.07	4.5889200
McPherson	188 04 46.00	8 05 51.91	4.3194832

PEAK, SANTA BARBARA COUNTY.

(Not occupied.)

This point is 2¾ miles a little north of west of primary station McPherson, and is the highest point on the range. It can be reached by traveling up the ridge westward from McPherson.

Station mark: Highest point of mountain.

[Latitude 34° 54′ 02.22″.   Longitude 119° 51′ 33.00″.]

To station—	Azimuth.			Back azimuth.			Log. distance.
	°	′	″	°	′	″	Meters.
Santa Ynez	14	48	03.03	194	43	56.49	4.6337473
Tepusquet	91	47	18.72	271	36	03.44	4.4767463
McPherson	289	46	42.42	109	48	14.50	3.6458659
San Rafael	349	03	42.49	169	05	14.41	4.3343919

SANTA YNEZ, SANTA BARBARA COUNTY.

On the highest point of the Santa Ynez Range. It can be reached from the Santa Ynez Valley or the coast via new road from Los Olivos to Santa Barbara. From the valley on north side of mountains, go from Los Olivos or Santa Ynez to Mahoney's ranch, thence by road to the top of divide, thence east along the ridge 5 miles to station.

Station mark: A rock 2 by 4 feet, found in place, with a hole 2½ inches deep drilled in it.

[Latitude 34° 31′ 31.79″.   Longitude 119° 58′ 43.93″.]

To station—	Azimuth.			Back azimuth.			Log. distance.
	°	′	″	°	′	″	Meters.
Gaviota	82	11	19.18	262	03	49.90	4.3100387
Tepusquet	155	53	58.83	335	46	52.14	4.6681901
McPherson	200	37	33.66	20	43	12.85	4.6322557
San Rafael	216	25	03.23	36	30	39.52	4.4044042
Pine	246	37	00.23	67	04	40.56	4.9075345
Reyes	259	35	41.90	79	59	25.73	4.8127423

ZACA, SANTA BARBARA COUNTY.

(Not occupied.)

A point locally well known as Zaca Peak, about 10 miles east of north from Los Olivos.

Station mark: A small tree on summit.

[Latitude 34° 45' 58.94".   Longitude 120° 01' 26.79".]

To station—	Azimuth.	Back azimuth.	Log. distance.
	° ' "	° ' "	*Meters.*
Tepusquet	136 40 59.81	316 35 23.85	4.3364840
McPherson	235 06 26.76	55 13 39.49	4.3702877
San Rafael	288 08 24.34	108 15 34.46	4.3056366
Santa Ynez	851 09 07.80	171 10 41.27	4.4320598

TEPUSQUET, SANTA BARBARA COUNTY.

A station of the United States Coast and Geodetic Survey on the highest peak of the Tepusquet Range. It can be reached from Goodchild's ranch in the Conyado Valley.

Station mark: A hole drilled in solid rock.

[Latitude 34° 54' 30.98".   Longitude 120 11' 13.14."]

To station—	Azimuth.	Back azimuth.	Log. distance.
	° ' "	° ' "	*Meters.*
Gaviota	1 24 42.75	181 24 17.54	4.6561948
Gaviota (by C. & G. S.)	1 24 39.76	181 24 14.86	4.6561948
McPherson	273 52 58.05	94 05 47.00	4.5341310
San Rafael	302 50 22.77	123 03 08.37	4.6087544
Santa Ynez	335 46 52.14	155 53 58.83	4.6681901

GAVIOTA, SANTA BARBARA COUNTY.

A station of the United States Coast and Geodetic Survey on one of the highest peaks to the eastward of Gaviota Pass. The peak is best reached through the canyon extending toward the eastward from the pass at a distance of about 1 mile from the wharf. The highest peaks in the vicinity (between 150 and 300 feet higher) are situated 1½ miles to the eastward.

Station mark: A copper bolt set in concrete, above which a hollow cement pier is erected.

[Latitude 34° 30' 01.01".   Longitude 120° 11' 56.89".]

(By Coast and Geodetic Survey, Yolo base data. Latitude 34 30' 00.83".   Longitude 120° 11' 56,89.")

To station—	Azimuth.	Back azimuth.	Log. distance.
	° ' "	° ' "	*Meters.*
Tepusquet	181 24 17.54	1 24 42.45	4.6561948
Tepusquet (by Coast and Geodetic Survey)	181 24 14.86	1 24 39.76	4.6561948
Santa Ynez	262 03 49.90	82 11 19.18	4.3100387

ALASKA (NOME DISTRICT).

Triangulation Stations.

The following geographic positions are dependent on the positions of Grave and Round triangulation stations, as furnished by the United States Coast and Geodetic Survey.

The field work was done by Mr. R. B. Robertson, with a Saegmuller 4-inch vernier theodolite reading to 30″, under the direction of Mr. E. C. Barnard, topographer.

Average closure error of triangles, 11″.

ROCKY.

On highest point of a rocky peak about 7 miles N. 73° W. from Chinik. There is no trail to station, but it can be reached by going in a straight line from Chinik. There is good grass and water on west side about 1½ miles distant.

Station mark: + cut in solid rock, over which is a small pile of rock.

[Latitude 64° 34′ 24.84″. Longitude 162° 48′ 10.84″.]

To station—	Azimuth.	Back azimuth.	Log. distance.
	° ′ ″	° ′ ″	*Meters.*
Round	12 46 14.4	192 43 23.4	4.06137
Town	73 43 30.5	253 31 42.9	4.03657
Lime	121 47 26.3	301 16 49.3	4.50053
Grave	45 35 47.9	225 28 55.6	4.17143

ROUND.

A station of the Coast and Geodetic Survey on a rounded point, about 1 mile north of the island on which the astronomic station was situated. It is about 1,000 feet from the edge of the bluff.

Station mark: A cross cut in the center of top of a rock flush with surface of ground.

[Latitude 64° 28′ 22.10″. Longitude 162° 51′ 21.38″.]

To station—	Azimuth.	Back azimuth.	Log. distance.
	° ′ ″	° ′ ″	*Meters.*
Boot	86 39 02.9	266 22 28.0	4.16917
Grave	95 58 35.1	275 49 30.9	3.90852
Town	135 58 30.9	315 49 35.6	4.05584
Rocky	192 43 22.4	12 46 14.4	4.06137

NATURAL ROCK.

(Not occupied.)

A prominent rock on ridge between Golofnin Bay and Quinnehuk River.

[Latitude 64° 45' 25.75''.   Longitude 162° 51' 40.00''.]

To station—	Azimuth.	Back azimuth.	Log. distance.
	° ′ ″	° ′ ″	Meters.
Town	18 01 39	197 58 00	4.39838
Rocky	352 15 06	172 18 15	4.31504

TOWN.

On sand spit at entrance to inner Golofnin Bay.
Station mark: Cross cut on large stone flush with surface of ground.

[Latitude 64° 32' 45.81''.   Longitude 163° 01' 14.42''.]

To station—	Azimuth.	Back azimuth.	Log. distance.
	° ′ ″	° ′ ″	Meters.
Grave	1 02 53.9	181 02 44.8	3.86542
Boot	36 56 29.9	216 48 50.0	4.05432
Lime	139 56 55.1	319 38 06.5	4.40989
Rocky	253 31 42.9	73 43 30.5	4.03637
Round	315 49 35.6	135 58 30.9	4.05584

GRAVE.

A station of the Coast and Geodetic Survey on a high, grassy point about 300 meters from the end of a rocky point on the west side of the bay (Golofnin). There are several Eskimo graves near by.

Station mark: A cross cut in center of top of a large stone set flush with surface of ground.

[Latitude 64° 28' 48.99'.   Longitude 163° 01' 24.47'.]

To station—	Azimuth.	Back azimuth.	Log. distance.
	° ′ ″	° ′ ″	Meters.
Town	181 02 44.8	1 02 53.9	3.86542
Rocky	225 23 55.6	45 35 47.9	4.17143
Round	275 49 30.9	95 58 35.1	3.90852

BOOT.

On highest part of ridge, about 7 miles S. 37° W. from Chinik. This ridge forms a narrow neck of land between Bering Sea and Golofnin Sound. It can be easily reached from any side on foot or with animals. There is plenty of water and some wood on the Golofnin side, and probably on other sides. There is a natural pile of rock about 100 yards east of station. This is also a triangulation station of the United States Coast and Geodetic Survey.

Station mark: A rock monument.

[Latitude 64° 27' 53.11". Longitude 163° 09' 43.96'.]

To station—	Azimuth.	Back azimuth.	Log. distance.
	° ' ''	° ' ''	Meters
Monument	124 07 51.5	303 39 15.6	4.48456
Lime	161 10 15.9	340 59 08.1	4.48186
Town	216 48 50.0	36 56 29.9	4.05432
Round	266 22 28.0	86 39 02.9	4.16917

LIME.

On a white hill about 3½ miles N. 13° E. of a white hill near Fish River, known as White Mountain, and about the same distance from the town of White Mountain. The station is on the third white hill, counting from White Mountain north. There is little choice of a route to the station from White Mountain, but it is probably best to go via White Mountain and thence from one white hill to the other until station is reached. Wood and water are in abundance about one-half mile east of station.

Station mark: "U. + S." on rock, over which is a spruce tree about 15 feet high.

[Latitude 64° 43' 19.55". Longitude 163° 22' 03.26".]

To station—	Azimuth.	Back azimuth.	Log. distance.
	° ' ''	° ' ''	Meters.
Monument	52 50 57.6	232 42 27.9	4.38622
Solomon	80 25 55.1	259 46 11.9	4.55163
Council	123 11 55.0	302 49 05.0	4.37768
Rocky	301 16 49.3	121 47 26.3	4.50053
Boot	340 59 03.1	161 10 15.9	4.48186
Town	319 38 06.5	139 56 55.1	4.45989

WHITE MOUNTAIN.

(Not occupied.)

A low limestone hill about 200 feet above sea level on north bank of Fish River, one-fourth mile below town of White Mountain.

[Latitude 64° 40′ 41.11″. Longitude 163° 23′ 25.04″.]

To station—	Azimuth.	Back azimuth.	Log. distance.
	° ′ ″	° ′ ″	*Meters.*
Town	309 35 47	129 55 49	4. 36198
Boot	335 12 39	155 25 01	4. 41790

MONUMENT.

On highest point of ridge which runs north and east from Bluff City (Topkok), and about 4 miles N. 34° E. therefrom.   A trail runs close to signal, coming from the south.   It is easily accessible from Bluff City.   There is good grass in the draws and water about 2 miles north of station.

Station mark: A rock monument about 9 feet high.

[Latitude 64° 37′ 02.65″. Longitude 163° 41′ 24.56″.]

To station—	Azimuth.	Back azimuth.	Log distance.
	° ′ ″	° ′ ″	*Meters.*
Solomon	105 53 38.2	285 31 15.7	4. 31164
Council	169 19 18.2	349 13 54.1	4. 39978
Lime	232 42 27.9	52 59 57.6	4. 28622
Boot	303 39 15.6	124 07 51.5	4. 48456

CHOWIK.

(Not occupied.)

A sharp peak about 3,500 feet above sea level, at head of Neukuluk River, Ophir Creek, and Parantulik River.

[Approximate position: Latitude 65° 08′ 34″. Longitude 163° 45′ 30″.]

To station—	Azimuth.	Back azimuth.	Log. distance.
	° ′ ″	° ′ ″	*Meters.*
Rocky	324 02 16	144 54 08	4. 89170
Town	331 54 24	152 34 29	4. 87628

COUNCIL.

A round, rocky point about 6 miles S. 42° W. of Council, being the nearest mountain south of Council.

Station mark: A rock marked "U. △ S.," above which is a rock monument 7 feet high, with a pine tree in the top.

[Latitude 64° 50′ 19.20″.   Longitude 163° 47′ 17.57″.]

To station—	Azimuth.	Back azimuth.	Log. distance.
	° ′ ″	″ ′ ″	*Meters*
Solomon	38 13 07.7	217 56 03.3	4.38542
Lime	302 49 05.0	123 11 55.0	4.37762
Monument......................	349 13 54.1	169 19 13.2	4.39972

TOPKOK.

(Not occupied.)

On promontory by that name—a United States Coast and Geodetic Survey station.

[Latitude 64° 33′ 25.57″.   Longitude 163° 57′ 58.22.″]

To station—	Azimuth.	Back azimuth.	Log. distance.
	° ′ ″	° ′ ″	*Meters.*
Solomon ....—	151 46 10	331 38 26	4.14420
Monument............................	242 48 31	68 03 24	4.16949
Boot.....	284 35 16	105 18 44	4.60108

SOLOMON.

A high ridge, sometimes called Thomson Mountain, between the Right Branch and Big Hurrah Creek, both tributaries of Solomon River, and about 12 miles northeast of the mouth of Solomon River, but not visible therefrom.   Ridge has three round points about the same height, the station being on the one which shows to be in the middle from nearly all directions.   The point farthest west has two little natural humps on top.   Station can be reached by going up Solomon River about 8 miles and thence across country a little north of east 8 or 9 miles.   It is possible that it can be more easily reached from the mouth of Topkok River.

Station mark: "U. △ S." cut on rock in place, over which is a rock monument about 8 feet high.

[Latitude 64° 40′ 01.81″.   Longitude 164° 06′ 10.18″.]

To station—	Azimuth.	Back azimuth.	Log. distance.
	° ′ ″	° ′ ″	*Meters.*
Council	217 56 03.3	38 13 07.7	4.38542
Monument........................... ...	285 31 15.7	105 53 38.2	4.31164
Topkok	331 38 26.0	151 46 10.0	4.14420
Lime	259 46 11.9	80 25 55.1	4.55163

INDEX.

229

O

CPSIA information can be obtained
at www.ICGtesting.com
Printed in the USA
BVHW04*1445140918
527538BV00006B/46/P

9 780331 688672